FINE FURNITURE
for the
Amateur Cabinetmaker

BY

A. W. MARLOW

PHOTOGRAPHY BY I. B. WARNER
OF SHADLE STUDIO, YORK, PA.

A SCARBOROUGH BOOK
STEIN AND DAY/*Publishers*/New York

First Scarborough Books Edition 1977

Fine Furniture for the Amateur Cabinetmaker was originally published
in hardcover by Macmillan Publishing Co., Inc., and is reprinted by
arrangement.

Printed in the United States of America
Stein and Day/*Publishers*/Scarborough House
Briarcliff Manor, N. Y. 10510
ISBN 0-8128-2250-1

FINE FURNITURE
for the
Amateur Cabinetmaker

Books by A. W. Marlow:

Fine Furniture for the Amateur Cabinetmaker
The Cabinetmaker's Treasury (with F. E. Hoard)
available in paperback as
Good Furniture You Can Make Yourself
The Early American Furnituremaker's Manual
Classic Furniture Projects

Contents

Introduction

This book is directed toward providing the average serious amateur craftsman with the means of making fine furniture that is within his ability. Nearly every beginner is surprised to find his doubts as to his ability to be groundless. Amateurs with a serious purpose but little experience will find here sympathetic understanding, and guidance that will help them steer clear of many pitfalls and mistakes. By following the directions, they can count on a measure of success that will amply reward them for the time spent. In addition the mental relaxation provided by creative manual effort is often an end in itself.

Successive photographs show in minute detail how a subject piece should look as the construction progresses. The photographs are grouped with the pertinent text and provide a step-by-step supplement to the text. In addition, each chapter has lists of materials, detailed drawings showing dimensions, and covers special problems that may be encountered in the project in hand. Pattern outlines, where required, are superimposed on scaled squares to simplify the transfer of designs. Instructions cover thoroughly design and structural problems on everything but the most elemental woodworking procedures.

The projects have been selected for practical appeal in present-day homes. The basic designs are structurally sound and feature various forms of carving to emphasize this specialized field. The combination of classic forms in carving with proper guidance in traditional joinery insures finished products that will have both form and substance. From start to finish of a piece of furniture, every conceivable problem is anticipated, explained, and shown, fulfilling the reader's desire for a self-contained book of furniture construction practices.

Numerous home shops are equipped only with basic machines. Therefore the photographs will show how many operations encountered in the course of construction can be accomplished with hand tools. Machine tools are indispensable for certain classes of work; but the projects set forth in "Fine Furniture" are so personalized that emphasis is placed more on hand tools. Also it should be remembered that the pinnacle of wood craftsmanship was attained before the advent of power-driven machine tools. Therefore, except for turned pieces, anyone with a modestly equipped workshop may start on any subject piece with full confidence of success.

CHAPTER I

Tools

SELECTION

Carving tools, with continued use, develop a personality. The owner ceases to think of their monetary cost and regards them with affection, so that a duplicate tool cannot equal the original in the satisfaction it gives. That being true you should treat your tools with esteem and respect, giving them safe and adequate care. Regardless of the number of tools, a case or bench drawer fitted with compartments for storage is advisable. Under no circumstance should they be left on the bench when not in use.

Four photographs illustrate one tool of each number: in photo 1, reading from left to right, Nos. 1, 2, and 3. Photo 2, Nos. 4, 5, and 6. Photo 3, Nos. 7, 9, and 10. Photo 4, Nos. 11, 41, and 42. No. 42 is similar to 41 except for the long-bend shank.

As an aid in selection, all carving tools deemed necessary are listed here, with sizes in fractions of an inch:

No. 1	2	3	4	5	6	7	9	11	41	42
¾	½	¾	½	½	½		½		⅜	⅛
½		½	¼		¼	¼		⅜		
¼		¼	⅛			⅛		¼	⅛	
³⁄₁₆		⅛						⅛		
⅛										

We must first familiarize ourselves with the terms used, so that a *chisel* will always mean to us a tool with a flat cutting edge. The No. 1 chisel is ground at right angles to the shaft, while the No. 2 is ground at an angle of about 25 degrees, forming a point at one side. The No. 3 is the first of a group of *gouges* which progress to the No. 11 tool. All gouges have a curved sweep on the cutting edge; the No. 3 has the longest radius, and as the number increases to 11 the radii become increasingly short, the No. 11 being a half-circle. If we exclude the half-circle gouges 10 and 11, it will be seen that the cutting edge describes a segment of a circle, and that two side cuts of a ¼-inch gouge could be about equaled with one cut of a ½-inch gouge. Accordingly, in order to minimize the original outlay for tools, our first selection may exclude the ¾-inch and even some of the ½-inch tools. Also, because most woodworkers have several standard wood chisels, the list of No. 1 tools may be screened for duplicates.

The last of the family of carving tools have a V-type cutting edge and are called *parting* tools, or *veiners*. Regardless of the variety chosen, it will be found that quality tools are the most economical and satisfactory. "Quality" here means but one thing: the ability to maintain the sharp edge essential for producing clean, splinterless cuts. Let us assume that the tools have been purchased with edges already ground and honed. A number of trial cuts should now be made on pieces of scrap wood. At this point, or after further use, we may find it necessary ourselves to grind and hone the cutting edges.

GRINDING

Line illustrations (page 3) of the same tools show in a graphic manner how each tool may be ground. No difference of opinion is expected with Nos. 1 and 2; but the grind of curved tools may vary, and each variation has its own supporters. The author prefers the method suggested here.

Chisel No. 1 is always ground straight across with a flat heel. No. 2 is also a flat chisel, but is ground on an angle of about 25 degrees, forming a forward point at one side. The purpose of this tool is to cut and clean out a corner more acute than a right angle. Dovetailing is an example. Because the tool must be used for both right and left corners, it is ground to cut with either flat surface resting on the work.

For the No. 3 gouges, widths from ⅛ to ⅜ inch may be ground with very little lateral curve (cutting edge from left to right), to facilitate removal of waste wood in small areas, sharp corners, and the frequent need for shallow concave surfaces on leaf parts ending abruptly under the preceding leaf. The ½- and ¾-inch sizes are used for many purposes, most commonly to remove wood from larger backgrounds. If both of these tools combine a lateral curve with the customary rounded heel, a lifting action as the tool cuts through will usually bring the cutting edge to the surface at the end of each stroke. If these two tools were ground on a straight line they would tend to twist and dig below the intended depth of cut. A common belief, proved by experience to be false, is that a flat chisel is required for cutting flat background. The use of a flat chisel in such a case can easily be detected afterward by the side tool-edge marks left in every stroke. Other uses for the No. 3 gouge will be suggested as the work progresses.

Gouges Nos. 4 and 5 may have a nearly straight lateral grind because their use is confined, in most cases, to particular concave surface cuts or vertical cuts outlining the design for later relief.

A suggested grind for Nos. 6 and 7 can follow the larger No. 3 tools, because a lifting action is also desired of them.

A "middle of the road" grind is selected for No. 9. This tool is seldom used for a cut of sufficient depth to warrant the lateral shape of No. 11. Because it will be chosen frequently for outlining, a straight lateral line produces the best results.

In the tool drawings on page 3 it will be observed that the high or side points of Nos. 11 and 41 are wholly unlike those of the shallower gouges. A seeming contradiction, until further study of what takes place as the tool cuts through the wood, brings to light a simple explanation. When we are channeling wood the foremost objective is a clean, unbroken side line. To accomplish it, the surface cut must precede the deeper parting; otherwise, pressure from below will break surface wood, and natural grain weakness in spots may cause the breakage to extend beyond the intended channel line. A recessed lower cutting edge on this group of tools will have the same effect, in one operation, as would result from preliminary surface parting on the line.

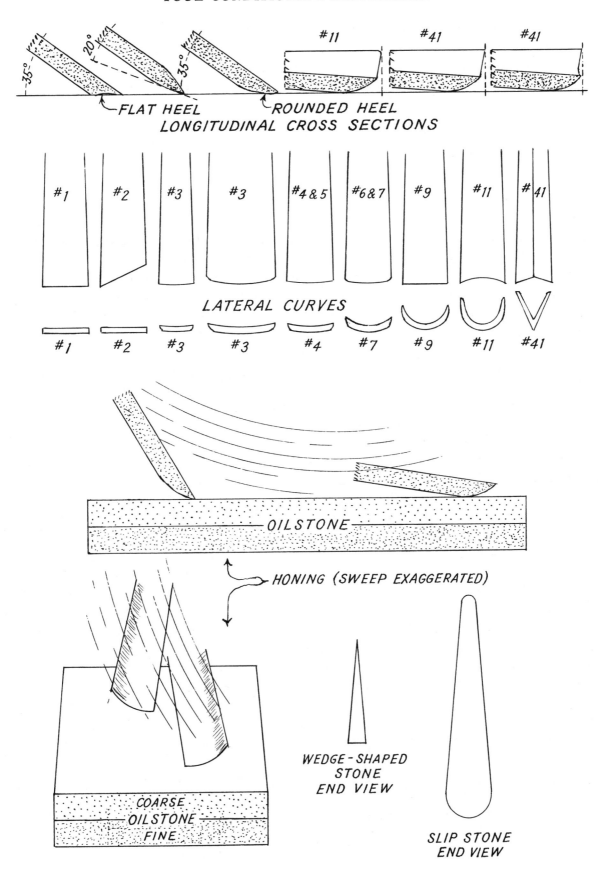

FLAT HEEL   ROUNDED HEEL
LONGITUDINAL CROSS SECTIONS

LATERAL CURVES

OILSTONE

HONING (SWEEP EXAGGERATED)

COARSE
OILSTONE
FINE

WEDGE-SHAPED
STONE
END VIEW

SLIP STONE
END VIEW

Two illustrations of No. 41 (longitudinal cross section) show, as a silhouette, first, how the tool should look after grinding, and secondly, how it probably will look until special and careful contact with the wheel takes away the projection of heavy metal always encountered at the base. Parting tools never make slick, clean, satisfactory cuts if there is even a trace of projecting steel where the sides meet. No. 42, ⅛ inch, is a long-bend parting tool necessary only when a line or vein is required inside a concave where straight-shank No. 41 would meet the surface on an angle too acute for controlled depth of cut.

HONING

Oilstones are manufactured by many companies. Size, shape, coarse or fine grit, and quality of materials used in manufacture should be considered by the buyer for his particular needs. Quality of material is less important in coarse stones than in finer hones. The price is usually indicative of quality. Carving tools are of cast steel, highly tempered, and final sharpening is accomplished best on a stone of razor-hone texture. One large flat stone that has one side coarse and the other fine is necessary. Two slip stones of fine grit will be sufficient, one large or most common in size, the other smaller and thinner for small-size gouges. To complete equipment for honing, a wedge-shaped stone with long tapered sides will remove burrs from the V-shaped tools.

After grinding, all wheel scratches must be removed from the tool's heel by repeated strokes over first the coarse, then the finer stone. Chisels, with a flat heel, are held on one correct angle (see drawing, page 3) throughout this phase of sharpening to retain the desired flatness. An added motion for No. 2 can be compared to a rocker gradually wearing away, refining the rounded surface so necessary for clean, sharp cuts. Simultaneously, a third motion is included for gouges: a slight twist of the wrist, as the tool is moved in a forward and backward rocker motion, results in a uniform, rounded heel laterally as well as longitudinally (Photo 4A).

At this stage of the conditioning process a heavy burr has been rolled on the upper surface. To remove this from No. 1, turn the tool over, lay it flat on the fine stone, and move it back and forth until the excess metal is abraded. Finally, one forward stroke on the heel angle, and then a forward stroke with the upper surface lying flat. Repeat until a satisfactory cutting edge is achieved.

Two heels constitute No. 2, and so final honing is accomplished by one forward stroke—first one side, then the other. Repeat.

For removing burrs from gouges and parting tools, use slip stones and the wedge in place of the flat oilstone. With that exception final honing is the same for chisels. Photo 4B illustrates the use of the slip stone to remove the burr on a gouge. Photo 4C shows the wedge-shaped stone in use on No. 41 veiner.

CONTROL

An explanation of tool control will immeasurably hasten its attainment. Carving with power by a mallet is comparatively simple, because control lies entirely in the left hand. The direction and angle of the tool as it receives the blow of the mallet determines its path and the depth of its cut. Curling the fingers of the left hand around the tool, with the thumb pointing upward and exerting opposite pressure, will assure a controlling grip. Place the hand in an area about half over the tool and half over the handle. Photo 5, taken from the Coffee Table series, illustrates this grip.

Most carving is done without a mallet, and so suggestions for tool handling will be helpful. The balance of the carver's body is important. For deep cuts, the power in the thrust must come from the feet upward. The artist should assume a stance that will preserve his balance when he puts pressure on the tool. Power flows from the body through the right arm, wrist, and hand, making the tool do what is intended. Direct control lies in this power system. The ability to stop a tool at an exact spot, to make cuts uniform in depth, to direct the tool properly without wavering, depends on muscular control and balance.

Hold the tool handle in your right hand so that the wrist can be twisted either to the right or to the left. Grip it firmly, muscles tense but not rigid. Depth of cut must always be governed by the tool's angle—never by downward pressure of the hand holding it. The left hand assists the right in many ways. Crooked fingers over the tool for heavy and medium cuts help control immensely. For short, light, precise cuts, rest the left hand close to the cutting area, curling the fingers around the tool so that the hand can pivot for a short distance while maintaining the support so necessary for complete control. Photo 6, reproduced from the Piecrust Table series, illustrates the instructions just given.

If these general directions are followed, progress in tool dexterity should be rapid.

LATHE WORK

One each of the following tools is necessary: ¾-inch skew, ⅛-inch parting tool, ¼-inch round-nose chisel, ¾-inch gouge, 1¼-inch gouge (Photo 6A).

Words are a poor substitute for experience in turning. Little that is effective can be said about tool handling. For good, clean turning, the tool must be sharp; the tool rest must be not more than one inch from the work; the handle must be gripped firmly yet pliably. Angle the tool in relation to the work so that it will make a clean cut rather than scrape off the wood. (Illustration 7, reproduced from the Covered Bowl series.)

There is no choice of methods for chucking except such small faceplate work as bowls. These pieces must be turned outside and inside. I prefer a wood screw-center faceplate because it is much faster, even though a boss has to be removed from the inside with hand tools and the center counter-bored and plugged.

By screw-center drive, turn the outside and the bottom of the bowl and sand them to finish smoothness. Before removing it to rechuck for inside turning, cut a center mark in the bottom. Rechuck to turn the inside and the top edge. Leave a column or boss of wood around the screw for support while sanding to a finish smoothness. Remove from the lathe. Cut away the boss—counterbore for ½-inch plugs inside and outside—insert the plugs with glue, and level with hand tools. Sand to finish smoothness.

One way to eliminate the center screw-hole and plugs is to attach a wood face to the metal plate. Glue the blank to be turned to the wood plate, with paper between. Turn the inside, then the top edge and the outside for a short distance down. Sandpaper with No. ½ and No. 3/0 paper. Remove from the plate. Measure accurately the top opening. Turn a shoulder on the plate, leaving a ¼-inch-high center to match exactly the bowl opening. Cut paper to fit neatly around the center rise; spread a thin line of glue around the shoulder; place the paper; spread a line of glue around the bowl opening at the highest point; and weight or clamp until glue sets. Turn the outside and the bottom, sanding to finish smoothness. Remove from the wood plate, and hand-sand the glued line around opening.

Lathe speeds for faceplate work and long stock are as follows:

DIAMETER FACEPLATE	R.P.M.	DIAMETER LEGS AND POSTS
Up to 8 in.	1,500	1 to 3 in.
9 to 12 in.	1,200	3 to 4 in.
13 to 18 in.	1,000/750	
19 to 24 in.	750/500	
25 to 36 in.	350/250	

Chapter XI contains a detailed explanation of contributory processes: sanding (flat work and carving), and finishing procedure. Also, "Where to Get It," with sources of materials and special tools.

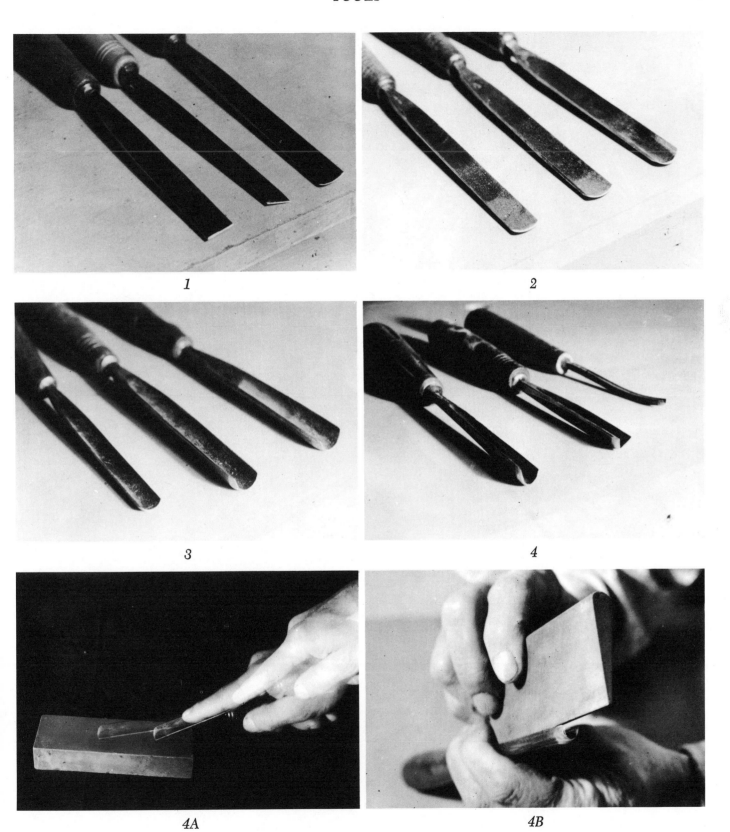

1

2

3

4

4A

4B

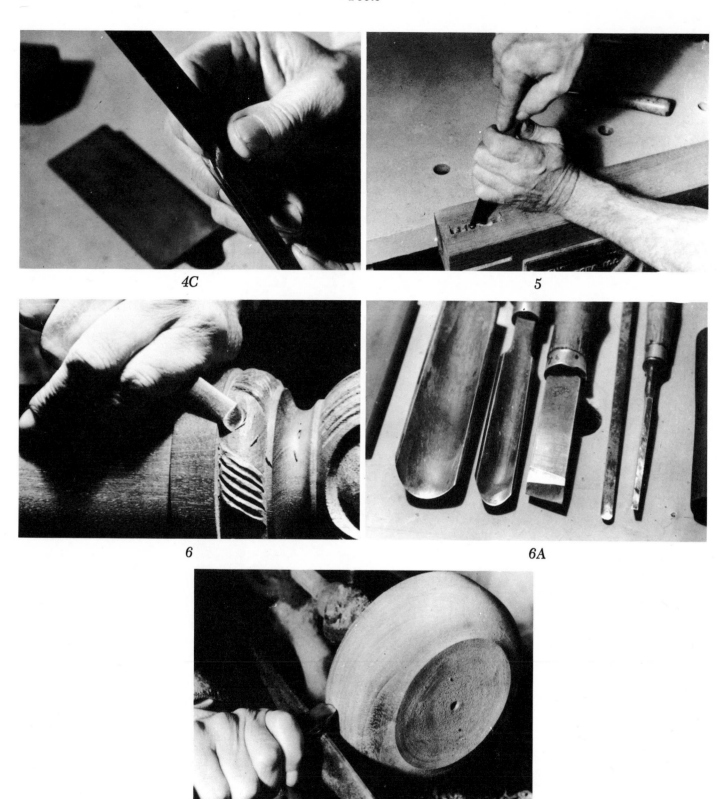

4C

5

6

6A

7

Subjects for Practice

PIECRUST TRAY

COVERED BOWL

RIBBON AND SCROLL TRAY

PAPER KNIFE

CHAPTER II

Subjects for Practice

This chapter offers inexperienced workers an opportunity to practice the use of tools with a definite goal. Errors in the first few attempts will cause little loss in material or work. The designs have been carefully worked out to show the fundamental use of the basic machine tools found in even the most modest hobby shop.

Although the pieces illustrated are primarily for practice, their usefulness and their decorative qualities make them desirable additions to any home. Mahogany is the wood chosen, because of its excellent response to hand tools; but native woods can be substituted.

Paper Knife

Presented first is a paper knife. A leaf design of simple carving constitutes the handle. The drawing on page 13 presents dimensions and pattern layout. The ideal material for small patterns is a tough, glazed "stencil paper," which can be cut to outline with scissors.

After preparing the pattern cut a blank of the wood selected, 1 by ½ inch by 8½ inches long, to size on the circular saw. Place the pattern, mark the outline, and position of center holes with a pencil. Bore ⅛-inch holes completely through the wood where they are indicated. Thread the jig- or fret-saw blade through each hole in turn, cutting to the egg-shaped line. Continue with the saw to follow the pencil line, forming the handle outline (Photo 8). Do not saw the blade to shape at this time, because the parallel sides offer good gripping surfaces to the vise while the handle is carved. The foreground of Photo 8 pictures a blank with pattern in position for marking. Under the jig-saw head another blank is being sawed to the outline.

Although there is neither back nor front (both sides are identical), the instructions will be clearer if we use these terms. Place the blank in the vise (Photo 9) as it comes from the jig saw. Choose a No. 3 carving tool to cut variable handle thickness on the edge outline as shown in the drawing on page 13. A band or jig saw can be used to make this cut; but the small volume of wood removed makes it impractical.

Crown the front and back (Photo 9), leaving untouched at the thickest part of the handle, about ¼ inch of rough edge wood. On the newly rounded surfaces, work guide lines for carving as in the drawing, page 13. The in-turned petals appearing to overlay the leaf must first be outline-cut in relief. Use No. 4, ⅛ inch, to part the wood around the petal tip by pressing the tool into the wood vertically. In Photo 10, the right side of the handle shows guide lines and the first parting cuts. The left side has No. 41, ⅛-inch veiner cuts made on all other lines. Next, give the overlay petals relief by sloping the surrounding wood down to their outline. The small area between the petals slopes off sharply from a central ridge. Round the surface of all other petals. Cut to a greater depth as you approach the tips, to put each petal on a different plane. The graceful effect of this procedure may be observed in Photo 11.

Attention is now centered on the in-turned petals. Channel or concave cuts down the inside edges can be made with No. 11, ¼ inch. Starting at the tips, sharp and fairly deep, the cuts should gradually become shallower, tailing off to nothing when each petal meets its opposite. The outside halves can now be rounded in the usual manner. Again using the No. 11, cut short channels in the centers of the petals immediately ahead of the in-turned ones (Photo 11). With the small No. 41, cut three veins in each adjoining petal to complete the handle.

Using the edge outline of the drawing on page 13 for guidance; draw blade thickness lines in pencil. Cut to the lines on the band or jig saw (Photo 11). Next, grip the handle carefully in the vise so that shaping cuts may be made with the ¾-inch No. 3. For its purpose, the blade's body need not be so thin as a metal one. Round the front and the back to approximately the shape illustrated in the drawing by "Cross Sections." Finally, round the guard or shield with a No. 3 gouge. Sand the entire piece for finish (Photo 12). Consult "Sanding," in Chapter XI.

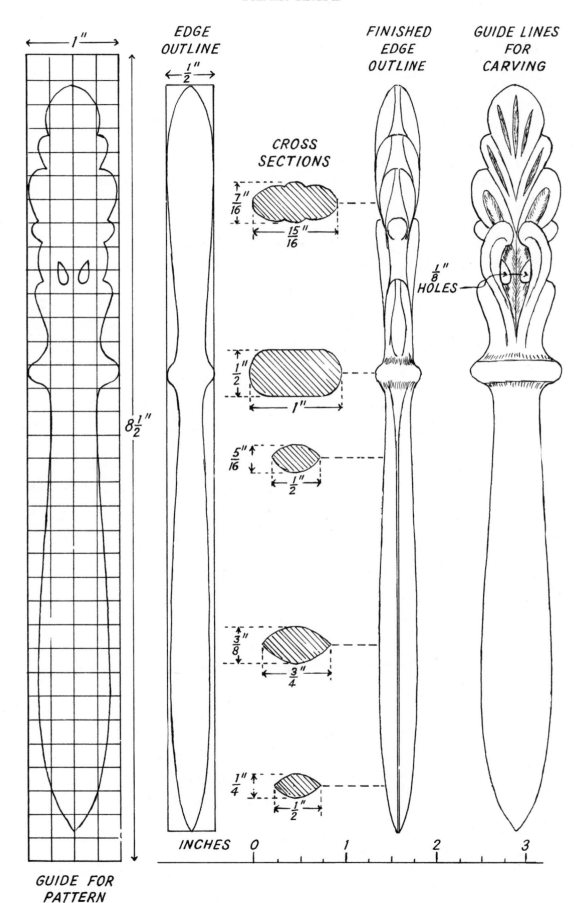

GUIDE FOR PATTERN

EDGE OUTLINE

FINISHED EDGE OUTLINE

GUIDE LINES FOR CARVING

CROSS SECTIONS

INCHES 0 1 2 3

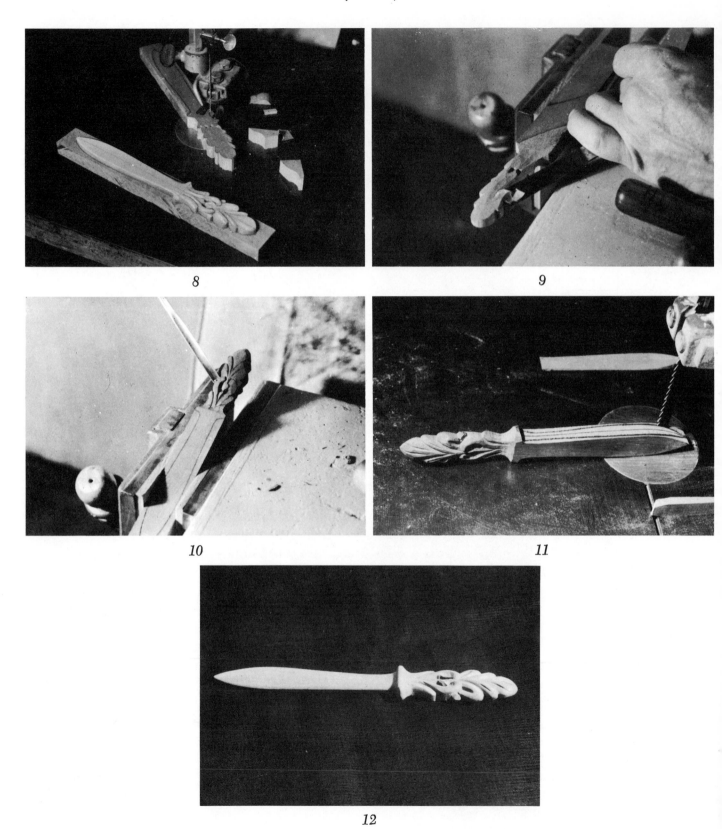

8

9

10

11

12

Piecrust Tray

(1720–1790)

Material: mahogany, 14 by 14 inches by $1\frac{3}{16}$ inch.

Trays of various sizes, decorated with innumerable interpretations of the piecrust edge, were made during the colonial era. Commonly adorning the mantel, they were often used to serve tidbits or refreshments.

Original trays were always made of one-board width; this characteristic is desirable but not necessary in reproductions. Should two or more pieces be glued together, match the grain as closely as possible.

Band-saw the board to a 14-inch circle. Mount the blank, as shown in the drawing on page 17, with six wood screws. Glue chucking with paper between is not recommended, because it may pull loose, and a whirling disc of this size is dangerous. The first step is to true up the circumference by holding a rest-supported gouge to true out all depressions. Swing the tool rest parallel to the face, and cut no more wood than is necessary for truing up. With a pencil, mark the disc while it is in motion, $\frac{1}{2}$ inch from the edge, as shown at the lower right of the drawing. With the parting tool, cut $\frac{1}{8}$ inch deep, inside the pencil line. Round the corners of the $\frac{1}{2}$-inch section with the skew, to form a wide flat bead. Holding the $\frac{3}{4}$-inch gouge firmly, cut the waste wood inside the parting-tool line to shape a small fillet. From that point to the center, turn to a straight line (Photo 13). A 12-inch straightedge may be used for the final true-up. Swing the tool rest around to the back for support and, with the $\frac{3}{4}$-inch gouge, turn to the approximate shape shown in the drawing, lower left.

To sand the flat surface, fold a $\frac{1}{4}$ sheet of No. $\frac{1}{2}$ sandpaper, over a cork or wood block, and press it against the work while it is in motion, moving the paper slowly back and forth. Crease the paper threefold and, with only finger pressure, sand the curved surface. Proceed in like manner with No. 3/0 paper. Remove the disc from the faceplate.

A pattern must be made for the next step. Lay a piece of pattern board on the bench or any flat surface. Set your compass for a 7-inch radius and draw the outside line. Without moving either the pattern material or the compass center, mark another line with $6\frac{3}{4}$-inch radius and a third with $6\frac{1}{2}$-inch radius. From the center of one uncut section to the center of the next a straight-line measurement should be five inches (drawing, page 17). Mark the typical piecrust curves in pencil. Indentations should not exceed $\frac{1}{4}$ inch nor cross the $6\frac{3}{4}$-inch radius line. Jig-saw the pattern. Place on turning and mark for trial only at the ends of the pattern. Place and mark ends for the full circle. In case of variation, either overlap or failure to meet, slight adjustment must be made at each section. Mark the complete outline. Photo 14 shows the tray on the jig saw with one section remaining to be sawed. Also prominently displayed is the sectional pattern placed for marking.

After sawing, draw a border line $\frac{1}{4}$ inch in from the edge, to outline the bead. Hold gouges of various curves vertically and, with one or two blows of the mallet, part the wood down to the fillet line (Photo 15). This may be done by sections, or the circle may be completed before removal of waste wood. Using ½-inch gouge No. 3, remove this waste (Photo 15). A ledge of varying width inside the roughed-out bead remains. Draw a line to follow the bead curvature ⅛ inch in from the bead. With No. 7 gouge, cut a fillet to follow the pencil line. No. 3, ½ inch, can be used to smooth the small areas which will extend the turned flat surface line. Photo 16 illustrates these cuts in small portions. In the foreground the wood is divided, and waste removed, to form the rough bead. The ledge is next worked and fillet-cut. A No. 3, ½ inch, is shown rounding the bead, outside and inside.

When the tray has been completed to this stage, grip it (Photo 17) in the vise, and cut away the right-angle edge left by the jig saw at every indentation. Shape these edges to match as closely as possible the uncut turned portions. The ¾-inch or ½-inch No. 3 is most suitable for this purpose.

Letter A on the drawing is a cross section at the largest diameter before cutting with saw or hand tools. B is the largest diameter with the bead cut in depth to the ledge. C is still the largest diameter with the fillet cut and the flat surface smoothed. D is the smallest diameter, with all cuts made. E shows how considerable weight may be removed from the tray by circular sawing, edge up, the full cut of the saw. Removal of waste wood to the center can be by a plane or hand tools, or by both plane and hand tools.

A fair question is: Why not start with wood of the final thickness? Then insufficient wood would remain for holding the tray with safety while turning. The lathe mounting screws should have a purchase of at least ⅜ inch. Whether or not to remove bottom wood is for the craftsman to decide.

Sand out all tool marks on the newly cut border, first with No. ½, then with No. 3/0. It is well to use No. 3/0 with a cork block on the flat surface, sanding in to the fillet and thus assuring an even continuation of the flat surface. Sand with the grain. A light sanding with No. 7/0 finishing paper completes the work. Photo 18 shows the tray ready for stain.

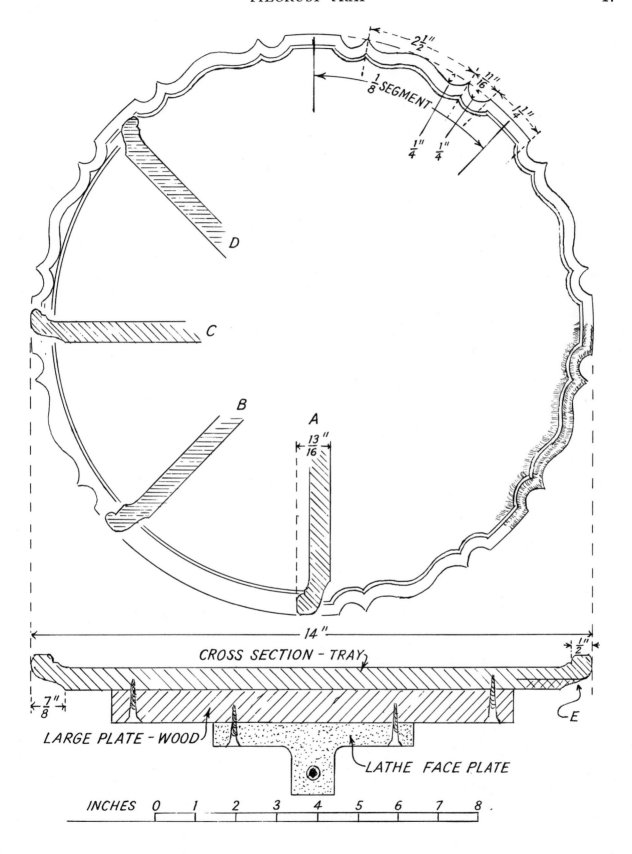

$2\frac{1}{2}''$

$\frac{1}{8}$ SEGMENT

$\frac{11}{16}''$

$1\frac{1}{4}''$

$\frac{1}{4}''$ $\frac{1}{4}''$

D

C

B

A

$\frac{13}{16}''$

$14''$

$\frac{1}{2}''$

CROSS SECTION - TRAY

$\frac{7}{8}''$

E

LARGE PLATE - WOOD

LATHE FACE PLATE

INCHES   0   1   2   3   4   5   6   7   8

Piecrust Tray

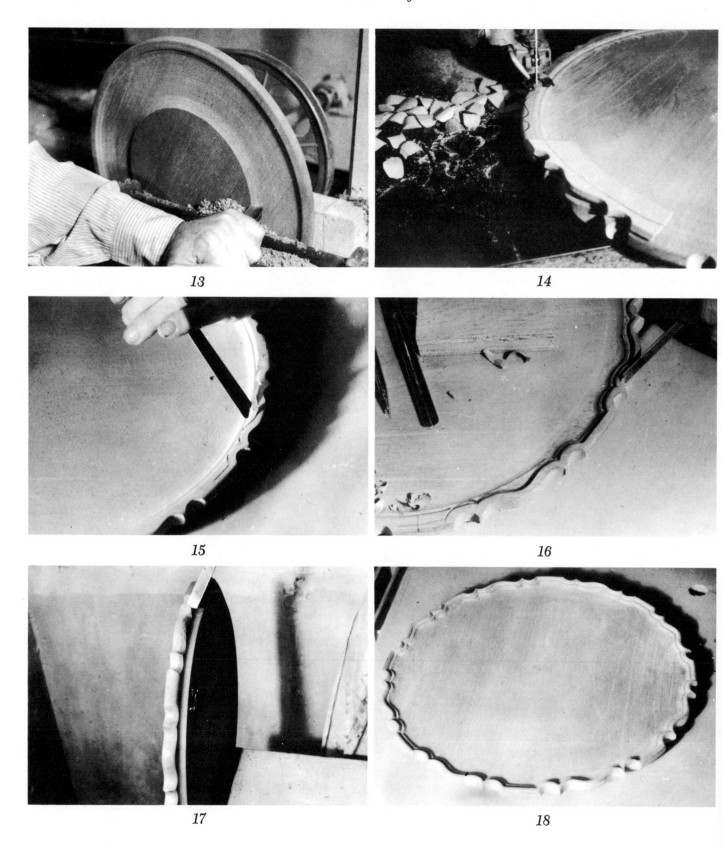

13

14

15

16

17

18

Covered Bowl

Materials: mahogany, 1 piece, 6½ by 6½ by 2 inches; 1 piece, 5¾ by 5¾ by $^{13}\!/_{16}$ inch; band inlay, 20 inches by ¼ inch.

Here is an attractive table decoration, for candy or salted nuts. The larger and deeper sizes are used as nut bowls. Two methods of faceplate turning are explained in Chapter I (under "Lathe Work"). The center-screw method is chosen for illustration in this book. Inlay may be purchased from one of the firms listed in "Where to Get It."

First, from the 6½-inch-square blank, band-saw a 6¼-inch-diameter circle. Bore a small pilot hole in the center. Attach to a screw-center faceplate by revolving the blank until it is tightly seated on the screw. Turn the bottom surface. This can be done easily by swinging the short tool rest parallel to the bottom. Hollow the bottom slightly toward the center, in order to insure a firm rest when the bowl is placed on a flat surface. With the parting tool, cut a substantial center mark. (For the hollowed bottom, see the drawing on page 21; for the center mark, Photo 19.)

Now swing the rest to a convenient angle, and start the curve that blends into the vertical side wall. Next, parallel the tool rest to the side, and finish cutting that surface (Photo 20). With coarse and fine paper, sand the bottom and about halfway up the side. Now, using the newly made center mark, reverse on the faceplate. A pilot hole in the center will make it easier to seat the blank accurately. Study the drawing on page 21 in conjunction with the photos. After the reversal, finish turning the bowl side. For this work, set the tool rest parallel to the lathe bed. Note a decided inward sweep to the side as it approaches the top edge. Next, swing the tool rest to parallel the top surface, and true up, removing as little wood as is possible.

With the lathe in motion, hold a scale to the top surface, measuring from the center outward a radius of 2⅝ inches, marking with a pencil. Check the pencil line for 5¼-inch diameter. With the parting tool at right angle to the top, cut inside the line to a depth of about ½ inch (Photo 21). The ½-inch depth is a matter of convenience, because all wood inside the parting cut must be removed: a deeper cut without side clearance would make the tool bind.

Remove the waste wood inside the bowl, resetting the tool rest frequently so that its tip remains near the cutting area. Use the ¾-inch gouge for this work (Photos 21, 22). In Photo 22, observe how the tool rest end extends into the bowl, making easy what might otherwise be difficult, the removal of waste wood under the top edge. Large calipers may be used to gauge wall thickness.

Now, with the parting tool, cut a channel in the outside wall for ¼-inch inlay, exercising extreme care so that the inlay will fit perfectly in both width and depth. In Photo 23, notice that a large area of waste wood still remains on the bottom. It may be removed at any time after the side wall has been cut to proper thickness.

Photo 24 illustrates the finish-turned bowl. A boss or dowel of wood is left unturned around the center screw, for support. Place the inlay in the channel provided (without glue). Hold the starting end with a spring clamp, and revolve the turning while channeling the inlay for the complete circle. Cut the inlay about ¼ inch longer than its fitted size. Remove the clamp and the inlay. Coat the under side of the inlay with glue, introduce one end of it into the channel, and clamp as before, placing the clamp so that the end of the inlay is visible. Slowly revolve the turning while carefully seating the inlay. In places, a gentle tap with a light hammer may be necessary. The band of inlay must be firmly seated around the complete circle. After completing the turn, lap over the excess inlay, and cut a butt joint with a sharp chisel. Press the newly cut end in place, and shift the clamp over the joint. Allow the glue to set overnight. Use coarse and fine sandpaper, inside and out. Remove the bowl from the faceplate.

If you are unfamiliar with the making and the use of plugs, follow these instructions: Purchase a ½-inch plug cutter. This is designed to fit the brace. Cut a random-width strip $\frac{5}{32}$ inch thick, and clamp it firmly on a substantial piece of unusable wood. Place the cutter and brace assembly vertically on the strip, and press and turn as with a bit. Continue turning until the plug is cut free from the surrounding wood. In the same way, cut the entire strip into plugs for future use.

Prepare for plugs to cover center holes by first removing the boss inside the bowl. Counterbore with a ½-inch bit. If the bit is of the "twist" type, cut only as deep as the outside cutting lip, and remove the center wood with a small No. 3 gouge. Repeat if necessary. Then counterbore the outside center. With glue, coat only the edges of the plugs; introduce them, and seat them gently because the wood separating the holes is thin. Allow overnight setting. Level off the surfaces with hand tools, and sand.

Turn the cover next. One faceplate setting is sufficient for this piece. Bore a pilot hole in the 5½-inch blank, and seat it firmly on the faceplate. First turn a shoulder $\frac{1}{16}$ inch wide, cutting toward the center and leaving $5\frac{3}{16}$-inch diameter on the under (faceplate) surface.

Start the outside design by turning the center button. A skew is the right tool for this portion. Follow with the small round-nose flat, to undercut for petal tips. With a ¾-inch gouge, rough down from the petal tips to the outside diameter. Work closely with the drawing on page 21. The next curve sweeps down from the petal tips and should be undercut slightly as it nears the lowest point, gently rising on the other side to a narrow flat terminating the curve (Photo 25). The most appropriate tool for this sweep is the small round-nose flat. A long ogee curve ending in a bead on the edge may be accomplished with the ¾-inch gouge. It is well to repeat a few words of caution: Have your tools sharp. Keep the tool rest close to the work. Sand to finish smoothness, to complete the lathe work. Do not remove the work from the faceplate. Detach the plate, and grip it in the vise for flower carving.

Mark off in pencil eight division lines around the flower circumference. Divide with a No. 3 gouge to the inside level depth. Make the cuts in the form of a V for tool clearance. Photo 26 shows these cuts, and the rounding of the tips of petals in the foreground to their final form. Also pictured here is a cover as it came from the lathe.

Photo 27 shows progressive cuts in sequence. In the left foreground is the petal division line in pencil. Next to the right, petals have been parted with the ⅛-inch No. 41, and one petal has the center rib marked in pencil. The next petal, counterclockwise, shows the rib cut in relief with the small No. 41. Please observe, none of these cuts is carried through to the center button; after reaching the high point, they end on a taper. The last series of cuts employ the ¼-inch No. 11 gouge shown at the top of Photo 27. The petal, at about "two o'clock," has had these channel cuts made. Although not very deep, they are necessary in order to break the flat surface of each petal. These channel cuts show in much better detail on Photo 28, which pictures the complete bowl and cover. Sand the flower carving with No. 3/0, and apply finishing materials to bowl and cover.

CROSS SECTION – COVER

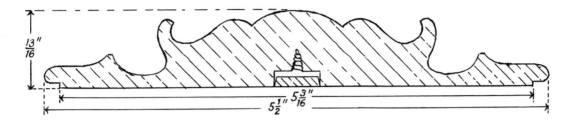

$\frac{13}{16}''$

$5\frac{1}{2}''$ $5\frac{3}{16}''$

CROSS SECTION – BOWL

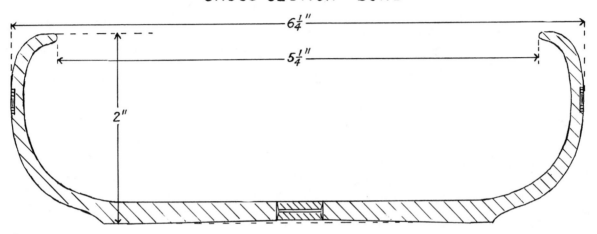

$6\frac{1}{4}''$

$5\frac{1}{4}''$

$2''$

PLAN OF HALF-COVER

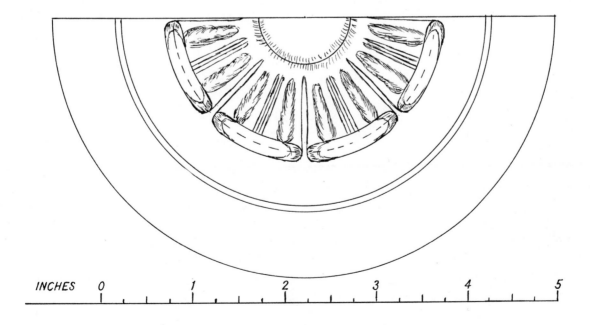

INCHES   0   1   2   3   4   5

19

20

21

22

23

24

25

26

27

28

Ribbon and Scroll Tray

Material: mahogany, 1 piece, 18 by 12 inches by $1\frac{3}{16}$ inch

Here, combined in tray form, are motifs frequently used in carving: border ribbons ending in scrolls, which overlap the versatile shell.

One-board-width wood is desirable for this tray but not necessary. Two or more pieces may be glued together to make the required 12-inch width. All four corners of the board used for these illustrations were cut back a uniform distance, to ease the positioning when it was dropped on the dado for hollowing.

The pattern may be made in one full-size piece as illustrated on Photo 29, or it may be a ¼ section (drawing, page 25). If the sectional pattern is used, it must be placed accurately over each quarter for marking. After the outline is transferred to the board, make an inside ribbon line ⅝ inch in from the border (Photo 31). Adjust the dado head for a ⅜-inch-deep cut. Bring the ripping fence close to the cutter, and mark the fence with a pencil where the cutting head first appears above the table. Mark also the exact point on the fence where the cutter disappears below the table top. These two pencil marks may be seen on the fence in Photo 30. They are the only visual indications of forward and backward cutting distance when the dado is covered.

The first dado cut will be down the middle of the board. Determine the distance from the corner points to where the cut should start and stop. Turn the board over, and, from both front and rear corners, mark this measurement on the bottom. Actual cutting may now begin. Slowly lower the board onto the cutter, constantly checking the mark on the board so it will match the forward fence mark when in its lowest position. Push the board forward until the rear corner mark meets the rear mark on the fence. Next, move the fence toward the dado slightly less than the width of the cutter. After the center cut is made the board should be reversed from side to side, two cuts being made for each set-up. When necessary, adjust the marks on the bottom for a longer or a shorter cutting distance to follow the penciled ribbon line. Photo 31 pictures the board marked with the inside ribbon line and dado work completed. Now cut to the outside pattern line on band or jig saw for final shape.

Study Photo 32 until you know what the next step is to accomplish. To the left, much of the waste wood is being chipped away roughly with the ¾-inch No. 3. This may be done over the whole circumference or by sections. Follow by chopping down in stages on the penciled outline of ribbon, scroll, and shell terminals with appropriate gouges to the depth of the dadoed bottom. Sloping cuts will be necessary in the waste wood, to allow clearance for each successive perpendicular gouge cut. As the desired depth is neared the remaining waste wood, to the true bottom level, may be removed with the large No. 3 gouge. By extending this level close to the border decorations, you will find it easy to gauge depth at the border line (Photo 32, upper left center).

Surface contouring of border carving in preparation for detail cuts comes next. Before study of Photo 33, return to 32 and observe the right uncut end—ribbon outlines continue into the scrolls. Relief cuts follow the outside lines because the inside lines have already been cut to the bottom

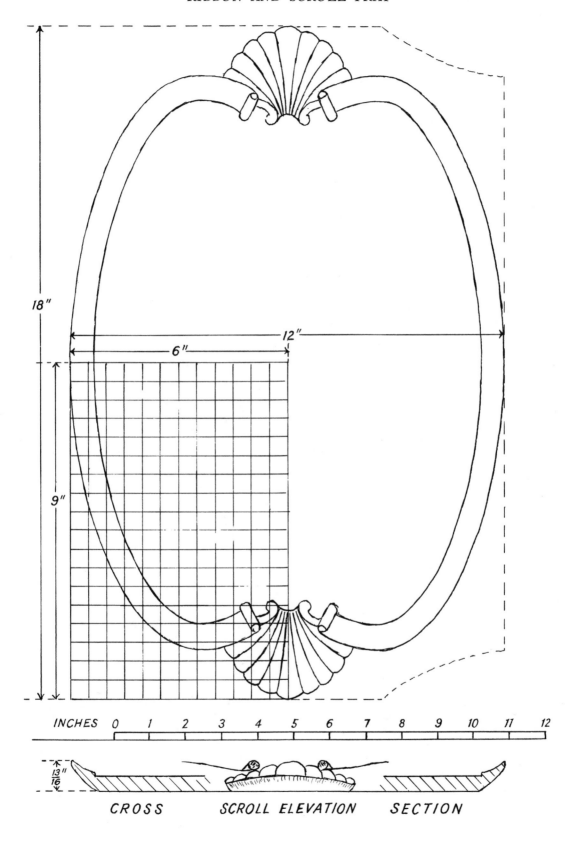

18"

12"

6"

9"

INCHES   0   1   2   3   4   5   6   7   8   9   10   11   12

13"/16

CROSS   SCROLL ELEVATION   SECTION

level. Crown the entire surface of the shells with a wide No. 3 gouge, the highest point being about ¾ inch from the outside edges. Slope the inside gradually to ⅛ inch above the bottom level.

Read carefully the explanations that follow, glancing frequently at Photo 33. For simplicity, the directions will refer in the singular to the shell, the scroll, etc. The scroll (upper left center) has been sloped from the highest point of the border wood to the thickness of the roll at and above the bottom level. This cut is rough and flat-topped—its purpose, simply to get the desired slope. Now the ribbon must also be sloped in to the perpendicular cut forming the width of the scroll. This operation is done roughly for the present. Now the scroll is nothing more than an elongated block approximately 1 inch long and ¼ inch thick.

Form the block into a roll by rounding the two top edges and slightly undercutting what could be considered as the under side of the roll. This has been done on the scroll (lower left) in Photo 33. The ribbon has also been cut to flow smoothly into the scroll. Give the scroll a final realistic touch by undercutting the top and bottom ends on an angle to simulate thin material unevenly rolled. Photo 37 pictures this clearly.

Next, cut the shell terminal in low relief as it emerges from under the scroll (Photos 33 and 34): as in all relief work, first a vertical chop on the outline and then sloping cuts on the lower surface. Draw in pencil the shell ribs, guided by drawing on page 25. Use small veiner No. 41 for initial separation cuts. Follow by cutting them deeper with a larger No. 41. Carefully round each rib with a No. 3 gouge. As a final clean-up cut, use No. 41 in each division to give the shell sharpness and a clean-cut appearance. Photo 34 illustrates on the left a shell completely cut, and on the right the first division cuts made. The uncut border ribbon may be finished last, to complete the tray-top carving.

Grip the tray in the vise as shown in Photo 35, using a space block to keep the vise jaw from pressing on the raised ribbon edge. Tool work underneath is purposely left in a rough state for contrast. Mark a border line on the bottom, about ¾ inch in from the edge and, if necessary, another on the edge ⅛ inch from the top. For sufficient finger space under the shell, draw the bottom line in an arc (Photo 35). Use a large No. 3 gouge and a mallet to cut away the waste wood. (For guidance in this work, turn to the cross section at the bottom of page 25.) Under the shell, cut a rather sharp concave for finger clearance. Do not remove the tool marks on the under edge with sandpaper. Sand the flat bottom to finish smoothness.

Before sanding the tray top, study the passage in Chapter XI on sanding. Photo 36 pictures the tray ready for sanding. Notice the cork block with sandpaper folded over it for the flat work. First, sand the entire border with No. ½ paper. Any unintentional cross scratches on the flat bottom surface can be sanded out when the cork is used. For the border, fold a small piece of paper, and use it as shown, keeping in mind the instructions in Chapter XI. The border is a type of carving where glove fingers should be worn.

After careful sanding of the border, the cork may be used with No. ½ paper. Sand as close as possible into the corners, but always sand with the grain. Remove all dado and hand-tool marks. For corners and other areas hard to get at, fold a piece of paper and use it as suggested for the border. Repeat with No. 3/0 finishing paper, until any coarse scratches resulting from the use of No. ½ paper are completely removed. The border under edge may have a cursory sanding with No. 3/0. A final sanding with No. 7/0 paper will prepare the piece for the finishing materials. Photo 37 shows the tray ready for finish.

29

30

31

32

33

34

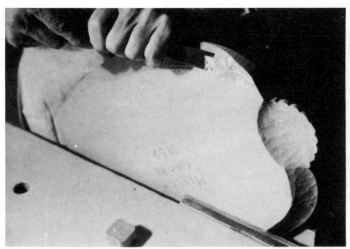

35

36

37

More Practice Subjects

DOUBLE PORTRAIT FRAME   SINGLE PORTRAIT FRAME
READING GLASS   CIGARETTE BOX

CHAPTER III

More Practice Subjects

Reading Glass

Materials

MAHOGANY

1 piece, 4½ inches by 4½ inches by ¾ inch.
1 piece, 4⅛ inches by 4⅛ inches by ¾ inch.
1 piece, 5½ inches by 2 inches by ½ inch.
1 magnifying glass, 3½ inches around.

Decoratively framed reading glasses are rare. For the amateur craftsman, a "glass" offers one of the most promising household opportunities to show his skill, by replacing the metal frame with a frame of mahogany.

The proposed design gives incentive for accurate and unusual turning. The handle should present no great difficulty, even though it looks elaborate.

Most reading glasses have an encircling metal band that must be removed first. The diameter and the thickness of the glass must be measured accurately at a point $\frac{5}{32}$ inch in from the edge, and the measurements must be noted for the final parting on the reverse side.

Study the ring-frame cross section in the drawing on page 33 until you realize their importance. Keep in mind, however, that any variation in glass size from that of the drawing will correspondingly alter these two measurements when you turn the main ring and secondary ring or glass retainer. When you press the two parts firmly together an inside channel for the glass is formed whose width should equal the thickness of the glass.

Band-saw one 4½-inch-square block to a 4½-inch circle for turning the main ring. Drill a pilot hole, and mount the block on the lathe faceplate. Consider the side toward the faceplate as the retaining-ring surface. True up the outside surface and edge. Disregard the extra wood thickness, which will be removed from the other side when the turning is reversed. Turn the surface and edge to match the drawing cross section. Using the parting tool, form the ring inside diameter exactly $\frac{5}{16}$ inch less than the glass diameter. Cut approximately in depth to the juncture point of what will be the glass channel when the turning is reversed. Continue checking with the cross section drawing. The progress to this point can be observed in Photo 38. Cut an adequate center mark for reversing. Sand the surface to finish smoothness, and remove the wood from the faceplate.

Drill a pilot hole in the newly made center, and mount the wood on the faceplate. For a short distance from the edge toward the center, cut away the waste wood, leaving ⅜-inch over-all thickness. Now cut accurately two offset grooves: the first, ¹⁄₁₆ inch deep with diameter of 3¾ inches; the second, 3½ inches in diameter with a depth approximately three-fourths the thickness of the glass rim. Observe on the drawing that the shoulder on which the glass rests is angled to correspond closely to the glass contour, Photo 39. The remaining one-fourth of the glass displacement will be cut into the retaining ring later. To complete the main ring, form a bead over the edge, leaving enough flat face surface to seat the retaining-ring overlap. Sand with coarse and fine paper from the groove cut over the bead to meet front sanding.

To part the ring completely from waste, set the lathe at its lowest speed. Pencil in a diameter to match exactly the inside ring measurement you determined and noted when turning the first side. With the parting tool, cut slowly on this line. As the wood becomes thinner, the tool makes a different sound, which is a warning to be ready for complete severance. Grip the tool firmly: otherwise the ring may bind and break. Remove waste wood from the lathe center.

Band-saw the 4⅛-inch square to a 4⅛-inch circle, and mount it on the faceplate. This will be the retaining ring. Turn it to match the corresponding face portion of the main ring (Photo 40). The considerable thickness of waste wood will be cut away when the turning is reversed. Make the outside diameter 4⅛ inches, inside the parting-tool cut to match that on the main ring. Turn a center mark for the reverse mounting. Sand to finish smoothness. Drill a pilot hole, and reverse the mount.

Study the drawing until you thoroughly understand this ring's function. Except for the center waste wood, turn the ring down to ³⁄₁₆-inch thickness. Pencil-mark a 3¾-inch diameter line. With the parting tool, cut outside this line to a depth equal to that of the groove in the main ring which will receive the resulting shoulder. Pencil-mark a 3½-inch diameter line. Inside this line, make a parting-depth cut somewhat less than the remaining one-fourth of the glass thickness (Photo 41).

A trial fitting may now be made (Photo 42). If the parts do not fit together perfectly, the error may be an oversized diameter shoulder which can be brought down to size with the parting tool. It is well to take this sizing process in stages—to avoid the danger of removing too much wood. When the parts have been fitted as in Photo 43, measure the glass channel accurately. Compare the opening with the glass thickness, and, if necessary, cut the retaining ring deeper and angle it to the glass contour for a neat fit. Photos 42 and 43 show a paper-thin edge of wood left on the ring when it is separated from the waste center. Repeat the severance process, to release the retaining ring.

Work on the handle next, first drawing its outline on stencil paper. (A scaled block outline is shown on page 33 to help in this.) Cut the paper to shape with scissors, then place the pattern on the 5½-by-2-inch block, and pencil-mark this. Saw the block to the pencil line on the jig saw (Photo 44—which also shows the handle pattern). Already a tenon for joining the handle and the ring has been cut to length and width, but not to thickness. Two radius lines show on the drawing, the larger one representing the outside ring diameter; the other, ³⁄₁₆ inch farther in to the center, should be drawn on the handle blank, to permit channeling to ³⁄₁₆-inch depth for firm ring seating. Tenon thickness of ⅛ inch is shown on the drawing (handle, side view) and is placed in the center of the handle thickness.

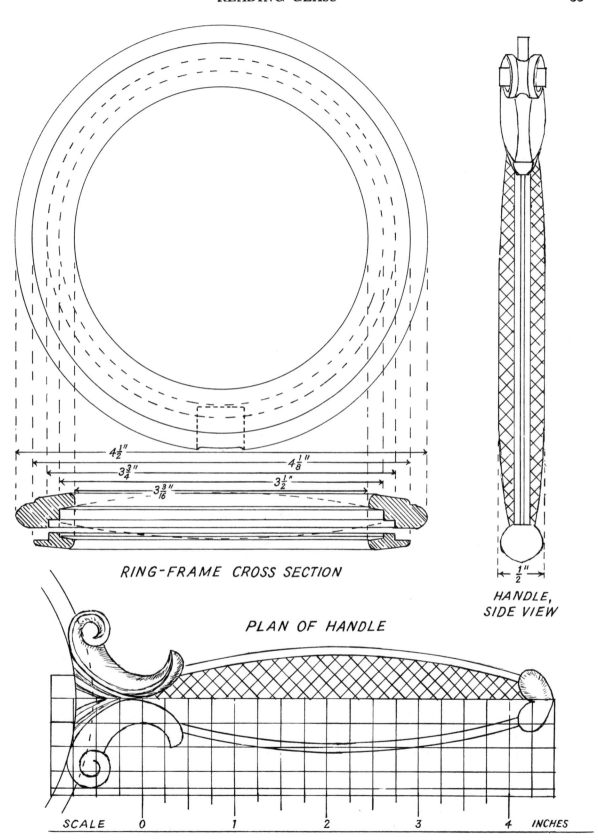

$4\frac{1}{2}''$

$4\frac{1}{8}''$

$3\frac{3}{4}''$

$3\frac{1}{2}''$

$3\frac{3}{16}''$

RING-FRAME CROSS SECTION

PLAN OF HANDLE

HANDLE,
SIDE VIEW

$\frac{1}{2}''$

SCALE   0   1   2   3   4   INCHES

Now cut a receiving slot in the main ring for the tenon. Scribe a line along the center of the ring thickness, ½ inch long. Drill a series of ⅛-inch holes completely through (Photo 45). Check the drill alignment for each hole. This is rather small work and you should take sufficient time for a satisfactory job. With a small chisel, complete the slot by cutting the sides in to a straight line.

Now cut the tenon to fit the ring slot by marking the top first with a center line then with one on each side for a total width of ⅛ inch. To avoid confusion, we will call the face sides of the handle front and back. Clamp the handle firmly on the bench with the front side up. Chop down vertically with No. 3 gouge on the inner radius line, and alternate with sloping cuts for tool clearance. Cut this shoulder to a depth that will join the finished tenon thickness. Repeat, on the back face. Grip the handle upright in the vise, and remove the tenon waste wood with a ¾-inch chisel. Keep a uniform thickness from top to bottom.

Now cut a ring-seating groove down to each edge of the tenon ³⁄₁₆ inch deep with the ¼-inch No. 11 gouge (Photo 46). This flute is to follow closely the same radius as that of the ring diameter. Frequent ring fittings are necessary for a satisfactory job. This means that, as the flute cut deepens, wood paralleling each long side of the tenon must be removed to form a continuous unobstructed groove (except for the tenon). For maximum strength when assembled, strive for a perfect fit. (Photo 47.)

Pencil in scrolls and tails (Photo 46). Clamp the piece firmly on the bench before carving the scrolls. Use appropriate gouges, held vertically, and part the wood on the pencil lines. Follow the same procedure as in all relief cutting; that is, follow each vertical parting cut with a sloping tool-clearance cut. From a high scroll center make a series of downward spiraling cuts, comparable to a miniature winding automobile ramp (Photo 48). The low point of the spiral is closest to the ring flute. From there the gradually rising edge swings into the long tail curve, reaching the high point where the two tails meet. The lower left scroll in Photo 48 has been cut thus far, and the upper right is in the forming process.

Still regarding the spiral as a ramp, bank the inner half of the road bed toward the inside curve (Photo 49). At the spiral base the banking slope broadens to take in the tail's full width. From the scroll base to the meeting of the tails, the highest point is the extreme outer edge of the curve. Now the ridge gradually swings over to what may be called the "middle of the road," which at the same time slopes down from the highest point to the tail's tip. The scroll side of the ridge is slightly concave; the opposite side, convex. Study Photo 49, noticing the rough relief cuts that border the tails to permit completion of the scroll carving. Now cut in relief the heart at the handle tip. Cut the back surface in like manner. Photo 49 shows a small penciled X between the scrolls, which corresponds to one marked on the front side of the ring.

Vise-grip the handle in convenient position for continuing around the scroll edge the flute cut started as a seat for the ring. (This cut also shows on Photo 49.) Even though the cut is much shallower, ¼-inch No. 11 is the tool to use.

Crown the front and back handle surfaces with a No. 3 gouge carefully, so that only light tool marks remain—leaving about ¹⁄₁₆ inch of edge wood untouched. Form the heart tip by making convex cuts with a small No. 3 gouge, heel up. Pencil in longitudinal border lines about ⅛ inch from the untouched edges, front and back. Using Photo 50 as a guide, cut to these lines with the ⅛-inch No. 41 tool. Now draw tangent lines about ³⁄₁₆ inch apart from top to tip, first from the right, then from the left, so that a diamond pattern results. With the veiner, carefully cut to these lines from one border cut to the other.

Photo 50 shows the smooth triangular recessed area between the scrolls, which now must be veined. With a ⅛-inch veiner, make four V cuts, two each from the right and the left of center. This work should be done before assembly. Photo 51 shows the final trial fitting and touch-up cuts with the veining tool to complete the carving. Here also the retaining ring has been laid casually on the frame. Sand the handle first with No. 3/0, and then with a No. 7/0 rub-off.

Coat the tenon and the ring slot with glue. Assemble the parts carefully, and firmly seat the ring on the handle. Allow overnight drying. Photo 52, a side-angle view, emphasizes the points that require careful attention. Notice also that the crown and diamond grip has been finished on one surface only. The views in Photos 53 and 54 show the frame ready for the finishing materials. Do not insert the glass and glue retaining ring permanently until all finishing materials have been applied. Before staining, press the retaining ring tightly in place without glue, and proceed in the usual manner. After material application, remove the retaining ring. Place the glass in the frame, glue-coat the ring shoulder, make a thin glue line on the overlap surface, and press in place. A weight evenly distributed over the entire ring for overnight pressure is recommended.

38

39

40

41

42

43

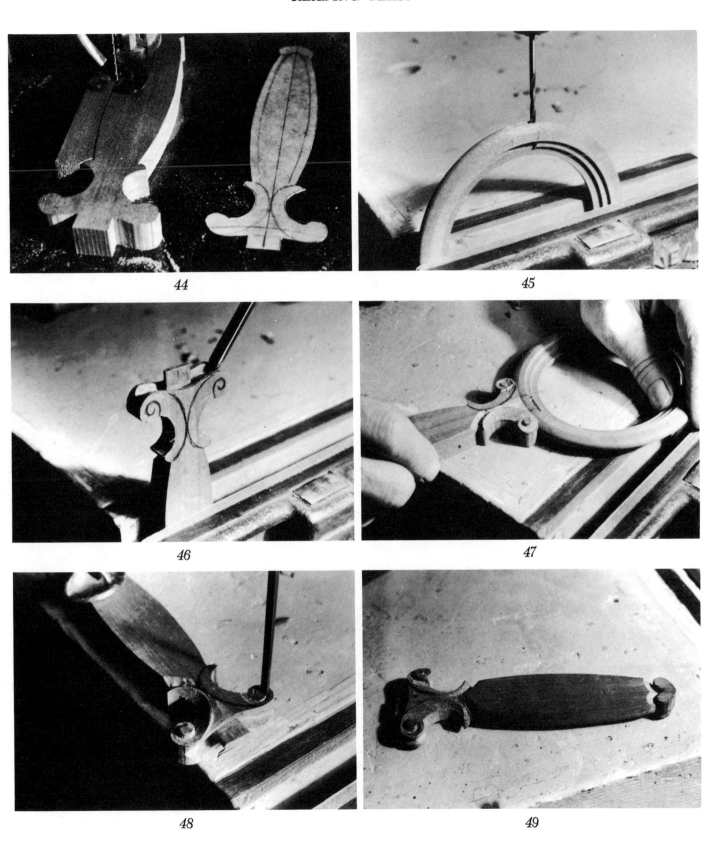

44

45

46

47

48

49

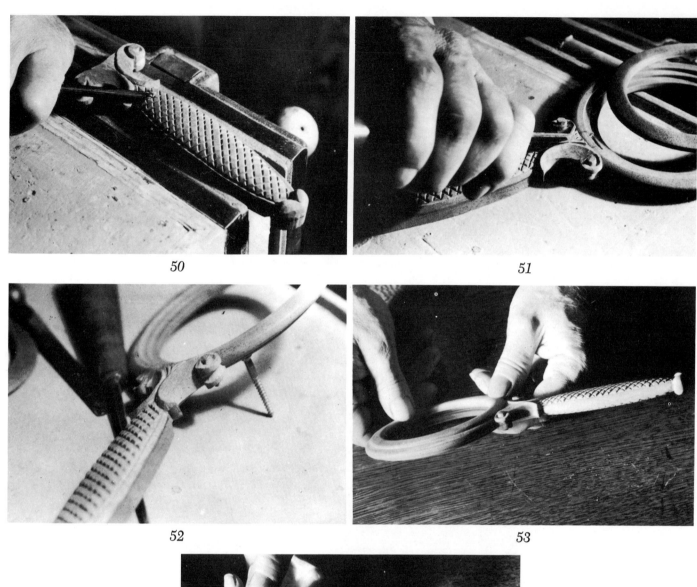

50

51

52

53

54

Cigarette Box

Materials

MAHOGANY

> 2 pieces, 9 inches by 4½ inches by ⅜ inch.
> 2 pieces, 9 inches by 2⅞ inches by ⅜ inch.
> 2 pieces, 4½ inches by 2⅞ inches by ⅜ inch.
> Wall liners, ⅛ inch thick.
> Divisions, 1/16 inch thick.
> Plastic: 2 pieces, 8¼ inches by 3¾ inches by 1/16 inch.
> Hinges: 1 pair, ¾ inch, narrow brass butts.

The cigarette box has become popular in recent years as an item of home décor. Boxes of various styles and prices may be purchased; but in many respects they are of a tiresome sameness. Illustrated in the following pages is a box of unquestionable distinction, with a pleasing geometric design ideally suited to the amateur craftsman. Except for the interlaced hearts, straight-line carving is the simplest style encountered in this book.

A word of advice prefacing instructions: Use, if available, a hollow-ground combination saw blade. It will give much cleaner sawed surfaces, especially across the grain. If the milling cuts are done accurately, assembly will not be troublesome.

Prepare side, top, and bottom panels of uniform ⅜-inch thickness. *All edges of these pieces are mitered to 45 degrees.* Cut the parts to the following sizes, with the saw tilted to 45 degrees (Photo 55): top and bottom, 9 by 4½ inches; ends, 4½ by 2⅞ inches; front and back, 9 by 2⅞ inches. Take extreme care when sizing to length, so that a true right-angle will result.

Next, leave the saw arbor set on 45 degrees, but change the blade to one making the thinnest cut: 1/16 inch is ideal. Study Photo 56. This set-up is calculated to slot all edges for splines. Set the ripping fence so that the blade will enter the mitered edges ⅛ inch from the panel's inside surface. Adjust the blade height for about ⅛-inch depth of slot. When the set-up is accurately made, slot all edges of every piece.

For splines, choose scrap mahogany—short ends but as wide as possible. Cut these scraps for resaw to convenient lengths (with the grain) about 1¼ inches. Set up the hollow-ground saw to resaw strips that will fit snugly into the slots. The importance of this milling cannot be overemphasized, nor can that of the next operation—sawing strips to length. Their length must be slightly less than the combined depth of two slots when placed for joining. Do not place strips nearer to corners than ¼ inch. Strips of this size are thin enough to break for desired widths. Photo 57 shows a top, front, and end panel ready for assembly. A spline strip has been introduced casually into a slot of the front panel. One also is pressed into the end panel so that it can be checked for size.

Spline stripping for one slot may be in any number of pieces. Use a slow-setting glue if possible. In preparation for gluing, shave the end of a stick so that it will fit easily into the slots. First coat all four slots of the bottom panel with glue. Next coat the lower half of the spline strips and introduce them into the prepared slots. Now coat the mitered edges and the protruding splines of the box bottom. Glue the end slots of the back panel, and introduce the splines; coat the bottom slot of the back panel; glue the end and bottom miters of the back panel; place them in position on the bottom panel. Do not press down tightly, because the sides must be manipulated in fitting the top into position. Repeat with the front panel. No splines are necessary in the end panels; therefore, coat with glue first the slots, then the end and bottom mitered surfaces. Place these in position. To prepare the top panel, follow the box bottom instructions. The upper slots and mitered surfaces of all four sides may now be coated with glue. Place the top panel in position; slant it outward slightly so that the sides and ends will allow the top splines to enter their receiving slots; press all parts together. Where necessary, apply clamp pressure for a closer fit. If an error has been made in milling, saw a tapered strip, coat it with glue, and tap it gently into the offending joint. Photo 58 shows the assembled box with clamps furnishing extra pressure where needed. Note: The lid will not be separated until all the carving is complete.

Refer to the drawing on page 41 for the stencil plan. A measurable time may be saved in pattern making by drawing only half of the panel width on stencil paper. Use scissors for the half-heart outline. Straight-line cuts are much sharper if made with a chisel. The pencil in Photo 59 is drawing in the interlaced lines of the heart on the box front. A separate pattern (not shown) is used for the upper design. Photo 60 shows all the lid design transferred, with the heart being filled in. No specific procedure is recommended for stenciling and carving. All surfaces may have their designs penciled in before carving; or each may be completed before another is started. Actual carving starts (Photo 61) with parting cuts made to the center of each triangle. Parting should be deepest in the center, where the three cuts meet. A mallet is not necessary. Division of the triangle with guide lines for parting is optional. The best tool for cutting triangles is the ½-inch No. 2. When parting, you will do well to place the forward point of the tool at the outer edge or at the inner edge, depending on the direction of the cut. To avoid changing position too often, cut one parting line in each triangle, choosing the more convenient direction of cut. Then shift position to cut the parting lines in the other direction. This suggestion may be applied to the next progressive cut—although, for illustrative purposes, Photo 62 shows triangles in various stages of completion. Some units of the design are only parted; others have been sliced down one side; still others, two sides. No. 2 chisel, having an angled cutting edge, slices the wood even when it is pushed straight ahead, and thus leaves a desirable glazed surface. Make tentative cuts on all three sides, lifting the waste wood which allows tool clearance for another, deeper cut. Continue until each plane meets its adjoining two. Experiments on a piece of scrap wood will determine the approximate angle at which to hold the tool. The deepest point of large triangles is about ⅛ inch. A uniform tool slant should be maintained on all triangles, large and small.

Heart designs should first have their outlines cut with the small No. 41 veiner. Follow with parting cuts (No. 2 chisel) as indicated in Photo 63 and the drawing on page 41. When forming heart-design depressions, follow the triangle technique. Photo 63 illustrates the lid with all triangles cut, the heart being carved, and two corners of the rectangle still uncut.

To complete the carving, use the small veiner tool to separate all design components (Photo 64). Sand only the uncut flat surfaces. Remove any sharp corners with sandpaper. Check all panels for cuts that may have been overlooked. The completely carved box is shown in Photo 64.

To separate the lid from the box, use a hollow-ground saw with a ¾-inch fence setting. Saw

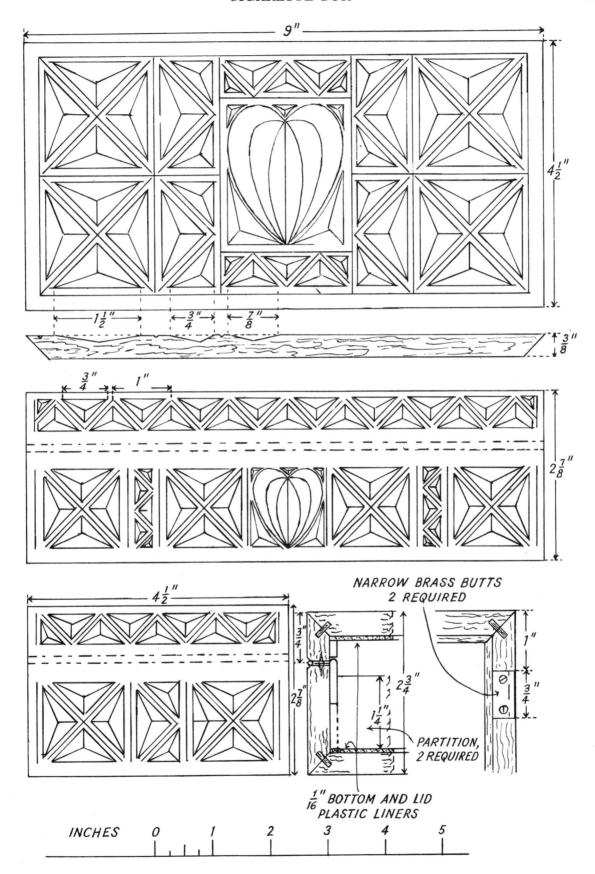

through all four sides (Photo 65). Sand the newly sawed surfaces, using a cork block covered with No. 3/0 sandpaper. A simple milling operation eliminates the necessity for metal lid supports when the box is opened. Cut a small, uniform chamfer (Photo 66) on the back edge of both the lid and the box. If the hinges are properly mounted (protruding slightly past the outside back surface) the chamfers will meet when lid is just past perpendicular. Photo 69 shows chamfers plainly.

If a ¾-inch dado head is part of the shop equipment, set it up to cut for hinges 1 inch in from the sides. Cut to a depth exactly half the thickness of the hinge when closed. (For the cut-outs to be made in both box and lid, see Photo 67.) In order to fit hinges without the use of a dado, two setups are necessary. Set the saw to 1 inch from the sides, raised to cut the proper depth. Set the fence for the second cut 1¾ inches from the sides. Intervening wood may be removed by a number of passes over the saw or with hand tools.

Photo 68 shows hinge mounting. It is done at this time only for trial purposes. The hinge should be removed when the cutouts and the hinge position have been checked.

For the box with interior completed, see Photo 69, which shows the supporting chamfers plus lid-carving detail from another angle.

Prepare sufficient wood for side liners, ⅛ inch thick. Cut strips in width to exactly the inside height of the box sides. When fitted on top of the 1⁄16-inch plastic bottom liner they will extend 1⁄16 inch above the box sides, acting as a seal when the lid is closed. Round the top edges of the strips with sandpaper. Also saw from ⅛-inch wood, strips ¼ inch wide to fit over the plastic liner in the lid. Do not round the edges of these pieces. Miter the ends of all four side pieces (Photo 70) to fit neatly into the box. While the saw is set for mitering, cut to length the ¼-inch strips to fit inside the lid.

Now divide the length of front and back strips into three equal parts. At the two division points saw slots (thickness of the saw in width) ¾ inch high. (Check with Photo 71 and the drawing detail on page 41.) Their purpose will be apparent in the next few photographs.

Now that the slots are ready for the division pieces, resaw wood to a thickness that, when sanded, will fit neatly into the previously sawed slots. Saw these pieces to 1¼-inch width, and round the top edges. Square the ends to fit from front to back inside the box. Attach to the cross cut gauge a stop block set to cut shoulders ⅛ inch wide (the thickness of side liners) by ½ inch high. When turned upright, this leaves full-length wood ¾ inch high to match slots (Photo 72).

All liner milling is now completed. Sand the exposed surfaces of these parts before trial assembly. Sanding the division pieces should be necessary before they will slide into the slots as prescribed. Photo 73 illustrates all liner parts for the box.

Make a trial assembly, seeing that the front and back liners are not held away from the bottom by division strip shoulders (Photo 74). Check the division strip lengths making sure that they will not bind when placed in the box (Photo 75).

For photographic purposes the lid is here attached (Photo 76); but it will be much more convenient to line both box and lid while they are separate. The photograph shows the plastic liners being seated in the lid and box. Before insertion, remove all chips and dust from surfaces to be covered with plastic.

For practical reasons, the directions and photographs will continue uninterrupted. However, an important point should be brought out: For neatness and a professional appearance, apply all finishing materials to the box, and finish the liner parts, before gluing them in place. If application of finishing materials is attempted after the lining is installed, a neat finishing job is nearly impossible.

Start lining the box first by spotting the inside back surface with glue (not too heavily) at about three places. Place the back liner in position. Introduce the division strips in their approximate position. Spot the front surface with glue. This liner must be slid into position vertically, because of division shoulders. Next, spot the end surfaces, and slide the parts into place. When lining the lid, coat strips lightly with glue instead of the lid sides Press them into place and, if necessary, clamp them with spring or small C clamps until the glue has set.

If the finish was applied before lining, the box will be complete after hinge installation.

55

56

57

58

59

60

61

62

63

64

65

66

67

68

69

70

71

72

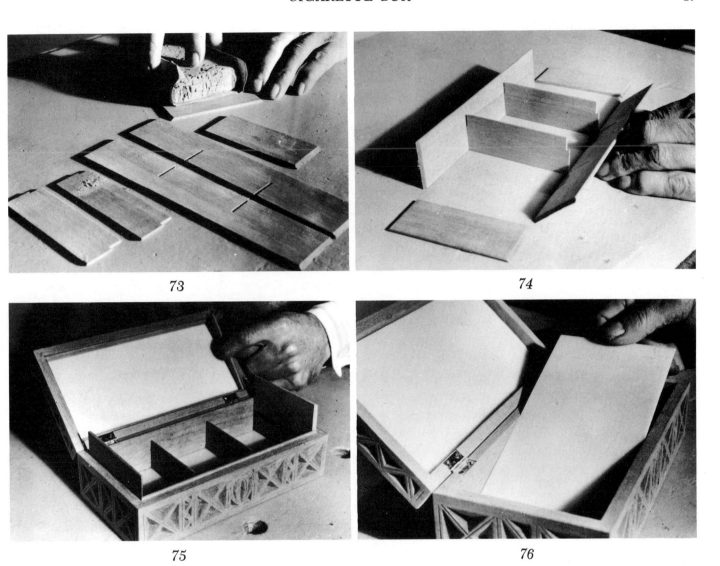

73

74

75

76

Portrait Frames

Materials

MAHOGANY

12 lineal feet, 1 inch by $^{11}\!/_{16}$ inch thick.
2 pieces, 4¼ inches by 2 inches by ¾ inch.
Hardware: 2 Soss invisible hinges, No. 100, 1 inch by ⅜ inch.
3 back panels, ⅛-inch tempered Masonite.

Modern home furnishings include 8-by-10-inch portrait frames, articles that were unknown before photography developed into a fine art. With no originals to copy, an effective design is suggested in this chapter. A chain of modified acanthus leaves is the featured decoration. Rope borders and stippled background complete the pattern.

It is assumed that a single and a double frame are to be made. First, check the drawing for the number of frame pieces and their dimensions. Saw the stock to 1 inch wide by $^{11}\!/_{16}$ inch thick: miter the ends to exact drawing lengths. Saw a groove in each end of every piece (width of saw blade) ⅜ inch deep. Saw splines to fit grooves snugly, with the grain running the short way. Saw one rabbet in each frame part for glass and picture, and another for the back panel (cross section drawing). Assemble without glue, to check the milling. Disassemble. For the double frame unit, choose two stiles (long upright pieces); carefully place them in right and left positions, and mark them for hinge mortises $^{15}\!/_{16}$ inch and $1^{15}\!/_{16}$ inches up from the bottom on the outside edges. Now measure down from the top, on the same edges, 1¼ inches and 2¼ inches. Scribe a line between the marks, $^{5}\!/_{16}$ inch in from the front edge. This measurement must be exact. The mortises are cut before carving, while a straight corner line remains from which to measure. Measure $^{3}\!/_{16}$ inch on the scribed line from each mark for the center of a ⅜-inch bit. Punch the centers with an awl. Bore each of these center points exactly ¼ inch deep. Between holes, bore another hole in each mortise, ½ inch deep, and cut away the waste wood for a straight-side wall line.

Mark the face of every frame part with sectional division lines, as in the drawing on page 49. Draw border lines for the ropes ⅛ inch from the inner and outer edges, the entire length of every piece. On stencil paper or other suitable material, draw the two leaf designs for patterns. Cut the pattern to the outline. Holding the center leaf pattern in the middle of each upper and lower frame part, start guide lines for carving. Place the repeat leaf pattern *properly and with care* (study the segment drawing) in a section next to the center, and mark. Turn the pattern over sidewise, place it in the following section, and mark. Repeat, to the end of the frame member. Mark in like manner all other top and bottom parts. When marking the stiles, place them in their upright position in pairs; compare the division lines with the segment drawing, start the chain-leaf design in the correct section, direction and proper side up. Rights will be opposite to lefts in the initial marking. Start with the first full section from the bottom.

Photo 77 illustrates in detail a right-hand stile. Note the spline groves in each end, the mortises

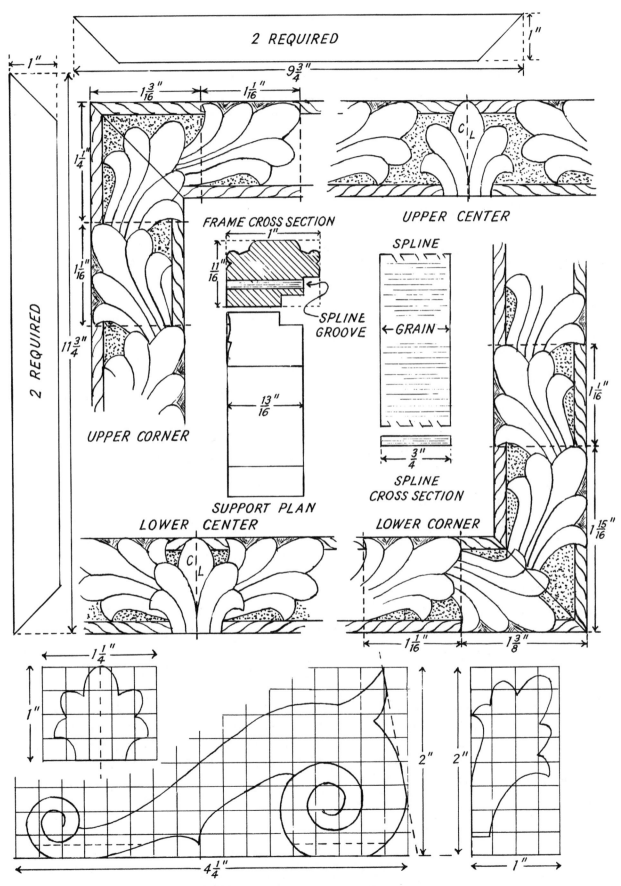

2 REQUIRED

1"

9 3/4"

1"

1 3/16"   1 1/16"

1 1/4"

C L

UPPER CENTER

1 1/16"

2 REQUIRED

11 3/4"

FRAME CROSS SECTION

1"

1 11/16"

SPLINE GROOVE

13/16"

SPLINE

← GRAIN →

3/4"

SPLINE CROSS SECTION

1 1/16"

1 15/16"

UPPER CORNER

SUPPORT PLAN

LOWER CENTER

C L

LOWER CORNER

1 1/16"   1 3/8"

1 1/4"

1"

2"

2"

1"

4 1/4"

PROJECT FOR PATTERNS

for hinges, and the fully marked face. Scribbled lines over the design at mortises are warnings not to carve too deeply in these sections. A repeat leaf pattern lies directly behind the stile.

Three frame parts illustrated in Photo 78 are, a top rail, a left stile with spline temporarily inserted, and a lower rail gripped in the vise. Tools were selected for width and curve to make parting outline cuts shown on the left side of each piece. Three different tools were used to complete the long S curves. Outline cuts are made by holding the tool in a vertical position on the design line, and tapping it once or twice with a mallet. Close scrutiny of Photo 78 reveals how the wood breaks away when short, close, edge cuts are made. This is waste wood, and so the breakage is unimportant. Breaks in the wood at the mitered edges, however, are to be avoided by discontinuing outline cuts about ½ inch from the edges. The corners are carved after the frame is assembled with glue, when one miter supports the other.

In the removal of the background wood to a depth of $\frac{3}{32}$ inch, a common mistake was made and photographed (Photo 79): a leaf tip was flicked off by pushing the ¼-inch No. 3 gouge a little too far, through carelessness (detached piece lying on leaf). Complete control of the tool should be maintained at all times. After photographing, the broken leaf tip was immediately glued in place and the frame part laid aside for a time (a good habit to acquire with unintentional cuts of this kind).

Background wood should be removed with care. Uniform depth and evenness lessen the difficulty encountered when rope cutting and stippling occur in their proper order.

Choose the ½-inch No. 3 gouge for leaf-surface relief (Photo 80). Start the gradual, downward cut about half the leaf's length, ending slightly higher than background depth. The central leaf on each lower rail is allowed to remain flat because the chain design, on each side, appears to spring from under it. On the top rails, the leaf's isolation creates no need for relief.

Now contoured, the leaf surfaces are ready for rib lines. Draw free hand, on every leaf, lines corresponding to those of the drawing. Used simply as guides, these lines need not be perfectly spaced nor curved. After the first few leaves are cut, smooth, flowing motions of wrist and arms will develop, to the point that guide lines may be unnecessary. From the group of tools, select No. 41, ⅛ inch. If this is sharpened properly, it will make the shallow cuts with ease. Part the ribs from leaf tip to next overlapping leaf. The tool must stop abruptly at this point, leaving a projection of waste wood—immediate removal is unnecessary. Cuts that are uneven in depth result from insufficient practice with the tool, and improvement will probably result if they are recut (Photo 81).

Study closely two frame parts in Photo 82. A top rail has all the ribs rounded, while a left stile (gripped in the vise) has the next operation added. To proceed with rib rounding, select ¼-inch No. 3. Depending on the direction of grain and the curve of rib, the tool's heel may be used up or down. Try it, reversing the direction of any cut you have started that tends to split deeply into the wood. Positive directions cannot be given for this operation, because you will encounter various grain patterns. General objectives include: changing flat-rib surfaces to rounded form; rounding rib tips.

The leaves have now lost much of their sharpness, temporarily. Rounding the ribs has lessened the apparent depth of division cuts; and waste wood projections at the leaf overlaps increase this sense of loss. To restore the sharp look, recut rib lines slightly deeper than they were originally divided, using ⅛-inch No. 41. Cut again leaf outlines where they lap over the next leaf in succession. To remove projections and clean out deep rib division ends, use a ⅛-inch or $\frac{3}{16}$-inch No. 1 chisel.

Hold the tool on a slant laterally, directly over the division, and press it. If necessary, lateral rocking motions may be used while exerting pressure.

To simulate curled tips, central ribs of leaves are cut in the following manner: Close to the outside edge and nearly parallel with frame line, cut a short ¼-inch No. 11 channel (an example can be seen in Photo 82, extreme left leaf). Follow with ¼-inch No. 3 heel up, molding the inside edge of channel into a long slope, and thus giving that leaf part the appearance of a gradual twist ending in a quick curl. Two light veins in this depression complete the leaf carving.

Background surfaces may now be marked with a pencil, ⅛ inch in from all edges, for rope carving. The right stile held in a vise (Photo 83) is marked, and parting with ⅛-inch No. 41 has partially taken place for illustrative purposes. Note the curl midway on the inside edge. The parting tool was stopped here, and the curl allowed to remain for the photograph. Held by hand, No. 41 is parting the top surface between leaves for eventual rope molding. After all the parts have been processed to this stage, surface background can be sloped in relief to the rope's edge. Most areas being small, ⅛-inch No. 3 will serve for this operation. Light, bevel cuts by ¼-inch No. 3, heel up, will remove each of three distinct corner projections from the rope mold, forming reasonably round surfaces for subsequent cuts.

At this time, the two supports for the single frame (Photo 83) can be explained in the order of operations. Make a pattern to the dimensions on the drawing; mark the outline in pencil on wood of ¾- or 1³⁄₁₆-inch thickness; band- or jig-saw to shape; sand the sawed edges; choose different gouges for parting scrolls, and proceed as directed for leaves (support to the right in the photo); rough out the relief of the scrolls by sloping the surface to the parting cut; make the parting deeper; finish the scroll relief; chamfer as indicated on the left support and the one shown in Photo 87— inside curves concave with No. 3, outside curves convex with No. 3, heel up. Where a double curve is encountered, the change from concave to convex is gradual. The left support has been bored, and a ³⁄₁₆-inch dowel introduced. The supports are fastened at the top by brass wood screws just under the small scrolls.

Check the rope-twist direction on the drawing and the photographs before starting this operation. Make frequent checks with Photo 88 for twist direction as work on the different frame parts proceeds, because it is easy to err in direction. Observation will show the outside rope twist is opposed to the inside, and is also opposed when starting from either side of central leaf on the bottom rail.

Again using ⅛-inch No. 41, start as though the twist is just emerging parallel to the rope direction. Cut slowly, swinging the tool more and more sidewise until the highest surface of the rope is reached. Reverse for the downward half: swing the tool the other way until parallel with rope—here the strands seem to twist out of sight. Repeat at about ⅛-inch intervals. An attempt to round each strand would be tedious and ineffective. Photo 84 illustrates a left stile, rope partly cut.

A stippling tool suitable for this operation (Photo 85) is an ordinary screw driver that has a blade ³⁄₁₆ inch wide, filed with an extra slim tapered file. Two V cuts leave three stippling points standing. File short bevels on the blade sides to bring them to a sharp ridge; short-bevel the blade edges to complete a three-point pyramidic tool.

Hold the tool vertically, and tap it once with a mallet hard enough to make a sharp, clear indentation. Move the tool, and tap it again. Repeat. Carefully, first stipple the outline of an area, then indent the center. As you lift the tool, turn it slightly to break possible directional lines.

The back of single frame, glued together, is shown in Photo 86. Note the spline extensions in opposite corners. To remove them, chop down vertically with the chisel; slant the next cut to make clearance for another vertical cut, and continue until you have cut completely through. Be sure no waste wood protrudes to interfere with the glass.

Because of grain direction, the chisels must start the removal of spline extensions on the outside at the corner, cutting toward the frame. Notice the hole, accurately placed to align support. This fastening is called a "blind dowel" and can be marked easily for boring. Drive a thin brad (about ¼ inch) into the support where it meets the frame, and cut the brad with wire cutters to within ³⁄₃₂ inch of the support. Stand the frame upright, slanting it backward to the approximate angle of support. Move the support (in its proper position) up to the frame, and press together. The brad marks a center for boring. Extract it, and bore each piece with ³⁄₁₆-inch bit ³⁄₈ inch deep. Repeat the procedure in the other support. This photograph also illustrates an invisible hinge held over the mortise of a stile.

For convenience in mounting the portrait after the frame is finished, note the ¼-inch rabbet ⅛ inch deep on the inside flat portions of support (plan drawing, below the frame cross section). When the supports are mounted flush with the outside edge of the frame, the supports extend over the back panel grooves, necessitating clearance for the insertion of the glass, the portrait, and the back panel.

The treatment of leaf ends that extend to the edge of the frame is clearly shown in Photo 87. A No. 3 tool slopes each rib tip to a V-shaped depression approximating the depth of lower rope line. A trial attachment, without glue, of the support to the completed frame is illustrated. The finishing materials can be applied with much greater ease if the supports are finished separately. Attach the support to the frame with glue and screws as the last operation.

Reenact all step-by-step operations to carve the corners. Glued joints should remain undisturbed at least overnight, until they thoroughly harden. Study Photo 88, which shows a permanently assembled frame with two corners cut, two uncut. When all the corners have been cut the frames are complete and ready for finish, unless sanding is contemplated.

Back panels of ⅛-inch Masonite cut to fit neatly, with their edges sanded, and with holes bored for small brass screws, can be processed at any convenient time. For the details of wood finishing, see Chapter XI.

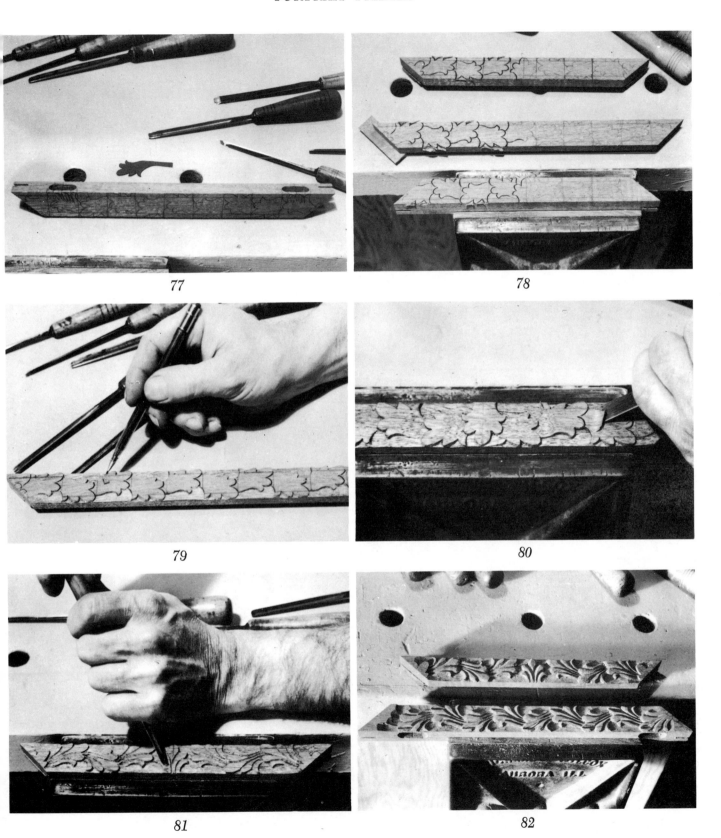

77

78

79

80

81

82

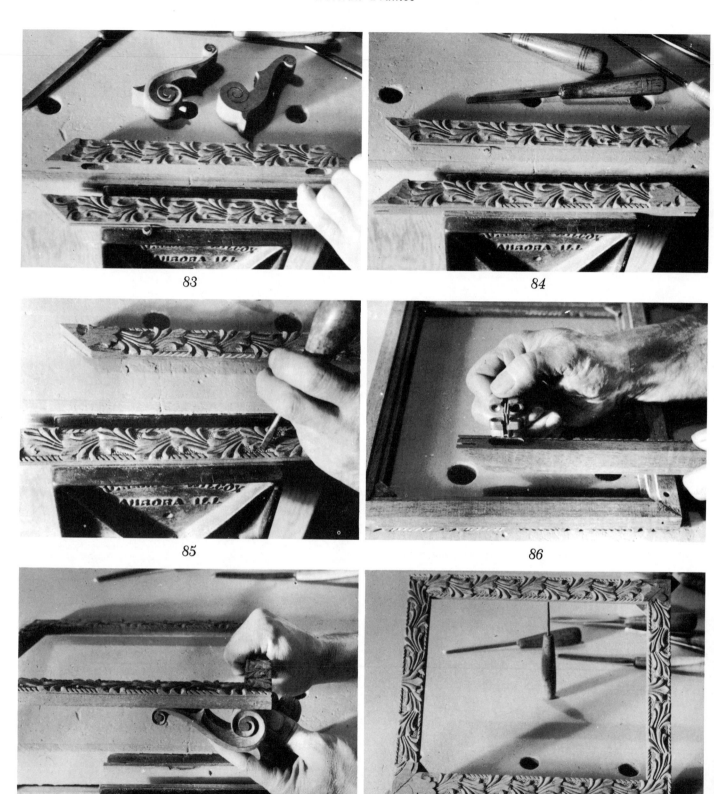

83

84

85

86

87

88

Rectangular Stool

CHAPTER IV

Rectangular Stool

PHILADELPHIA ORIGIN, 1730–1750

Materials

WALNUT

4 pieces, 2¾ inches by 2¾ inches by 17 inches.
2 pieces, 2⅝ inches by 18⅞ inches by ¹³⁄₁₆ inch.
2 pieces, 2⅝ inches by 13¼ inches by ¹³⁄₁₆ inch.
Upholstery covering: needlepoint, damask, or brocatelle, 23 by 17 inches.

A walnut stool from Philadelphia, where much of our valued furniture originated, has been selected for Chapter IV. In each period, stool design generally conformed in style to the front legs of chairs. This example has the Queen Anne characteristics. Graceful lines and simple, effective knee carving are features always in good taste. Web treatment on the spoon feet is a variation not ordinarily found around 1740.

Before construction is begun, a pattern must be made for the entire length of the legs. Patterns of this size may be made of any available material: Beaverboard, Masonite, plywood, or even solid wood, provided there is no warp or twist to cause difficulty when marking the leg blocks. For marking convenience, the material should be not more than ¼ inch thick.

As shown in the drawing on page 59, the pattern board is measured to size, 17 by 2¾ inches, then laid off in ½-inch squares to facilitate drawing the leg outline. (In Photo 89 a sample leg pattern has been laid out in ¼-inch blocks. The drawing calls for ½-inch squares, which take but half the time and are equally effective for this purpose.) Draw in the leg outline. Saw the board to size on band or jig saw to make the finished pattern.

Prepare four leg blocks 17 by 2¾ by 2¾ inches. Place the pattern first on the outside surface, and mark this with a sharp pencil. Turn the pattern over, and place it on the right-angle surface that will make both knee protrusions meet on the corner (illustrated on Photo 89). Mark in pencil. Repeat on the remaining three legs.

For the rail mortise, mark a center boring line with the scratch or marking gauge on each right-angle inside surface. Set the gauge to 1¼ inches, and mark from the inside corner. Bear in mind that the leg block will be band-sawed to 1¾ by 1¾ inches at the mortise area. A center boring line for a ⅜-inch bit, placed 1¼ inches from the inside corner, permits a ¹³⁄₁₆-inch rail to be milled thus: ⁵⁄₁₆-inch outside shoulder, ⅜-inch tenon and a ⅛-inch shoulder on the inside. For height, start the mortise ½ inch from the top of the leg. Pencil-mark the mortise end at 2⅝ inches from the top.

57

Photo 90 shows one inside surface bored for mortise, and the adjacent front surface marked to pattern outline for band sawing. Photo 91 illustrates the use of chisels for finishing the mortise to size. Shown here are the two inside surfaces bored for mortises. Mortising before band sawing is suggested so that the piece may be conveniently held for boring. The straight sides of the leg blocks provide good gripping surfaces for the vise; and if a drill press is used under blocking is not required for accurate alignment.

Band sawing to outline is the next operation. Study Photo 92, where one face side has been turned upward and sawed to the line. The method adopted here is to stop sawing before the waste piece is severed: back the saw out of the cut and repeat on other lines until the entire outline is sawed, but with waste wood still held in place by a small portion of uncut wood. This method makes it unnecessary to nail waste wood back in place. Shaping a cabriole leg is not at all difficult if you keep in mind the leg as it should look when completely sawed. In Photo 92 all the outlines have been sawed on the first face side. Remember, this includes not only one front profile but one back. If you fail to understand this important detail, only confusion will result when you attempt to reconcile in mind two surface cuts with four profiles. On the right-angle front surface may be seen the penciled outline for the next band-saw operation.

Turn the leg block over so that the second face side is up. The second cutting differs from the first in only one respect: waste wood is completely severed, because retention of penciled lines is no longer necessary. Photo 93 affords an excellent view of the operation. Notice the dark lines of the first cuts, stopping just short of completion, and the progress of the second cutting to the back profile. Waste wood from the front profile lies on the saw table opposite the leg.

After the second face side is cut, turn the leg back to its original position and sever the waste pieces of the first cut. Guide lines are no longer necessary, because the saw has so short a distance to travel. Photo 94 shows the result of work on the band saw. Waste wood lies close to the leg, for realism. Follow the same procedure with the remaining legs.

Prepare four rails: two of them $1\frac{3}{16}$ inch by $2\frac{5}{8}$ by $18\frac{7}{8}$ inches, and two $1\frac{3}{16}$ inch by $2\frac{5}{8}$ by $13\frac{1}{4}$ inches. On the ends, mill tenons $\frac{3}{8}$ inch by $\frac{7}{8}$ inch long, and place them as mentioned before, $\frac{5}{16}$-inch outside shoulder, $\frac{3}{8}$-inch tenon and $\frac{1}{8}$-inch inside shoulder. Rabbet the inside of the rail top edges $\frac{3}{8}$ by $\frac{3}{8}$ inch to receive a seat board. The upper part of the tenons alone must be removed to a depth of $\frac{1}{2}$ inch, so that they end $\frac{1}{8}$ inch below the seat-board rabbet. In final dimensions the tenons should match the leg mortises. Photo 95 illustrates a rail tenon entering a mortise.

Return now to the work on the legs which was interrupted to take up the seat rails. Follow Photo 96 by holding a leg upright to pencil-mark a spoon shape on the foot. It is a mere guide line, but one of importance inasmuch as the natural tendency is to draw the line in too close to the ankle. View the line in perspective, to be sure of a fairly true arc. Do the same with the remaining legs.

Hold a leg firmly between vise and bench stop-block (Photo 97). Chip away waste wood to the spoon-shaped line. Taper toward the bottom on a slight arc. Later photographs illustrate this detail clearly. Next, remove the square corner on the front and on each side with a No. 3 gouge. Because of grain direction, work from the foot toward the ankle (Photo 98). Sufficient waste wood should be cut away on the front corner to leave an unbroken spoon-rim line (check again with Photo 98). Each side corner is to be rounded; but cutting must be started at the point where the penciled spoon line meets the corner. Cut at first with a feather edge, gradually increasing the

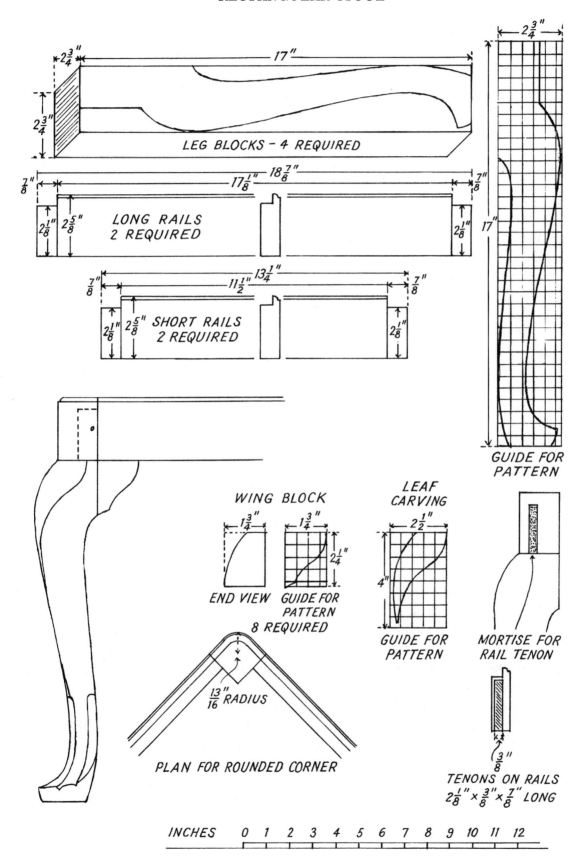

2¾"

17"

LEG BLOCKS - 4 REQUIRED

2¾"

2¾"

17"

GUIDE FOR PATTERN

⅞"   17⅛"   18⅞"   ⅞"

LONG RAILS
2 REQUIRED

2⅛"   2⅝"   2⅛"

⅞"   11½"   13¼"   ⅞"

2⅛"   2⅝"   SHORT RAILS
2 REQUIRED   2⅛"

WING BLOCK

1¾"   1¾"

2¼"

END VIEW   GUIDE FOR
PATTERN
8 REQUIRED

LEAF CARVING

2½"

4"

GUIDE FOR
PATTERN

MORTISE FOR
RAIL TENON

13/16" RADIUS

PLAN FOR ROUNDED CORNER

⅜"

TENONS ON RAILS
2⅛" × ⅜" × ⅞" LONG

INCHES   0 1 2 3 4 5 6 7 8 9 10 11 12

depth of cut approximately to a ¼-inch radius. A taper on each side increases the spoon flair so necessary for pleasing proportion (Photo 98).

With a drawknife, remove saw marks from all band-sawed surfaces (Photo 99). Include in this operation rounding the back corner of each leg to a ¼-inch radius as far as the ankle. From there to the foot end, the radius increases to about ¾ inch. Do not use the drawknife, or round any corners on front surfaces above the knee, at this time. Round the front corner on each leg from the knee to the ankle, and each side corner from a point below the wing-block attachment line to the ankle. With a No. 3 gouge, blend the conjunction of drawknife and gouge cuts into a smooth flowing line (Photo 100).

Measure from foot end upward 4½ inches, and mark for web ending. Draw in web division guide lines. Space the lines as indicated on Photo 101, the center section being the widest at the spoon rim. As the lines continue up the leg, they become equidistant.

A long-bend No. 42 veiner serves especially well in this web dividing job. Divide it as illustrated in Photo 102. Use of a mallet on the tool handle for first rough cuts will probably give better control in following the lines. Cut them approximately ⅛ inch deep.

To sink alternate webs, select a No. 3 gouge and start cutting at the spoon rim. Cut to the full depth at the division or side lines, less deep toward the centers. Results show pronounced convex surfaces at the rims. As cutting proceeds to the ankles, gradually flatten the surfaces to full uniform depth. Because of grain direction, cutting must be reversed at a variable point on each leg (Photo 103). Round the top of each raised web with a No. 5 or No. 7 gouge, chopping vertically and cutting away the wood above it for relief. Wood removal, even though of slight depth, must continue up the leg two inches more or less, tapering off so that the cabriole curve will not be deformed.

Photo 104 is a close-up of all tool work completed. All band-saw marks have been removed from the raised center vein with a No. 3 gouge. Sandpaper requires much less effort for obliteration of gouge marks than for removal of saw marks. Before sanding, resurface the side veins in like manner.

Sand first the sunken webs, touching and smoothing the edges of the raised veins (Photo 105). Sand next the raised portions. Cover the sand block or cork with paper to smooth the wood below the spoon rims. Strokes should be made with the grain and in an arc motion to follow the curve of the portion sanded.

Next, with the cork and paper, sand the legs from the webs to the knees, including rounded corners. Caution: Do not dull the sharp corners to which the wing blocks will be attached. So far, sanding instructions have applied only to the leg fronts. The two back surfaces of each leg have uninterrupted curves from bottom to wing attachment points that make special instructions unnecessary. Sanding only with No. ½ paper at this time is preferable. Should slight marks appear on the sanded surfaces later, sanding with No. 3/0 on completion will remove them.

Assemble the legs and rails without glue, to be sure of perfect joinery. Separate the parts for final assembly. Hold together two legs, with end-rail mortises upward. Coat all mortise surfaces with glue. Coat the tenons of one end rail with glue. Assemble and draw tight with a bar clamp. Glue the other end, and clamp it. Taking first one end assembly, glue the side-rail mortises; then do the same with the other end. Next coat all tenons on the two side rails. Assemble all parts into one unit. Turn the stool upside down on the work table; place clamps spanning the two clamps that hold the end assemblies, and draw them tight (Photo 106). Turn the stool upright, and check it with a large square. Should any adjustment be necessary, shift off parallel either one or both of the last placed clamps. Allow the glue to harden overnight.

Remove clamps. Bore ³⁄₁₆-inch or ¼-inch holes about an inch deep through the joints for pins (Photo 107). Coat the holes with glue, and drive in dowel pins precut to 1¼ inches long.

Set a compass to 1³⁄₁₆-inch radius, and mark the top of all four legs as illustrated in Photo 108. Reset the compass to ⁷⁄₁₆-inch radius, and, using the same center, scribe another quarter-circle inside the 1³⁄₁₆-inch for the seat board insert line.

Before shaping the outside radii with hand tools as illustrated in Photo 109, hand-saw a quarter-circle at the juncture of each knee and rail line. These saw cuts, approximating the outer scribed lines on the leg tops, will allow chips from the rounding process to fall free when parted the full distance. Because of varying grain direction, it may be necessary to chip off the waste wood from the knee upward.

To continue the seat board depth line over the leg tops, clamp the tool firmly to the bench top (Photo 110). Chop across grain with ½-inch chisel and mallet to the depth of rail rabbet as illustrated in the photograph. Remove waste wood by small bites rather than wide, thick cuts. This method lessens the resistance, and the shock to the joints with each mallet blow. Chop to the actual depth required, but only roughly to the side lines. Place the stool in an upright position and finish the cutouts with a chisel (on the straight lines) and appropriate gouge for the curves.

Mill eight wing blocks, sized to 1¾ by 1¾ inches by 2¼ inches long. Hold each in place (Photo 111), square with the bottom of the rail and flush with the outward curvature of the knee. Mark the knee curve on the block in pencil. Because of possible band-saw variation when shaping the legs originally, number each block and its intended leg surface. Band-saw all blocks to these pencil lines. Next, hold each block in place (matching numbers), and draw a line continuing the leg curve over onto the wing block (Photo 112). Individual marking of each block at this point is also advisable because of original band-saw variation.

Make a pattern of stencil board for the wing block outline. A guide for this pattern is on the drawing on page 59. Mark each wing block on the front surface, holding the pattern parallel to the edge that will be glued to the leg. As shown in Photo 113, the pattern should meet the continuing leg line previously marked on the wing block. There are four right-hand and four left-hand blocks.

Match numbers and glue blocks to the legs. Clamps cannot be used because of the block's shape, and therefore they must be rubbed on in the following manner. Apply preferably hot glue to the block surface only. Do not coat the leg surface nor the top block surface which will touch the rail. Press the block against the leg, moving it into position by short back-and-forth motions. When it seems to "catch," release all hand pressure. Repeat until all the blocks are attached. Allow overnight drying. Photo 114 illustrates wing blocks glued to one leg.

Remove any band-saw marks and any surface plane variation at the joint areas with a draw-knife. This tool will not cut entirely in to the juncture of knee and rail; the remainder must be worked with a No. 3 gouge (Photo 115). Note that the shoulder at the radius base has been left standing for convenience in pattern marking.

Follow the pattern layout drawing, page 59, when preparing for tongue-shaped knee carving. Enlarge the space blocks on the stencil board, draw in the outline, and cut with scissors. Place the pattern at the knee ridge of one leg, as shown in Photo 116. First, mark one side in pencil; then, reverse the pattern and mark the other side. Do the same with the other three legs. The dividing knee ridges may now be removed by rounding all knee surfaces to meet the rail corner radii.

Tongue carving may be completed on each leg before you proceed to the next. Start with a veiner tool No. 41 by parting the design outline. Note the right side of Photo 117. Note also the veiner part way up the left side. This cut may be deepened and leveled to a uniform depth when background wood is removed for relief purposes. Channel along the right and left sides with the ½-inch No. 11 gouge, leaving edges about ³⁄₃₂ inch wide. The gouge is shown on the right side of the carving, Photo 117. Cut away the inside wall of the channel on a gradual slope toward the tongue center. This is illustrated in Photo 118.

Relieve the carving by gently sloping the surrounding wood with a large No. 3 gouge (Photo 118). This will complete all tool work on the pilot leg. Complete the remaining three legs. Photo 119 pictures the knee carving finished and ready for sanding.

Top-edge molding is the final machine operation. If a shaper is not available for this work, a circular saw may be used. Then, because of knee overhang, a board about ¾ inch thick must be used in place of the higher saw-table fence (Photo 120). Place the board so that only the saw-blade width will cut the rails to a depth of ¼ inch. Place the stool upside-down on the saw table. While holding it against the temporary fence, pass each rail over the saw (Photo 120). It is possible, and not too difficult, to swing the stool around each corner radius while you hold it to the fence, and thereby to cut the shoulder on the curved corners as well as the straight sides.

On the work table in an upright position (Photo 121), the stool is ready to have the molding rounded with a plane. Choose a small block plane, and quarter-round from the upholstered board rabbet down to the newly cut shoulder (Photo 122). Short plane strokes around the corners will finish all the tool work.

Use a molded sanding block, first with No. ½ paper and then with No. 3/0, to smooth this molding for finish (Photo 123). Sand all surfaces (including the rails) not previously sanded with No. ½ paper. Sand thoroughly, making sure that all marks are erased. Now go over the entire stool with No. 3/0 paper, bearing in mind that sanding can make the product look either professional or mediocre. Finally, rub off the entire stool with No. 7/0, preparing for the application of finish materials.

If you wish to fasten the upholstered board in place, attach to the center of each long rail a block about 3 inches by ¾ by ¾ inch on the inside face ⅛ inch down from the upholstery rabbet. Coat the block with glue and rub it, like a rub block, on the rail. After overnight drying, bore through the blocks vertically for wood screws.

Prepare a ½-inch-thick plywood board for upholstery by sawing it to ³⁄₁₆ inch less than the opening in length and width. Radius each corner, allowing uniform clearance all around. Block-plane the upper sharp edge to a decided quarter-round (Photo 124). If you wish to upholster the board yourself, follow these suggestions: Purchase a piece of foam rubber one inch thick by the board size. Trim all edges neatly—bevel the top edge with scissors on about a 45-degree angle, half the rubber thickness. Stretch unbleached muslin over the rubber, and tack on the board edges, placing the tacks about 1 inch apart. Cut away the waste muslin at the bottom edge of the board. Stretch the covering material in like manner, but tack this piece to the bottom of the board about 1 inch in from the edge. Pleat the material around the corners. Fit black cambric to the board bottom, allowing for lap under, and tack every 3 inches. When the stool is ready for use, insert the upholstered unit and fasten it with screws.

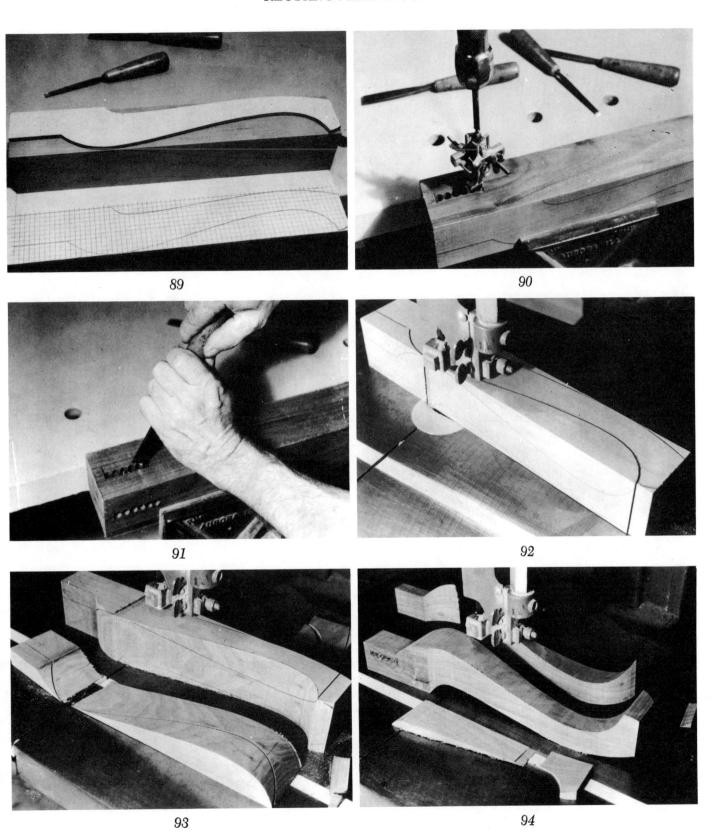

89

90

91

92

93

94

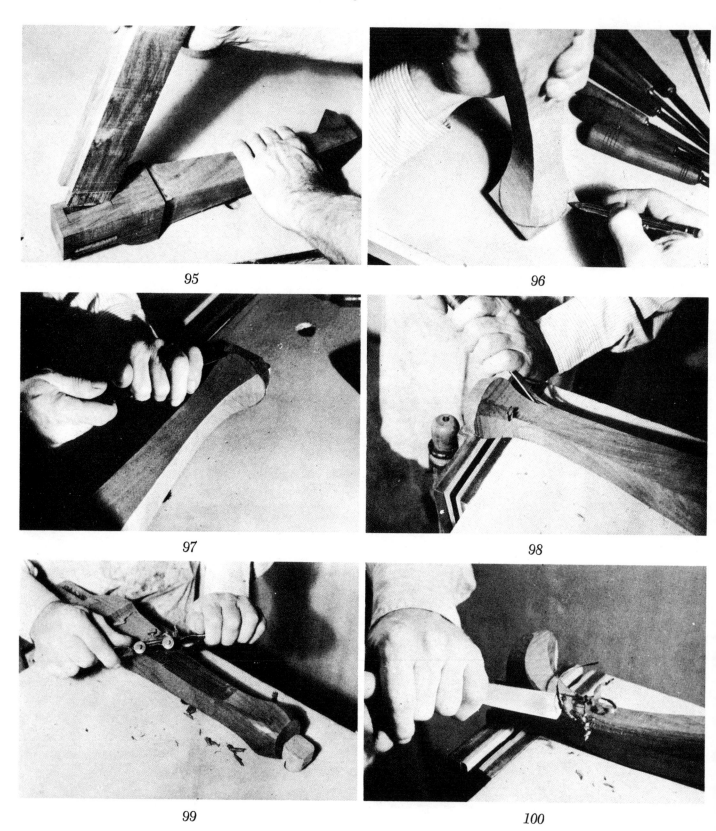

95

96

97

98

99

100

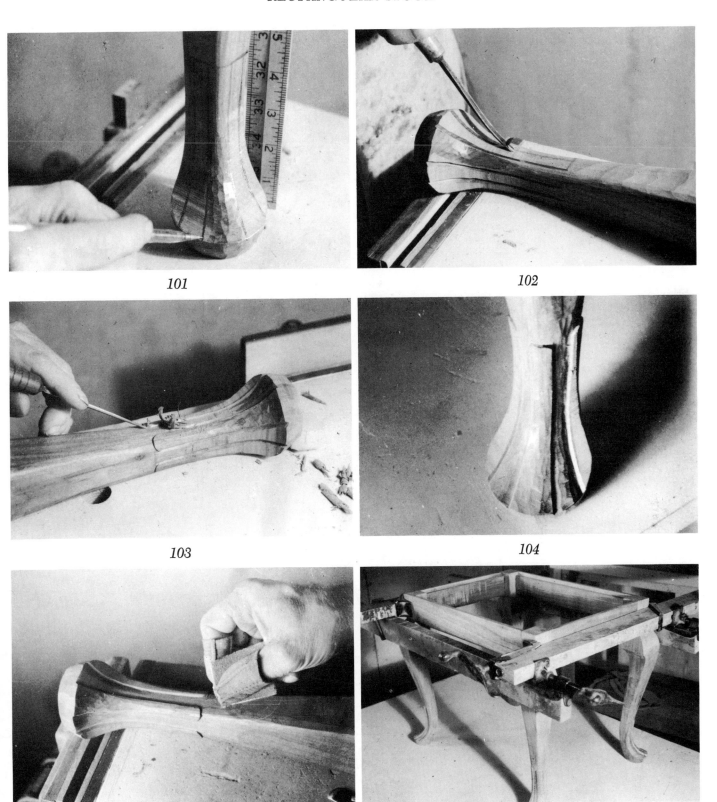

101

102

103

104

105

106

107

108

109

110

111

112

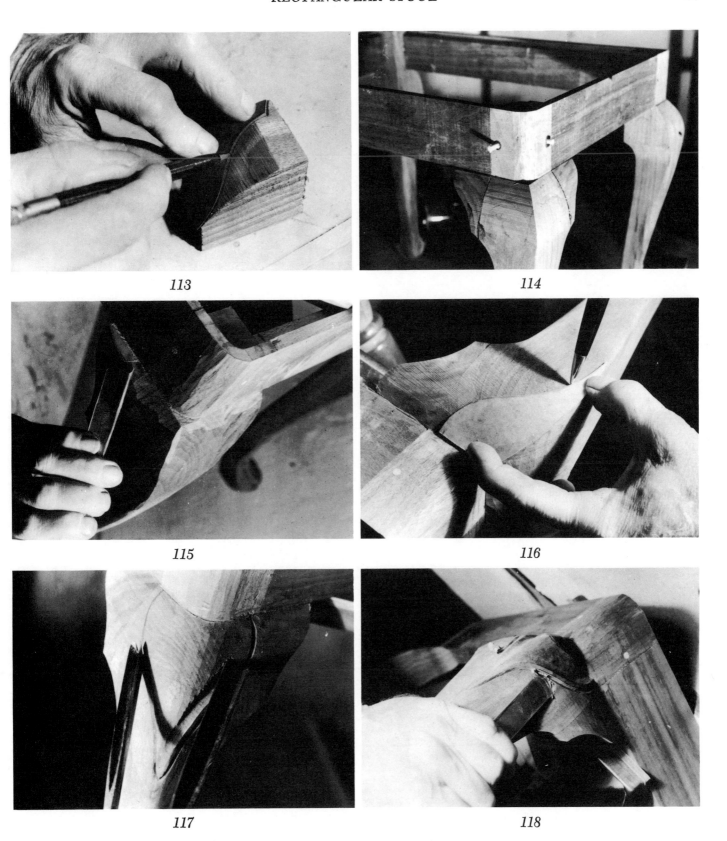

113

114

115

116

117

118

119

120

121

122

123

124

Oval Stool

CHAPTER V

Oval Stool

PHILADELPHIA ORIGIN, 1760

Materials

MAHOGANY

4 pieces, 15⅝ inches long, 2¾ inches wide, 2¾ inches thick.
1 piece, 13⁹⁄₁₆ inches long, 11 inches wide, 3 inches thick.
8 pieces, 2¾ inches long, 2 inches wide, 2 inches thick.
1-inch sponge rubber, 16 by 20 inches.
½-inch plywood, 16 by 20 inches.
Covering material: choice of needlepoint, brocade, silk damask, etc., 19 by 23 inches.

This oval stool, typical of the Philadelphia influence in its stout structure and style of carving, is a fine example of colonial cabinetmaking. The originator accepted the more difficult method of design execution in preference to sacrificing fine points. For example, he could have solved the problem of excess knee-area wood by arranging the legs with face parallel to the oval curve instead of with corners protruding. Legs so arranged are much less attractive because of the flat face on the knees that results. Also, they would terminate in unrealistic ball-and-claw feet, with two front and two back claws on each foot.

Before starting work on the stool, lay out the full-size oval on paper (Photo 126). Sizes and radius lines may be taken from the drawing, page 73. Note that where the short radius lines reach the long rail a freehand pencil line must allow one curve to flow smoothly into the other. When the plan is completed, lay the pattern board (covered with carbon paper) under a short and a long rail of the drawing. Transfer these lines to the pattern board, using a hard pencil. Thus, the drawing remains intact for future reference. Saw the board to the outline.

Measure ½-inch squares on the pattern board for the leg outline. A guide is provided for this purpose on the drawing, page 73. Draw in the leg outline, and saw the board to shape.

Start construction by milling four squares 2¾ by 2¾ inches by 15⅝ inches long. Choose two right-angle surfaces of each leg for the front. Place the pattern first on one front surface, making sure that the knee edge of the pattern meets the front corner (Photo 127), and outline it in pencil. Turn the pattern over, place it on the other front surface, knee edge to knee edge, and outline it. Do the same with the remaining three legs. Before any further work is done on the leg blocks, rough out the four rails.

By nesting the rail patterns, you can save a few inches of wood when you saw the rails (Photo

71

128). Square a 3-inch-thick block to 13¾₁₆ inches long by not less than 11 inches wide. First, place the long rail pattern with its outside curve touching the long side of the block. Carefully measure both pattern ends for distance from the block edge. Unless they are equidistant, the rail will lose its square ends. Outline the pattern on the block in pencil. Lay the same pattern close to the first marking for the second long rail, allowing enough space for a saw-cut width. Measure from pattern to the block edge, to keep ends square. Mark the block in pencil. Mark the remainder of the block with two parallel squared lines 8⅝ inches apart for the short rails, employing the same procedure.

Band-saw the two long rails, whose ends were squared before marking. Now carefully band-saw to the squared lines, the ends of the short rails; and follow this by sawing on the curved lines. The progress of band-sawing in Photo 128 shows the first straight-edge waste piece lying in the foreground. Next, a long rail completely cut and the piece of waste wood that lies between the two long rails. If the 3-inch block from which the rails were cut was in a rough state, smooth either the top or the bottom edge of the rails by hand plane or jointer. Set the circular saw fence to 2½ inches, and saw the four rails to the prescribed height.

As indicated in Photo 129, it is more convenient to band-saw the legs to shape after their dowel holes have been bored. Determine the back corner of each leg block by facing the pattern-marked surfaces front. Starting at the top mark toward the foot end, scribe boring center lines 1 inch from the back corner on each right-angle side surface. Measuring from the top, mark for dowel-hole centers (across the scribed lines) with a pointed awl ⅝ inch, 1⅜ inches, and 2⅛ inches.

Set the stop on a ⅜-inch bit to bore holes 13⁄₁₆ inch deep. Place a leg block in the vise (Photo 129), and bore three holes on each inside surface, taking care to align the brace and bit for an accurate fit when the stool is assembled. Do the same on the two side surfaces of each leg.

Now mark for matching holes in the rails. Set the marking gauge to scribe boring center lines on all rail ends (from top to bottom) ⁹⁄₁₆ inch from the inside corner. Make a mark that will distinguish the top of each rail and prevent any mistake as you mark down from the top ⅝ inch, 1⅜ inches, and 2⅛ inches. Make awl marks for the bit centers. Grip each rail in the vise vertically (Photo 130). Align the brace and bit, and bore the three matching holes 13⁄₁₆ inch deep. Do the same on all rail ends.

Band-sawing the legs is the same as in the Walnut Stool (Chapter IV). An important difference is that waste wood above the knees remains until after assembly, when you remove it with a hand saw. Another variation is the foot shape. Cuts on the first marked surface are shown in Photo 131. The cut that will give the back of the leg its shape has been made but not carried completely through. This method leaves the waste wood in place for a solid bearing surface when the leg block is one-quarter turned to make the second set of cuts. Note also that the cut forming the front claw has been sawed within ¼ inch of severance. On all saw cuts stopped before completion, the blade must be backed out to the starting point. For safety in backing the blade, stop the saw's motion first. In Photo 131 the saw has cut the front curve to the stopping point and has lost all motion. Next the blade will be backed out.

Photo 132 shows the second marked surface turned up for sawing. Waste wood from the front claw, and waste severed by the long leg curve cut, lie on the saw table. The saw blade has cut about half the distance required to form the back curve.

Make a one-quarter turn, bringing the leg back to its first position on the saw table. Thread the blade through the incomplete cuts, one after another, put the saw in motion, and finish sawing

PLAN OF STOOL

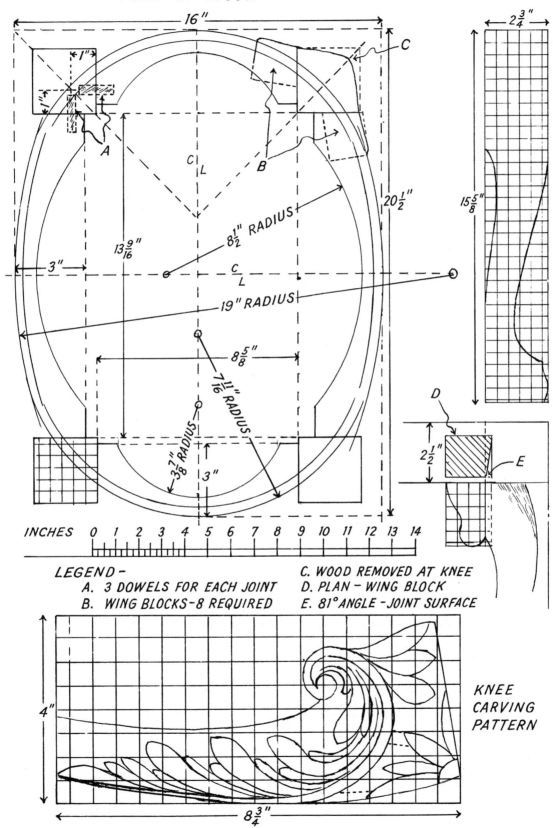

16"

1"

1"

A

C
L

C
L

B

C

20½"

13 9/16"

3"

8½" RADIUS

19" RADIUS

8 5/8"

7 11/16" RADIUS

3 7/8" RADIUS

3"

2¾"

15 5/8"

D

2½"

E

INCHES 0 1 2 3 4 5 6 7 8 9 10 11 12 13 14

LEGEND —
A. 3 DOWELS FOR EACH JOINT
B. WING BLOCKS-8 REQUIRED
C. WOOD REMOVED AT KNEE
D. PLAN – WING BLOCK
E. 81° ANGLE - JOINT SURFACE

4"

KNEE
CARVING
PATTERN

8¾"

each cut. Photo 133 shows a leg completely sawed to shape. The waste pieces lie on the table just as they fell away from the leg when parted.

Prepare the feet for carving by drawing pencil lines parallel to the corners, far enough from the peak to make a total claw width of about 7/16 inch. These are only guide lines for making relief cuts and need not be too accurate. Lines should extend upward to the small ankle. If you hold a pencil in your normal way you will find that the middle fingernail will slide along the right-angle surface and thus act as a uniform spacing auxiliary. A leg with claw lines drawn is illustrated in Photo 134.

Before carving, make a convenient bench set-up to hold the leg rigidly. The most common arrangement is to equip the vise with a dog which may be raised for use. The other leg end is held by a peg slipped into one of a line of holes in the bench top. For the first cut, use a large No. 41 tool and a mallet. Cut to a depth of about 3/16 inch on each line (back claw included). Because of grain direction, cut from the high point toward the ankle, as illustrated in Photo 135. Reverse the direction when cutting to the foot end.

The areas between the claws must now be rough-cut with the large No. 3 gouge, to an approximate ball. Keep in mind that the claws when finally shaped will have more relief, permitting further refinement of the ball shape. Study Photo 136. At about the upper knuckles the ball shape gradually turns to a concave curve. This area will develop into a realistic-looking web. As the claws near the ankle, they come closer together and narrow the area between. Use a smaller No. 3 gouge here to further the claw relief. When the ball and web areas have had their preliminary shaping cuts, deepen the relief with a No. 11 gouge (Photo 136), which forms a rounded fillet instead of a sharp groove where claws meet ball and web. Use this tool at the same time to shape the claws to width. Make the knuckles about 7/16 inch across and, by cutting curves from knuckle to knuckle on each side of the claws, bring the width of the intervening bone down to about 5/16 inch. Photo 137 shows clean-up cuts with No. 11, and also the gradual tapering off of relief cuts when they approach the ankle area.

Foot appearance from the bottom at this point of progress may be studied in Photo 138, where the back claw is in the high foreground and the top quarter-section of ball and web is being roughed out. Note that the ball is fairly round and satisfactory from the average carver's standpoint. An earlier caution will stand repeating: Allow for the grain direction, and aim carving tools to cut with the grain. Thus you will avoid splintering the wood.

Take a long look at Photos 139 and 140. The next process is to form the claws and nails. Round the top of each claw from the ankle down, using a ½-inch No. 3 gouge. When you reach the lower knuckle the claw will protrude too far, and you will have to remove progressively more and more wood, to the end of what will be the nail. You will readily understand this profile change by studying Photo 140. When you are forming the nails, chop straight in with a No. 6 gouge, 3/8 inch up from the bottom, holding the concave side of the tool toward the nail. First, make sloping cuts on the nail (Photo 139, left); then, slope the cuticle. From the cuticle to the first joint, a concave curve must show in profile. This is also the case between the first and second joints. When changing profile, recut the claw to the desired round form. Round the top of each knuckle by cutting away the decided sharp edge with a No. 3 gouge.

Photo 140 is a close-up of the top foot shown in 139. Notice the shape and the position of the web end. This is a comparatively simple operation. First, pencil in a guide line; then, choose either a No. 5 or a No. 6, ½ inch, gouge (whichever matches the pencil line better) and chop in to a depth of $\frac{1}{16}$ inch. Using a No. 3 gouge, heel up, work the ball shape down to this relief line. Photo 140 is a clear illustration of before and after. The upper web has been chop-parted, while the lower one has the relief cuts made. The claw portions below the web line seem to grip the ball tightly, so that a round fillet here is not desirable. The deeper flute cut left on the ball by gouge No. 11 is eliminated by the final shaping of the ball with a No. 3 gouge. Continue the web relief cut down each side of the claw to form a sharp corner or juncture of claw and ball.

Comments on the work progress shown in Photo 139 are as follows: The lower claw on the left foot is still in the rough. The middle or front claw is completely cut. The top one shows the nail being formed. The right foot is nearly complete. As soon as the four web ends are cut in relief, this foot will be ready for sanding. The back claw consists of a nail, cuticle, and lower joint (Photo 144). If only one foot has been worked on, as a pilot, carve the remaining three in like manner.

Round all four corners of each leg with a drawknife. At the same time, remove any band-saw marks from flat surfaces up to the knees. Do not disturb the sharp edge that will receive a wing block after assembly. Round corners to what may be judged a $\frac{5}{16}$-inch radius (Photo 141).

Sanding carved parts is explained in detail in Chapter XI, but a reminder of the most important points will not be amiss. The sandpaper must not be allowed to dull edges that should remain sharp. Press lightly on all high spots, because they are the places that receive the hardest cutting action. Sand first with No. ½ paper, and after assembly with No. 3/0. Photo 142 shows the top quarter of a foot sanded with No. ½; the lower section is about to be sanded.

Much work remains to be done, and the necessary handling of the parts entails a constant risk of rub-marks, bumps, and scratches. Therefore it is well to give the feet only a preliminary sanding now, and to postpone the removal of the blemishes mentioned to the final No. 3/0 sanding of the finished stool. Photo 143 shows a sanded foot: back claw at the top, side claw in the center, and front claw at the bottom. Notice that the glove fingers protect the fingernails from the sandpaper.

Cut ⅜-inch dowels 1½ inches long. Coat the receiving holes in the rails with glue, then insert the dowels and tap them with a hammer to seat them firmly. Test-assemble each rail and leg for hole alignment and spacing (Photo 144). You can make the final assembly easier by numbering each leg surface and each fitted rail end.

All is now ready for assembly. Arrange the legs and the short rails in order, so that no time will be lost matching numbers. Coat the three holes in one leg with glue, and insert the dowels which have already been glued into the rail. Glue-coat the holes in the leg numbered for the other end of this rail. Insert the dowels. Place the newly created unit in a bar clamp, and draw it tight, making sure that the rail ends are seated properly against the legs. A problem in bar-clamping oddly shaped units like this stool end is the danger of exerting unbalanced pressure. Place the clamp so that the pressure centers over the middle dowel. Photo 145 shows how wooden blocks can be centered on the proposed pressure area so that the part of the clamp pad nearest the bar will not bear against the work, causing unbalanced pressure. The other end unit should be similarly protected. Allow overnight setting in the clamps.

Treat the long rails as you have just finished treating the short ones. All the unfilled dowel holes must be coated with glue, and both rails placed for clamping in one operation.

After the overnight setting in the clamps you are ready for the assembly of all the parts to form the completed stool. Place the clamps and the wood blocks as illustrated in Photo 145. Draw them tight, and examine the joints to make certain that they are perfect. Stand the stool on a level floor, and see to it that all four feet touch it at the same time. If one or more joints are imperfect the stool will rock on two opposite legs. This condition may be remedied by loosening, shifting, and retightening the clamps.

The next operation is to remove unwanted leg wood at the rail line with a handsaw. Draw a freehand pencil line across the leg tops to make the oval curve continuous. Square a pencil line with the bottom of the rails on each front surface. Handsaw to about the depth of the rail curvature (Photo 146). Do not saw too deeply. After you have made the vertical saw cut it is simple to reinsert the saw in its slot and deepen the cut if necessary.

Illustrated in Photo 147 is the vertical hand-saw cut. Start the saw well outside of the penciled curve. As the cut deepens, check to be sure it does not curve inward. Combine this cut to meet the horizontal one.

Prepare eight wing blocks 2¾ inches long by 2 inches wide by 1¾ inches thick—or one piece 2 inches wide by 1¾ inches thick of sufficient length for cutting the eight blocks. Study the wing-block detail on the drawing (page 73). Set a hollow-ground saw to 81 degrees—cut this angle on one 1¾ inch-side of each block. The hollow-ground saw will leave a sufficiently smooth surface for rub-block gluing to the legs. The lesser width surface is intended for the face side.

Make an outline pattern for the wing blocks, using the guide provided in the drawing, page 73. Mark the blocks for band-sawing on the face side. Keep one side of the pattern upward for marking four blocks, and turn it over for marking the remaining four. This procedure provides rights and lefts. Band-saw to the outline. If desired, the band-sawed surfaces may be sanded before attaching blocks to the legs. Coat with glue the angled block surface alone. Press it against the leg, and rub it into position, instantly releasing it when the glue seems to "catch." The block's position may be ascertained from Photo 148.

Between the knees and the rail line (Photo 149), much wood must be removed. Start chipping below the knee high point with a large No. 3 gouge and mallet, and remove more and more wood as you approach the rail line. Study subsequent illustrations that show profile development. Of course, whenever wood is worked by hand the article must be held rigidly in the vise. When you rough-shape the knees, as in Photo 149, grip a rail in the vise close to the leg on which you are at work.

After you have chipped off most of the waste wood, use a sharp drawknife to get the desired knee curve. In Photo 150 you can tell how much wood has been removed from the left face by noticing how far the crest line veers to the right. Excess leg wood may be removed at this time to form an uninterrupted oval on the rail area.

Unlike the knees of a rectangular stool, which may retain their full band-sawed curve, the knees of an oval stool must have their protrusion modified. A primary reason for this is the extra swell given to the knees by cutting the square (rail area wood) back to the oval line. It should be noted also that, from wing-block joining edge to center crest, there is a tapering of the wood removed. Photo 151 presents the leg's appearance after the right face has been reshaped. When sufficient wood is removed, a decided crest line will form down the center.

Photo 152 presents a 90-degree side view of the leg. Compare the surface widths. The left, or back, surface is considerably wider than the right, or face, surface, indicating how much wood was removed to lessen the swell.

Before preparing the knee-carving stencil paper pattern, draw a freehand pencil line down the center of the leg, for a twofold purpose. First, it is necessary when placing the finished pattern; secondly, it makes easier marking of the over-all pattern outline, as evidenced in Photo 153. Place a piece of pattern material on the leg, covering completely the area to be carved. Mark and trim the top edge to match the lower rail line. Hold the material in this position, bending the stencil paper to follow the leg curvature. Draw an approximately straight line from the top of the paper to the bottom. This will be the center line of the pattern. Without moving the stencil paper, press it flat against the front surface of the leg and mark the outline of the leg, including the wing block, on the under side.

Now mark the under side of the stencil paper with ½-inch squares. Should you find a variation when comparing this full-size outline with the smaller one in the drawing on page 73, follow the full-size on the wing-block area. Below the wing, draw in the leaf outline, by following the scale-block drawing, page 73. Be guided by this drawing when you fill in the leaf petals with smoothly flowing division lines. Note that the sunflower in the top position remains attached to the main pattern by two tabs (drawing, page 73, and Photo 154).

After all details are drawn on the pattern material, cut it with scissors to the outline. Place the pattern on one leg face, using the center line and the junction point of leg and rail as a guide. Check the pattern for proper placement at the wing-block edge. Transfer the design to the leg surface in pencil (Photo 154). Turn over the pattern, check the three borders, and mark. Do the same for the other legs.

With the various tool shapes and sizes, chop in the outlines of the entire design, including the top side of the long curved rib extending from the wing-block scroll to the center line. (In Photo 155 all parting chop cuts have been made in the left half of the leg.) Cut away the background wood to a depth of about 3/32 inch. For most of these small, oddly shaped areas, a ⅛-inch to ¼-inch No. 3 gouge will serve best. A directive worth repeating: Keep the background surfaces uniform in depth, leaving only light tool marks to be removed with sandpaper. Background relief cuts bordering the lower part of the leaf design are made on a long taper in order to retain an uninterrupted leg line.

The heavy, long curve border rib starts at the wing-block scroll. It is approximately ¼ inch wide and, in the center, merges with its opposite into one, tapering in width to a point at the lower leaf tip (Photo 156). The upper sides of these ribs were formed when the background wood was removed. The lower sides should now be relief-cut with a ⅜-inch No. 41. Relief extends the entire length from scroll to lower leaf tip—on both leg surfaces. Slope the leaf wood in to meet this relief cut, as shown in the lower part of Photo 156. The gouge held in cutting position is a No. 3, ½-inch, heel up. The sloping leaf division lines, the sunflower petals, and the wing-block leaves are marked and cut. (See the drawing, page 73.) The leg pictured in Photo 156 has progressed beyond this point.

The flower center, or button, is half of a 1-inch circle and should be chopped in for sharp relief.

The lower half of the leg pictured in Photo 156 has the leaf petals divided by cuts with ⅜-inch No. 41 on the penciled guide lines. Tail out the No. 41 cuts when you near the border rib. Leave the scroll centers square-edged, but slope off all leaf and flower edges slightly with a No. 3 gouge, heel up. Observe the leaves (upper half of Photo 156). The broad centers are dished out with a ½-inch-wide No. 6 gouge. Flower petals are treated in like manner—the center one has been cut half its length. The end leaves of each cluster of three, topping the wing-block scrolls, are dished out; the center leaf remains convex. All concave petals, plus the center leaf just mentioned, are further decorated with a No. 41 veiner cut down the center. The ⅛-inch No. 41 tool in Photo 156 is veining the second concave leaf. To complete the carving, slope both edges of the border ribs with No. 3 gouge, heel up.

The ball and claw feet and parts of the legs have been sanded with coarse paper. Sand the remaining unsanded leg surfaces with No. ½ paper. Sand the knee carvings with No. 3/0 only, carefully retaining sharpness. Sand all four feet and legs with No. 3/0.

To mold the top rail edge, clamp a spacing board against the circular saw fence. Adjust the fence so that the spacer barely touches the blade, which should be set to a cutting height of 5/16 inch (Photo 157). Invert the stool, press the rail against the spacer board, and pass over the saw. Move the stool back and forth, combining this movement with a circular motion so that no areas will remain uncut. Turn the stool to its upright position and mark a pencil line 5/16 inch in from the newly cut shoulder. You can make the line a uniform measurement around the circumference by using your middle finger as a guide. This line represents the seat-board recess.

Mark another line around the inside of the rails ⅜ inch down from the top edge for the depth of the recess. Choose the largest No. 3 gouge, and chop down vertically on the 5/16-inch line for its entire length. Using the same tool, chip off the inside waste wood to a depth about the same as that of the chop cut. Repeat chop and chip cuts, gradually removing the waste wood to the desired ⅜-inch depth (Photo 158). It is advisable, when recessing over the legs, to place the outside leg surface solidly on the bench and chop across the grain.

Form the ¼-inch round molding on the top edge with a small hand plane (Photo 159). Reverse the plane direction when necessary to avoid cutting against the grain. A shaped sanding block will not serve too well on this curved molding. Therefore, crease a ¼ sheet of No. ½ paper in three folds, and sand first the 5/16-inch shoulder. Next, sand the quarter-round, removing all plane marks. Finish-sand the molding with 3/0 paper.

The last sanding to be done is the outside rail surface (Photo 160). Using a cork block to support the No. ½ sandpaper, sand it sufficiently long to remove all tool marks. As you reach the rail area adjacent to the knee carving, discard the paper-covered block and take up again the No. ½ paper in three folds used earlier on the molding. Sand with it up to the carving. Thus you will avoid cross-scratching the carved leaves. Repeat with No. 3/0 paper, taking particular care to remove the coarse No. ½ paper scratches which cross the leg wood. Deep scratches across the grain will show prominently when the finishing materials are applied.

Process the ½-inch plywood seat board next. Laying this on a work table, invert the stool and center it on the board. Pencil-line the board by following the outside oval stool curve, and cut it to this line on the band saw. Measure the total width of the top molding (it will probably be a scant 7/16 inch). Add another 1/16 inch, and circumscribe a line on the seat board (about ½ inch) in from the band-sawed edge. Band-saw to the new line. Clearance of 1/16 inch all around is sufficient for the weight of ordinary covering material. If you wish to use needlepoint, make the clearance ⅛ inch. Round the top edge of board with a hand plane to about a ¼-inch radius. (Detailed instructions for upholstering the seat board are given in Chapter IV). Give the entire stool a final combination inspection and No. 7/0 finishing paper rub-off. Photo 161 shows the completed stool ready for finishing materials.

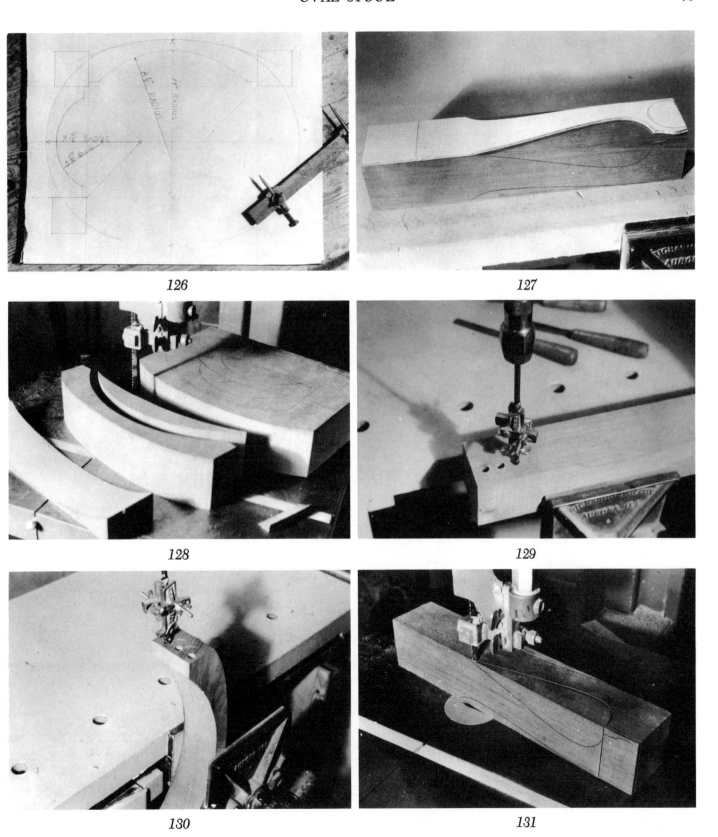

126

127

128

129

130

131

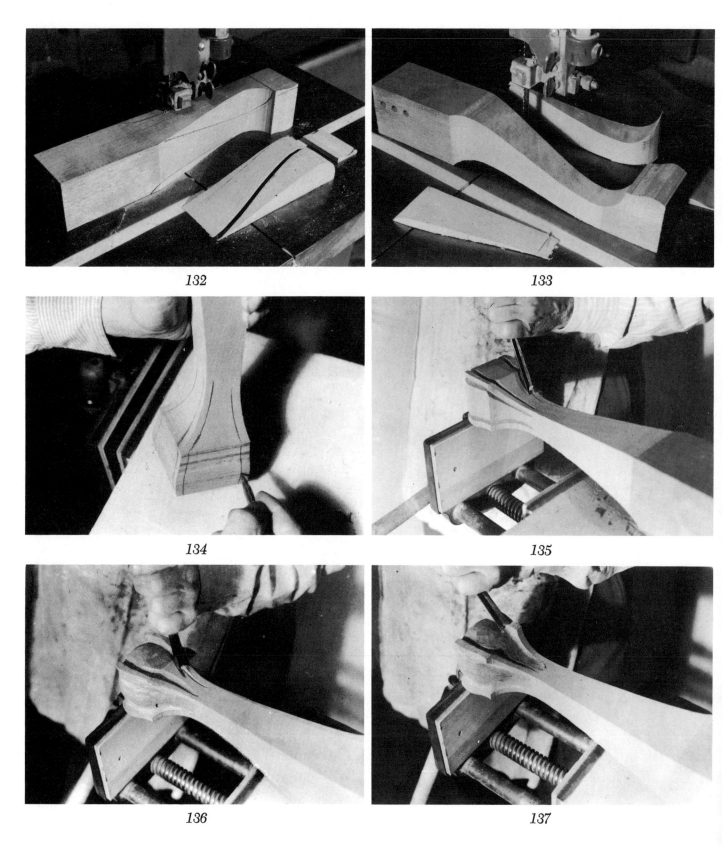

132

133

134

135

136

137

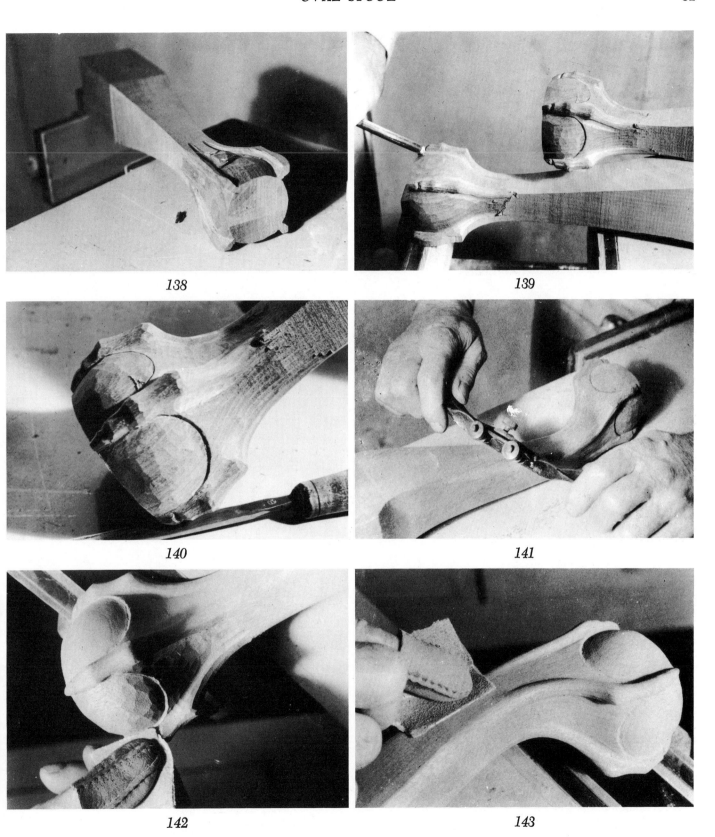

138

139

140

141

142

143

Oval Stool

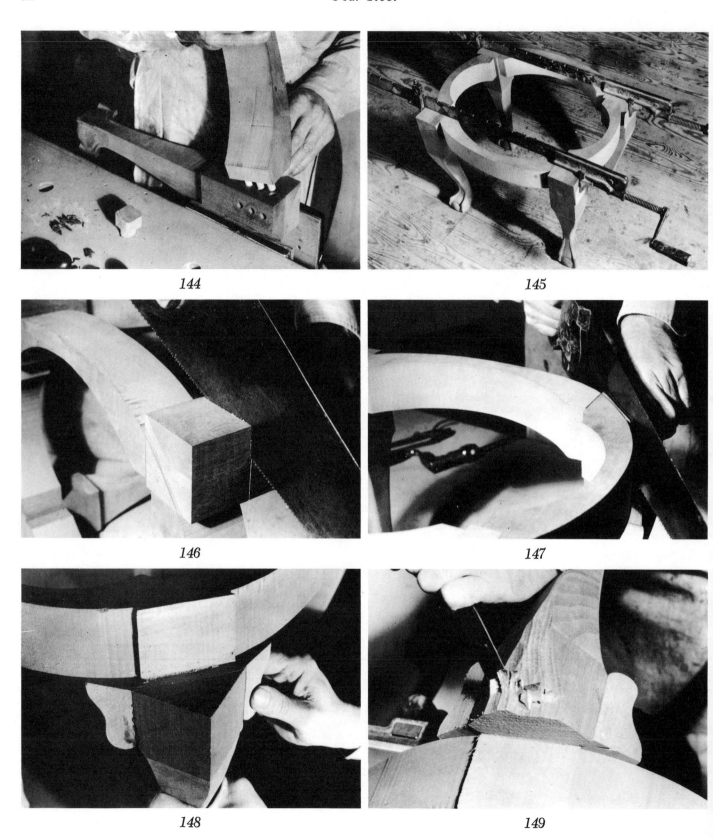

144

145

146

147

148

149

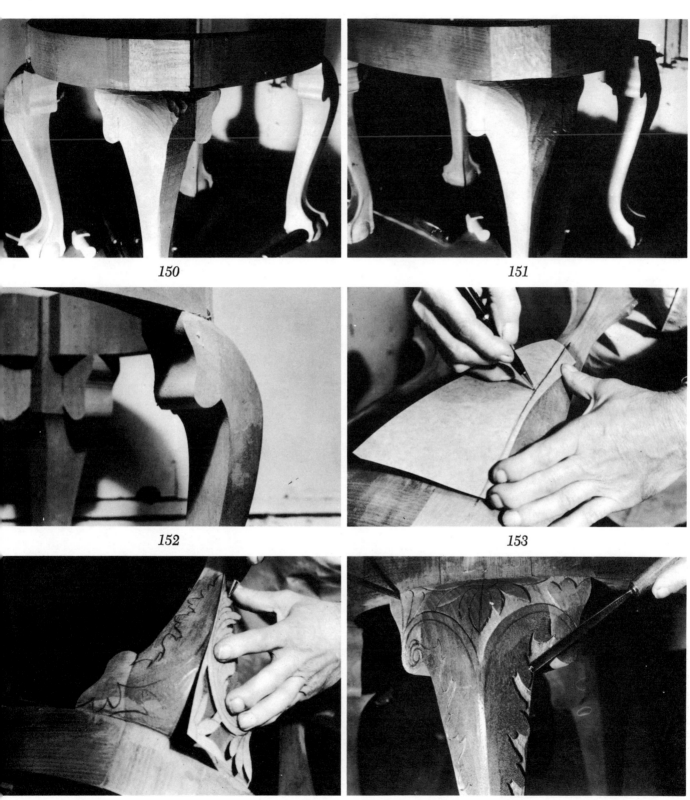

150

151

152

153

154

155

156

157

158

159

160

161

Candlestand

CHAPTER VI

Candlestand

MASSACHUSETTS ORIGIN, ABOUT 1775

Materials, for one pair: mahogany, 2 pieces 35 by 3 by 3 inches thick, 1 piece (for 6 legs) 16½ by 7½ by 3 inches thick, 2 pieces 11 by 11 by $1\frac{3}{16}$ inch thick, 2 pieces 6 by 6 by $1\frac{3}{16}$ inch thick.

Candlestands are popular home furnishings. Although not often used as they were originally intended, they are admirably suited to the modern use as plant stands. The stand selected for illustration here is well designed from top to bottom. Cabinetmakers of New England were much more partial to the rat claw and ball (or egg—which the shape more readily suggests) than were those of New York and Philadelphia. The appeal of this foot is the long, graceful lines, which are in keeping with the tall slender proportions of the stand. Candlestands are particularly desirable in pairs, and so the material list calls for sufficient wood to build two stands.

It seems natural, probably because parts are added to each end, to start with the column, or post. In using 3-by-3-inch posts it is not necessary to smooth the wood, because they will be turned all over. Set a marking gauge, and mark the exact center on each column end. Press a pointed awl into the centers for true balance, and mount a post in the lathe.

Too many cautions about turning tend to increase the feeling of uncertainty about the job ahead. Lathe work is really one of the lesser problems of furniture building. All will go well if you take these few elementary precautions for safety: Check the driving and tail-stock centers—they should be embedded sufficiently far in the wood to prevent slippage. Predetermine the proper speed for a piece of this size. Have the tool rest reasonably close to the turning, and hold the tools firmly but without tenseness.

In Photo 162 the blank is being turned to a round shape. Should it develop a slight longitudinal bow after leaving the saw, considerable vibration will result at a high speed. If this happens, slow down the r.p.m. until the corners are cut and the balance is restored. As indicated on the measured drawing, page 89, the entire column length is to be cylindrical and of 2⅞-inch diameter.

While the post is in motion, measure and mark in pencil two parting lines: one, 3⅝ inches up from the base; the other, ½ inch farther up (the base end is to the left in Photo 163). Set the calipers to 2¾ inches. Keeping the parting tool on the base side of the 3⅝-inch line, part the wood to the caliper setting. Also part the extreme end to a 2¾-inch diameter. Remove the wood between the parting cuts with a gouge, carefully checking with the calipers at various points to avoid cutting too deeply. For a uniform diameter, right up to the shoulder, lay the skew flat on the tool rest, and scrape to uniform size. Hold the parting tool on the upper side of the second line, and part to a depth of 2⅜ inches. Mark a temporary line about 7 inches up from the base, and keep within these marks when gouging out a valley for the 2-inch dividing cusp diameter. (See the drawing on page 89.) The longitudinal and diameter parting-cut measurements are the most important part of turning, because all intervening curves start and end at these points.

After you have done the preliminary gouge work on the 2-inch cusp area, determine the distance and diameters (from the scaled drawing) of the parting cuts to the vase bottom (Photo 163). Keep in mind that the parting tool must be placed on the correct side of the penciled mark for dimensional accuracy. As an illustration: Suppose that, in parting for the 2-inch cusp, a ⅛-inch parting tool were placed on the wrong side of one mark. The result would be a cusp ⅛ inch wide instead of a ¼ inch wide. Read the drawing in the following manner: After the ½-inch cap which will cover the leg dovetails, make a ½-inch S curve to the next parting cut; then a ⅞-inch cove (parting flats included) to the ¼-inch cusp. From cusp to vase bottom, 1¼ inches. Use the parting tool at the vase bottom for diameter only, without allowing any flat to remain at this point of curve change. Next, measure up 3⅛ inches for vase, a parting cut, a ⁷⁄₁₆-inch S curve—parting cut and fillet to the long taper. In cutting S curves, use a ¼-inch round-nose or ¾-inch gouge for concave, and a skew for convex. The deeper and wider coves may be turned with the ¾-inch gouge. Experiment with this proposed technique: Turn the gouge on its side, with the heel toward the area that is *not* to be cut. Give the tool thrust, and twist it to an upright position, moving it no farther than what will be the deepest part of the cove. Repeat on the other cove side. Avoid cutting too deeply on any one cut. Instead, make successive cuts on each side until the cove takes the desired depth and contour. Before turning the cove between the cusp and the vase, reduce the vase to rough size for the clearance of tools used in the cove work.

Photo 164 shows a post finished-turned to the long taper. The skew on the left is placed for turning one side of the cusp. The ¾-inch gouge on the right is placed for making the concave part of the S curve. The fillet flowing into the taper may be made with either the round-nose flat or the ¾-inch gouge.

Shift the tool rest to the top end of the turning. Mark about 2 inches down from the end. Gouge out to a diameter of 1⅞ inches, from the mark downward a distance of about 6 inches. By removing waste wood at this time, you can avoid unnecessarily deep parting cuts for the two beads indicated on the drawing for this area. Make a pencil mark down from the end 1³⁄₁₆ inch. This end section will finish to 1³⁄₁₆ and provide a dowel for the supporting disc. Next, measure ½ inch and mark for a double bead, and follow with another ½ inch for an S curve. Check the drawing to be sure on which side of each line to place parting tool. Place it accordingly, and part the wood to the proper depth (Photo 165).

Photo 166 shows the progress of the lathe work, with the double bead and the S curve finished. Now, measure 1⅝ inches to the first of two beads, ¼ inch for the bead, and 1¾ inches to the next ¼-inch bead. After the second bead, a shallow fillet will flow into the long taper. Size the beads for width with the parting tool, cutting to 1⅝-inch diameter. Photo 166 illustrates the use of the skew to round the beads.

The only parts that remain to be turned on the top end are the sections between the beads and below the S curve, and the 1-inch dowel (Photo 167). Use the ¾-inch gouge to work the dowel down to rough size. Finish to an accurate 1-inch diameter with the skew. The parting-tool cut,

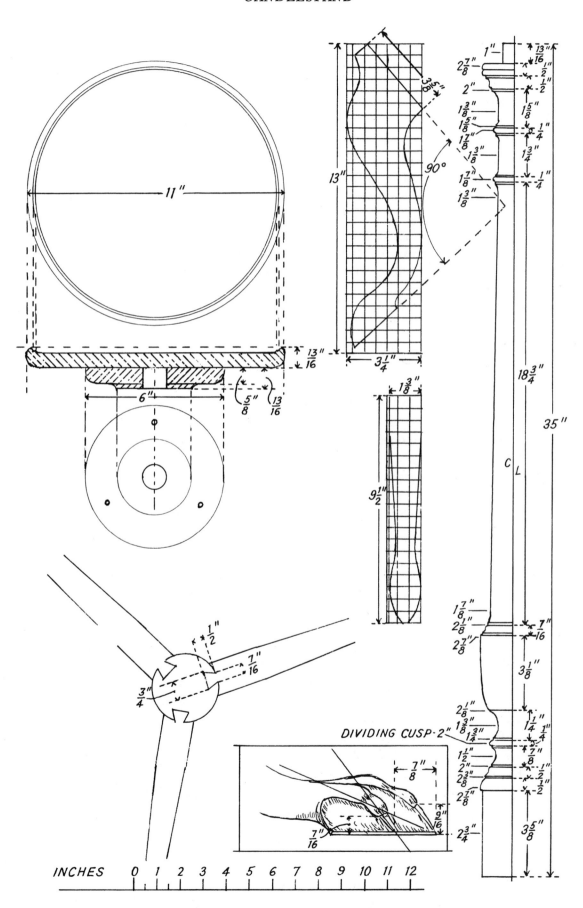

DIVIDING CUSP-2"

INCHES 0 1 2 3 4 5 6 7 8 9 10 11 12

from the double bead in to the dowel, forms the resting surface for the supporting disc and should be slightly undercut in order to insure disc seating on the periphery, where strength and rigidity lie. For turning between the beads and up to the S curve, use the ¾-inch gouge. Both these sections and the top end of the long taper have a small diameter of 1⅜ inches. Shallow fillets connect small diameters with the parting-tool flats except below the S curve, where a much deeper fillet joins two diameters.

To complete the turning, work the long taper down to size. You can do it best with the large gouge. For its length, the turning is now rather slender and may "whip" unless there is some steadying influence. Avoid the usual left-hand grip on the tool, and place your thumb in the tool concave about ½ inch from the cutting edge. Rest your fingers lightly on the turning, and bend them to follow the contour. You will find you can control and propel the tool quite satisfactorily with the thumb in this position. As you move the tool, move the fingers to maintain their steadying effect on the turning. Sand the entire turning (dowel excepted) first with folded No. ½ paper, carefully retaining all sharp high points. Keep the sandpaper moving along the turned surface, back and forth. (If the paper remains on one spot it will cut deep scratches into the wood.) Repeat with No. 3/0 paper. Before removing the post, mark pencil lines about ½ inch from the long taper ends. These indicate the start and stop for flutes. Photo 168 shows the finished turning.

A small bench shaper is a desirable piece of shop equipment. A substitute is a shaper attachment for the drill press. Except that its spindle is inverted, this performs in much the same manner as the conventional machine.

A simple adjustable jig for fluting and reeding is now required. Start with a bedboard of poplar or pine about 45 inches long by 6 inches wide, and 1¾ inches thick to give rigidity. Photo 169 shows the head, or indexing, end. Channeled into the bed and fastened permanently is a cross arm 8½ by 2½ by 1¼ inches with a ¾-inch hole centered 2 inches above the shaper table. Make a narrow slot with a hack-saw blade directly above the ¾-inch hole. Insert, and pin-hinge, a piece of sheet metal or part of a hack-saw blade.

Turn a few interchangeable indexing heads on the lathe. These turnings consist of ¾-inch shafts, 2⅜-inch diameter heads ½ inch thick. Drive a nail in each head center, and cut off the nail, leaving ⅛ inch protruding and filing this to a point. Then place two more nails in each head opposite each other about ½ inch from the center, file to points. These prevent the work from slipping. On one indexing head, lay off the circumference with twelve equally spaced division lines. Slot these with a saw for hinged hack-saw blade to drop in when aligned. The extra heads may be kept in reserve for differently numbered divisions.

Starting about 20 inches from the head, channel the bed (¾ inch by 1¼ inches) every few inches for variable measurements between centers. A tail arm (equal in size to the head) has a ⅜-inch hole centered to match the ¾-inch head hole (Photo 170). Equip this arm with a pointed ⅜-by-6-inch bolt for tail stock center. Bore the arm for two wood screws that will hold it in place when fitted in any one of the channels.

Shaper blade sets made of high-speed steel with 60-degree edges and ground to the desired shape are much more versatile than solid cutters. For this type of cutter, a number of spacing collars must be available. Two of the collars have two 60-degree parallel grooves on the flats of each. When the collar on top is inverted, two 60-degree shaper cutters will fit snugly in the grooves of the two collars. A pair of cutters may be made from ¼-inch to 1-inch width shaper steel. When the spindle nut is tightened, the cutters are locked firmly in place. Their versatility lies in the fact that they may be set to protrude much or little. Also, the collars act as a stop for depth of cut when shaping curved surfaces.

Flutes are half-round depressions, or channels, extending any given distance on a material surface. Photo 171 shows a post mounted in the jig and fluted all the way around. The shaper spindle is equipped with ¼-inch high-speed steel, ends ground to a half-round arc. The distance these cutters are allowed to protrude past the collars determines the depth of the flutes.

Reeds, as applied to furniture and architecture, are half-round beads of indefinite length. The perfect reed is a true half-circle; but in many cases perfection is impractical. When there is a considerable variation in diameters the width of each reed will vary with the diameter change. Another determining factor involved in the vase (Photo 172) is that the number of reeds should equal the number of flutes above them.

Instead of the shaper cutters forming one complete reed (as they do when fluting), the two cutters are ground to arrow points. When in use they cut a dividing line between two beads, forming the right side of one and the left side of the other. Starting with ¼-inch shaper steel, arcs are ground from the center to each edge. When you are grinding cutters for the shaper, hold the steel against the wheel at an angle of about 60 degrees for heel clearance. If the angle approached 90 degrees the arc described by the shaper spindle would bring the cutter heel into contact with the wood and would make smooth, cleanly cut work impossible. Set up the reed cutters in shaper collars, and cut reed divisions.

For sanding flutes and reeds, grip the jig in the vise without removing the post. It is the most convenient way to hold the turning and still revolve it as sanding progresses. Photo 173 shows a round-edged block covered with sandpaper for flute work. It is well to sand all flutes with No. ½ paper before changing to No. 3/0. A sanding block for reeds has an edge similar to the reeding shaper tools. Sand reeds by starting the paper-covered block down in each division and working up to the apex. Note the pencil line that marks the flute ends. After flute and reed sanding, replace the post in the lathe for pencil-mark removal and a final No. 7/0 finishing paper sanding.

The next six photographs illustrate leg progression. Mark ½-inch squares on the pattern board. Follow the previously explained practice of transferring the leg outline from the drawing (page 89) to the pattern board. Band-saw the pattern to shape. Use 3-inch-thick wood from the list of materials, which will be band-sawed to outline. Two legs 1⅜ inches thick will be obtained from one band-sawed outline. Place the pattern (as indicated in Photo 174) on the 3-inch-thick block. Mark three complete outlines, nesting the pattern as shown for minimum waste.

In Photo 175 waste wood has been sawed from the bottom curve and dovetail surface of the first leg outline. Be especially careful to keep on a straight line when sawing the foot bottom and dovetail (or post juncture) lines. The relationship of these lines, one to the other, is 90 degrees (check with the drawing, page 89). Photo 175 also shows the saw starting the upper curve cut.

A leg outline, completely sawed from the block, lies on the band-saw table in Photo 176. The penciled outlines of two more legs show clearly on the block. When all three are band-sawed, enough material has been prepared for six legs.

One side of each double-width leg blank must be smoothed either by the jointer or by the hand plane for resawing (Photo 177). Set the circular saw fence to 1⅜ inches plus about 1/32 inch for saw-mark removal. For safety, have the saw blade raised to little more than half the necessary height. Make this cut, and turn the leg blank end over end to cut the remaining half. The smoothed side of the leg blank is, of course, placed against the fence (Photo 178).

The blank remaining after the first $1\frac{3}{8}$-inch width was resawed now has two rough sides. Smooth one side with plane or jointer, and size to width (Photo 179). Repeat with the other two double-width leg blanks. Smooth the sawed side of each of the six legs.

Next, cut dovetails on the straight $3\frac{5}{8}$-inch surfaces. These operations call for a series of photographs and related textual instructions identical to those given for the Piecrust Table. For instructions, turn to pages 170–171 (Photos 348–357).

After completing the dovetails, mark a piece of stencil paper $9\frac{1}{2}$ inches long by $1\frac{3}{8}$ inches wide with $\frac{1}{2}$-inch squares for side profile pattern. (An outline guide for this purpose is scaled down in the drawing on page 89.) Cut the pattern to shape with scissors. Hold the pattern as in Photo 180, keeping the pattern tip on the forward end of the leg blank. Mark the outline with a pencil. Band-saw to these lines while holding the leg so that the foot pad is solidly on the saw table. When the saw cuts to the ankle area (Photo 181), lower the leg for convenient sawing of the remaining taper. Repeat on the other five legs.

A helpful piece of shop equipment (not shown in Photo 182) is a leg-supporting prop of wood about bench height. Make it $2\frac{1}{2}$ inchs wide by $\frac{1}{2}$ to $\frac{3}{4}$ inch thick with a square-edged flat bottom channel $\frac{1}{2}$ inch deep by $1\frac{1}{2}$ inches wide cut in one end. When a leg is gripped in the vise at the dovetail end so that the overhanging end rests in the prop channel, solid support is assured. The prop's main purpose, however, is to allow unobstructed working space above and on each side of the foot.

Draw a center line freehand on the top of a foot from its tip past the ankle area. Round the foot from center line to side profile with a large No. 3 gouge (Photo 182). The tool cutting direction is from the highest point toward the tip; then it is reversed to cut toward the ankle. Continue the rounding process past the ankle until the grain direction necessitates another tool reversal.

Change the vise grip on the leg to bring the bottom surface upward. Round the corners of the under side from the ankle to and including some of the foot pad. The foot bottom surface should now be roughly egg-shaped, as in Photo 183.

In the box drawing (page 89) pertinent measurements and claw positions are marked on a shaded drawing. The height of the side "nails" is $\frac{7}{16}$ inch, while the main front nail reaches to $\frac{9}{16}$ inch. Space the lines parallel with the bottom surface upward $\frac{7}{16}$ inch on the sides (Photo 184) and one $\frac{9}{16}$ inch across the front. If necessary, re-mark the center line from tip to ankle. The box drawing shows the side claws starting $\frac{7}{8}$ inch back from the tip. The nails taper in width from about $\frac{5}{32}$ inch at the top to a $\frac{1}{16}$-inch tip. Side knuckles adjoining the nails may be drawn $\frac{1}{4}$ inch wide by $\frac{3}{8}$ inch long; the front knuckle, $\frac{1}{4}$ inch wide by about $\frac{1}{2}$ inch long. These figures are by no means fixed: they only indicate proportions and claw position. Some variation may well add a distinctive touch to the feet. Draw three claws on each foot, as in Photo 184.

Veiner relief cuts follow the claw lines. Use the $\frac{1}{4}$-inch No. 41, cutting only as deep as tool control permits without the use of a mallet (Photo 185). A deeper cut may be made after the egg has been cut down to rough size and shape. An important difference between rat claws and bird claws is the absence of webs on the rat's foot. Side claws on the rat's foot angle up to meet the central one at about the high point of the foot. Depth of relief for claws should not exceed $\frac{3}{16}$ inch at any point, and should become quite shallow when nearing the base line. An average reduction of egg size when carrying through claw relief is about $\frac{1}{16}$ inch at the base, deepening to $\frac{3}{16}$ inch where the claws join. Use No. 3 gouges of various widths for egg shaping.

Carve the claws to finish shape next, giving them a smooth, rounded appearance. Use a No. 41 veiner to shape the claws and sharpen the juncture line where they grip the egg. All rounding and contour work can be done with a $\frac{1}{2}$-inch No. 3 gouge. There is only one distinct break in the smooth-flowing claw line—where the nail and the knuckle meet (Photo 186).

The last cuts on the feet are made with a veiner. Photo 187 shows a parting cut that separates the egg from a $\frac{1}{8}$-inch-thick pad. Remove the severed nail ends from the pad edge with a No. 3 gouge.

Photo 188 pictures a leg held at the dovetail end in the vise. It is supported by the prop already described in this chapter. Before the next operation of rounding the leg, an important condition should be noted. When you were shaping the egg below the side claws, you removed considerable wood. This left heavy shoulders on the under side of the ankle (Photo 187) which must be reduced to a narrow shoulder of about $\frac{3}{32}$ inch. Use a drawknife for both this operation and rounding the leg. Observe on Photo 188 that the leg rounding does not extend above the knee. It does, however, continue up the leg on the under side, tapering off at the dovetail.

Sand the legs and feet first with No. $\frac{1}{2}$ paper. Sand the sides and the undersides in their entirety, the tops only as far as the knees. Sand with the grain on flat side surfaces. Very light pressure on coarse paper when you are sanding the feet will retain the carved sharpness. Repeat with No. 3/0 paper (Photo 189).

Dovetailed legs, having been previously fitted, may now be attached permanently to the posts. Coat the sides and bottom of a channel with glue. Choose the corresponding leg number, and glue-coat the dovetail. Enter and slide the leg upward in its channel (Photo 190). Reasonable force to seat the leg solidly may be applied with a hammer or mallet to the underside of the leg. If any leg should fit loosely at the top, make a wedge-shaped piece of wood about $\frac{1}{2}$ inch long, running with the grain from a feather edge to $\frac{1}{8}$ inch. Glue-coat both sides, and place it against one side of the channel (heavy end upward) before seating the leg. Should a wedge be needed at the bottom end, introduce a glued wedge and drive it in with a hammer after the leg has been seated.

Photo 191 shows one leg of the stand held in the vise while work is done on the other two. From the knees to the tops, the legs are still in a rough, oversize state. Use a large No. 3 gouge, and chip downward from the turned cap as far as the grain direction permits. Reverse the tool direction, and chip upward from the knee. Gouge work is not intended to leave a finished surface but only to remove most of the excess waste wood. The crowned contour worked on the legs below the knees is to continue up to the cap. The two visible legs in Photo 191 are being shaped to near finish size.

Photo 192 illustrates the use of a round-bed drawknife. Drawknives are designed with either a flat or a rounded bed. Usually the one with a flat bed is the larger and has an adjustment screw at each end of the knife. This tool is for use on either flat or convex surfaces, whereas the round-bed type is for concave work. Blend the crown shape of the lower leg area into the newly cut knee and up to the cap. Process all the legs to this point.

The top leg surfaces are quite prominent, especially when finished; exercise care in sanding, and remove even the smallest blemishes. Examine each leg after sanding, for possible unevenness that could mar the smooth-flowing lines. Sand each leg thoroughly with No. $\frac{1}{2}$ paper, then with No. 3/0. Sand the other legs in like manner.

Scribe a 6-inch circle on the 6-by-6-by-1³⁄₁₆-inch block provided for the supporting disc, and band-saw to this line. Bore a pilot hole for the lathe screw center-face plate. Mount the blank on the face plate. First true up the edge, removing all band-saw marks. True up the bottom face, cutting away only as much wood as is necessary. Leaving a 3¼-inch diameter bottom face, cut a fillet ³⁄₁₆ inch deep, and carry this lower level out to the edge on a straight line. Use the ¾-inch gouge for this entire turning (Photo 194). Round the corner to about a ½-inch radius. Mark a true center with the parting tool for boring a 1-inch receiving hole for the post dowel. Sand first with No. ½ paper, keeping it in motion laterally, to avoid deep scratches. Follow with No. 3/0 sandpaper. Repeat with the second supporting disc. These turnings do not have to be reversed, because the top faces have been planed. Bore 1-inch center holes for the post dowels. When boring, clamp the turnings to the level bench top—align the brace and bit for true 90-degree holes. Bore three screw clearance holes in each disc for attaching tops.

Through the center of the post dowels, cut a longitudinal band-saw slot (blade width). Prepare two wedges about 1¼ inches long by 1 inch wide, tapering them from ¹⁄₁₆ to ¼ inch. Coat the 1-inch hole of one disc with glue. Place the disc over the dowel so that the slot is at right angles to the wood grain. Press the disc down over the dowel, tapping it with a hammer if necessary for solid seating. Coat with glue, both sides of a wedge, introduce it in the slot, and drive it in tightly with a hammer. Take the precaution of holding the stand off the floor when driving in the wedge. Allow overnight drying. Cut off the protruding wedge wood to the level disc surface with a large No. 3 gouge (Photo 195).

Mark two circles on each of the 11-by-11-by-1³⁄₁₆-inch pieces. The larger, outside diameters, are to be 11 inches. Inside circles should be scribed to the wood face-plate diameter of the lathe. Use these smaller circles as guides when centering and attaching the lathe faceplate. Band-saw to the larger diameter (Photo 196).

Photo 197 shows the steel faceplate fastened to the larger wood plate with screws. Four screws near the wood-plate perimeter hold the top firmly while it is turning. Center the wood faceplate accurately on the inner circle, and drive in the screws. Choose a screw ⅜ inch longer than the thickness of the wood faceplate. Mount this assembly on the lathe spindle.

Check the lathe speed chart in Chapter I for the proper r.p.m. of a disc this size. First, true up the edge, removing all band-saw marks with the ¾-inch gouge. Round the bottom surface corner to a ½-inch radius—this is the surface attached to the faceplate (Photo 198). Keep the tool rest very close to the work, because in one revolution the tool cuts two alternate cycles, with the grain and against it. This condition needs more effort for tool control.

Swing the tool rest parallel to the top surface, setting it quite close to the work (Photo 199). True out the top surface, removing no more wood than is necessary. Cut a groove ⅛ inch deep with the parting tool, leaving ¼ inch of wood on the outer edge for a bead. Form the bead by laying the skew flat on the tool rest and scraping the wood to the desired shape. This will not leave as smooth a surface as would result were the skew pointed in and made to cut instead of scrape. Because of the alternate grain direction, point cutting is not safe (Photo 200).

From the parting-tool flat, which is ⅛ inch deep, cut a shallow fillet another ⅛ inch deep with the ¾-inch gouge (Photo 201). This new level should be held as the turning progresses toward the disc center. As in Photo 201, use of the ¾-inch gouge extends only far enough to give clearance to the larger gouge.

Cut away the remaining waste wood of the top with the large gouge (Photo 202). When nearing the desired level, have a straight-edged stick about 9 inches long to touch against the top surface. Gradually turn down the high points, frequently checking with the stick for a straight surface. Handle the gouge cautiously at the exact center of the turning. It is better to leave a slight rise here than to undercut.

Sand the outside edge, bead, and fillet with folded No. ½ paper. Use a block covered with No. ½ paper for the flat top surface. As before, keep the block in motion. Otherwise, deep scratches extremely hard to work out will result. Repeat with No. 3/0 paper, sanding longer than seems necessary for positive removal of coarse scratches. Take the faceplate assembly from the lathe, remove the top, and burn in the screw holes with stick shellac, or fill them with other material. Sand the bottom surface first with coarse, then with fine sandpaper, using the block with each number grit. Repeat with the other top.

Place the supporting disc on the inverted top as in Photo 203. Direct the grain of support at right angles to the grain of the top. Measure from the support block to the edge of the top at about four points of the circle to center the base. Use three screws as illustrated—their length not to exceed ⅜ inch plus supporting disc thickness at the screw-hole area. Seat the screws, and bring the other stand to completion.

After a quick rub-off with No. 7/0 finishing paper and a careful examination for flaws, the stands are ready for finishing materials.

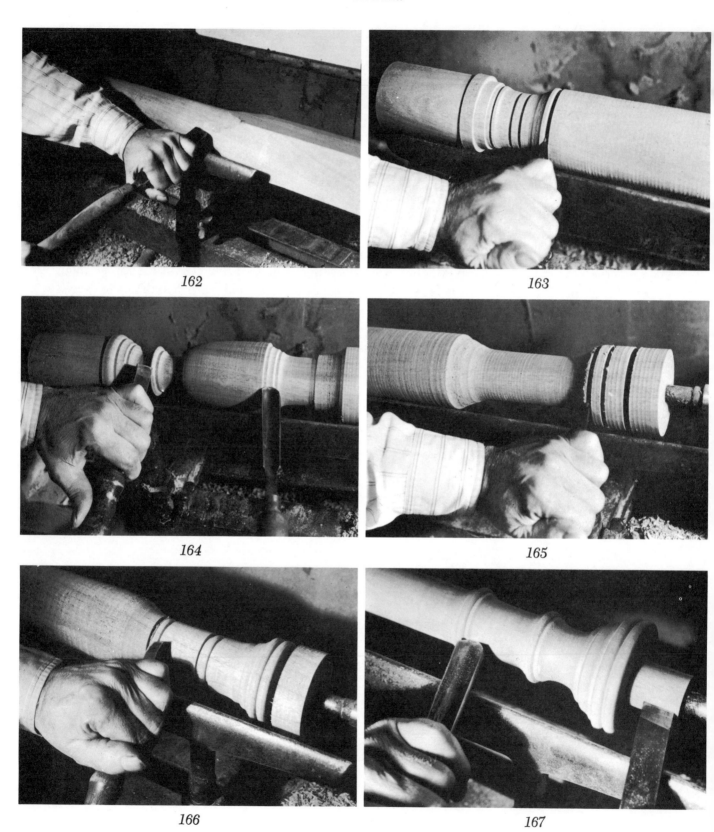

162

163

164

165

166

167

168

169

170

171

172

173

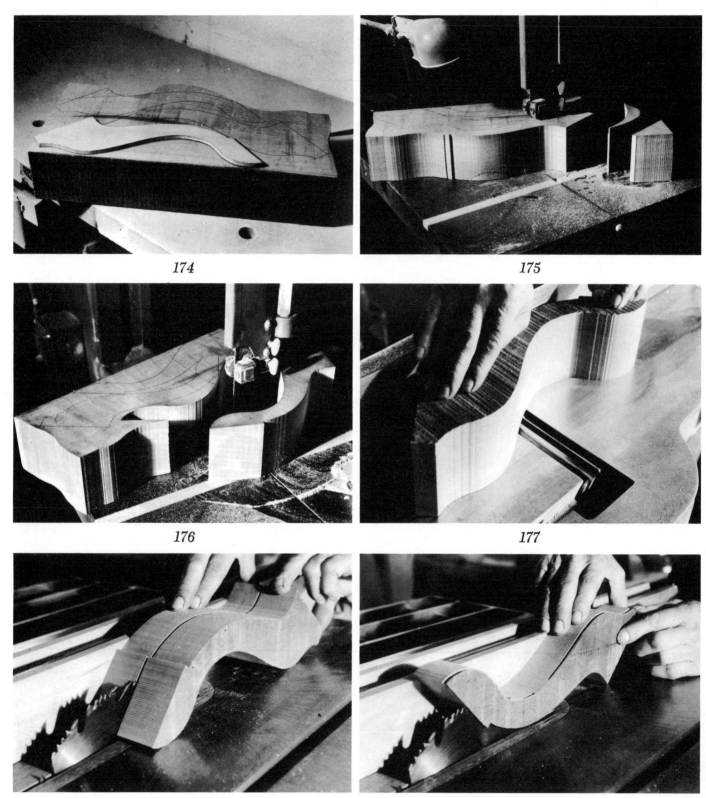

174

175

176

177

178

179

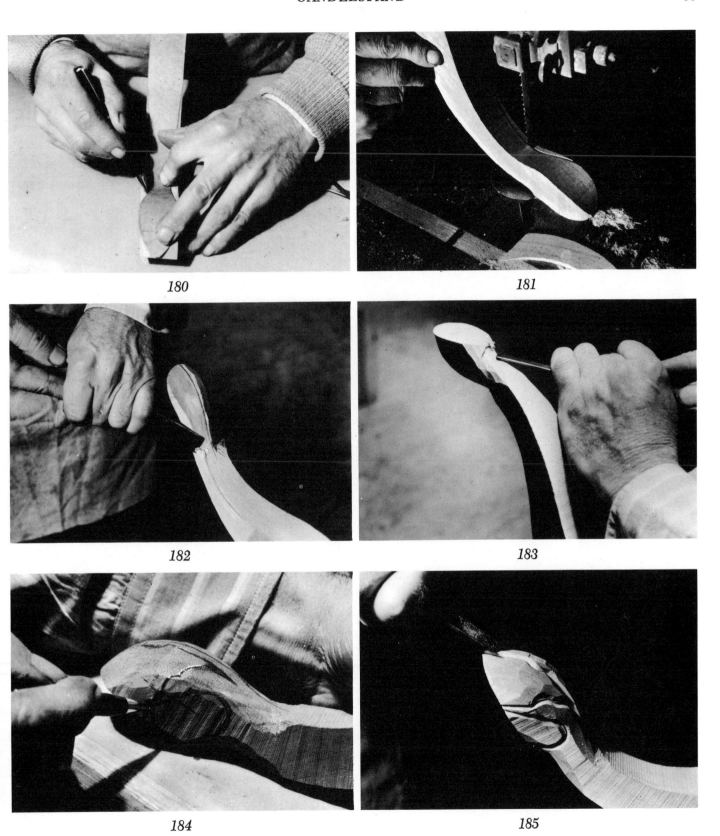

180

181

182

183

184

185

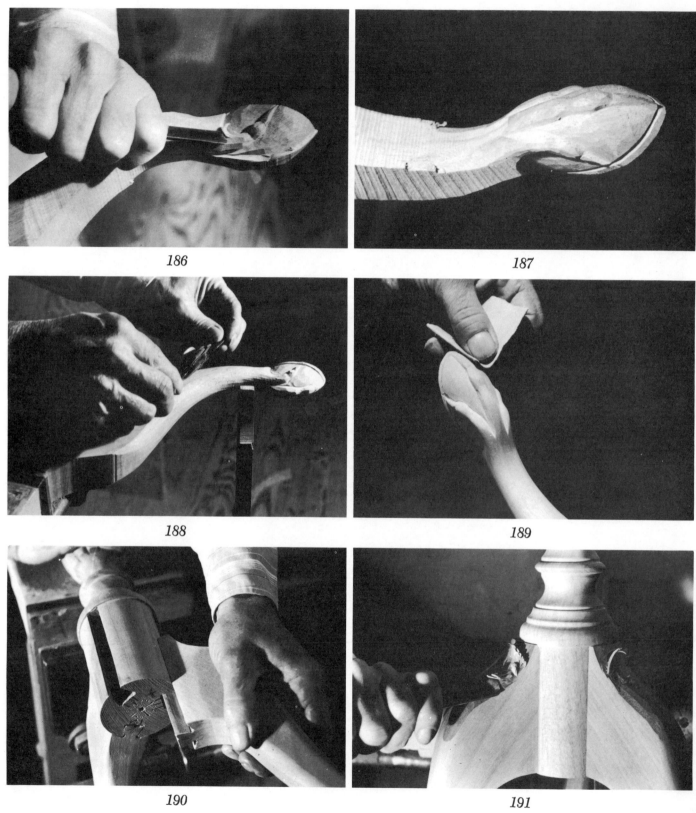

186

187

188

189

190

191

192

193

194

195

196

197

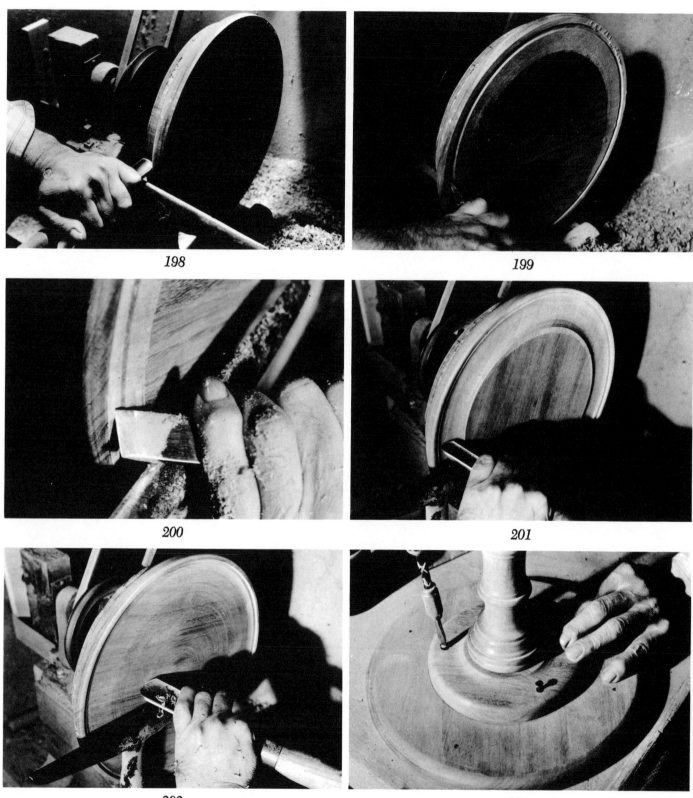

198

199

200

201

202

203

Walnut Mirror Frame

CHAPTER VII

Walnut Mirror Frame

CONNECTICUT ORIGIN, 1720

Materials (Measures in Inches)

WALNUT	LENGTH	WIDTH	THICKNESS
2 pieces	29	2⁹⁄₁₆	¹³⁄₁₆
1 piece	18⅞	1½	¹³⁄₁₆
1 piece	16¾	3¼	¹³⁄₁₆
1 piece	16	6½	⅝

1 piece ¼-inch silvered plate glass cut to fit the glass rabbet.
1 piece ⅛-inch Masonite cut to fit the back rabbet.

Mirror frames of 1720 were necessarily small. Sheet-glass manufacture and the silver coating process were crude and expensive; consequently, glass was restricted to a few square feet in area Quality was never equal to that of flat glass today. Bubbles and waves were the most common imperfections. The glass size of the original frame reproduced and enlarged for this chapter is only 10⅛ by 16⅞ inches.

Three different widths and lengths make up the parts for this frame. Study the drawing (page 107) to become familiar with the positions of top and bottom rails in relation to the stiles. Dotted lines represent the size each frame part must measure to saw accurate end miters. The drawing shows two stiles (frame side pieces) with over-all measurements of 29 by 2⁹⁄₁₆ inches. The ends of both pieces are mitered, holding to the 29-inch outside length. All four frame parts are ¹³⁄₁₆ inch thick. The bottom rail is the only frame part that can be sawed directly to the finish width and mitered to 18⅞ inches length. The top rail as shown on the drawing should be 3¼ inches wide and squared to 16¾ inches length. Observe the miters on this piece. Instead of starting the 45-degree cuts at the top corners, measure from the top 2 inches downward on the squared ends, and mark with a pencil. Start the miter cuts at these points. After the miter work is completed, choose a surface of each frame part for the face side, and mark it prominently in pencil. Also mark the top ends of the stiles so that they will be milled, right and left, for splines.

Mount the ¼-inch dado head on the circular saw arbor, and raise it to cut a strong ½ inch in height. Set the fence ⁷⁄₁₆ inch from the near side of the cutter. Channel all mitered ends for splines as in Photo 206. Place the marked face sides against the saw fence.

Mill the splines from scrap pieces of walnut not less than 3½ inches wide. Depending on the wood thickness, provide enough for four splines. Use a hollow-ground saw if it is part of the shop equipment. Saw the wood for splines to 1-inch lengths. Reset the saw fence so that ¼-inch-thick pieces can be cut from these blocks. Because the block in Photo 207 is so small it is pushed past the saw with a notched stick for safety. Try the first spline in a channel for size. It should not be so tight that it has to be seated with hammer or mallet blows; nor should it fit loosely. If necessary, make fence adjustments and complete spline sizing.

Top corner patterns are needed now. Follow the usual procedure of laying off ½-inch squares on pattern board and penciling in the outline provided in the drawing (page 107). They may be made separately or combined into one (as shown on Photo 208). Band-saw to outline.

Assemble the frame, complete with splines but without glue. The bottom rail ends are fitted to meet the outside stile edges, which means that the over-all frame width, at the bottom, will measure 18⅞ inches. To determine the position of the top rail, measure down the stile miters 1½ inches and mark in pencil. Start the upper end of the top rail miters at these points. Press all joints together, seating them firmly. Check the frame with a large square. Now check the frame width at the top; it should be 18⅞ inches. If there is a variation, either raise or lower the top rail to correct the measurement. In that case, change the pencil marks denoting the top rail position.

Place the corner pattern on the frame as in Photo 208. Keep the outside straight edges flush with the frame edges. If the pattern is in its proper position, the pencil line representing the mitered joint will be directly over the frame joint (Photo 208). It is necessary to mark only the inside curves at this time because the outside will be marked and band-sawed after the frame parts are glued together.

Separate the frame parts, at the same time removing the splines. Set the hollow-ground saw to cut 1½ inches wide, and saw the stiles to a point near where they break into curves (Photo 209). The left stile can be started into the saw at the bottom end. The right side piece must be lowered onto the saw at the curve, and cut completely through the lower mitered end. The top rail (having drop curves at both ends) must be lowered onto the saw at the left side and stopped when near the right curve. Before removing, stop the saw motion for safety.

Photo 210 shows the band saw completing the top-rail curve cuts. Start the band saw at one end, cut to the pencil line blending the curve cut into the straight one made by the circular saw. Carefully pass the rail (in the straight saw-cut channel) to the other end curve. Saw to this line, completing the shape of the inside top rail. Band-saw to the inside lines drawn on the stiles.

Place two bar clamps on the work table, paralleling them about the frame width. Glue-coat the dado channels of both stiles. Coat with glue the half of each spline that will be entered into the stile channels. Enter and seat the splines, positioning them for removal of waste wood inside and out. Now glue the channels of the top and bottom rails. Glue-coat the remaining portions of the splines, and assemble the frame. Place it on the bar clamps, but do not draw the clamps tight yet. Adjust two more clamps for the frame width, and place them on top of the frame at the top and bottom ends (Photo 211). Now exert pressure, a little at a time, on all clamps. Vary the pressure of some clamps to allow each frame joint to slide into its exact position. Check with a large square. Allow overnight drying.

Remove the clamps. Cut off the waste spline extensions on the four inside corners. Place the corner pattern in position, and mark for the outside curve (Photo 212). Repeat at the other top corner. Band-saw to outlines (Photo 213).

The waste spline wood will be removed from the outside top corners when you band-saw them to

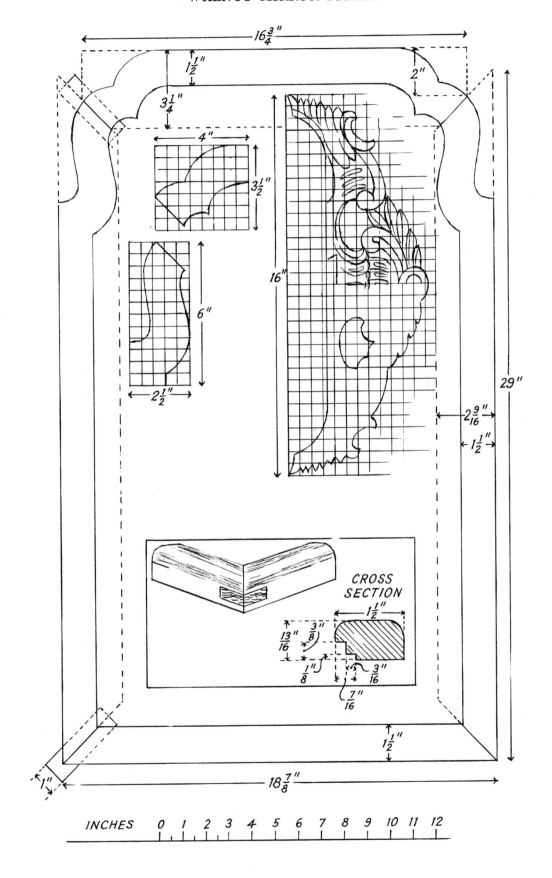

CROSS SECTION

INCHES 0 1 2 3 4 5 6 7 8 9 10 11 12

outline. The lower spline extensions must be chipped off with a No. 3 gouge (Photo 214). As illustrated in the photograph, the grain direction makes it necessary to start the chipping at the corner and move along the frame.

Set up the shaper with the cutters ground to about a ½-inch radius. Position them in the grooved collars so that the cutting starts just above the lower collar (Photo 215). When the cutters are set as directed, the lower collar acts as a stop for cutting depth. Adjust the spindle for height, place the frame on the shaper table face side up, and round the corners, inside and out. At all indented curve breaks, the shaper will cut only to its radius (Photo 215). Sharp divisions to follow the outline must be cut in with hand tools. It is presumed that a shaper is part of the shop equipment. If it is not, hand tools can be used; but they consume much more time.

In Photo 216 the shaper is mounted with one square-edged cutter for glass and back grooving. The use of two cutters is preferable; but if only one can be used a piece of the same-width steel must fill the opposite groove. Set the cutter for a ¼-inch-wide rabbet. Turn the frame over (face down), and adjust the shaper spindle to cut ⅜ inch from the wood height downward (check with the drawing cross section, page 107). This is the glass groove in depth and width. Reset the square-edged cutter to ⁷⁄₁₆ inch, and adjust the height to cut only ⅛ inch downward. This cut will provide a seating groove for the ⅛-inch Masonite back.

The same radius corners result when shaping the back rabbets, as explained for the front rounding. Photo 217 shows a bottom corner being squared out with a chisel and mallet. Make a number of narrow cuts rather than subject the corner to too great shock. If you do not have a shaper you can cut the straight-line portions of grooves on the circular saw. In this case, saw the grooves before assembly to eliminate squaring out lower corners.

Photo 218 shows the corner on the right squared out, and (center) the manner in which the top curve is treated. Cutting glass to an indented point is impractical if not impossible. This problem is solved by cutting the glass and back channels in a straight line from wide point to wide point.

Turn the frame face up, and clamp it to the bench top for hand-tool rounding of the indentations. Chop-cut a parting line up and over the round with a ¾-inch chisel, holding the tool in line with the opposite point. Using a large No. 3 gouge, chip the wood as illustrated on the left of Photo 219, forming a continuation of the round into the parting cut. Progress of this work in Photo 219 shows the indentation on the right parted, and one side rounded. On the left of the photograph, the parting cut has been made, one side rounded, and the gouge is chipping the other side.

Next, make a pattern for the crest carving. For this size pattern, the use of rigid material is suggested. Divide it into ½-inch squares in the usual manner. Instead of following the guide line in the drawing (page 107) for the lower or frame matching outline, place the frame on the pattern board and mark its outline. Follow the drawing guide for all other design lines. Jig-saw the pattern to outline, including the two internal cut-outs. Marking one half of the pattern with the over-all design, as shown in Photo 220, will make the carver increasingly familiar with its curves and proportions. Mark the pattern outline on the 16-by-6½-by-⅝-inch panel, as shown in Photo 220. Because of short radius curves, saw this panel on the jig rather than the band saw. After jig-sawing, place the panel in position on the frame for trial fitting. If necessary, remove wood at the indicated areas with hand tools for a satisfactory fit.

The craftsman should start this crest carving with the right idea. Whereas the carved decorations in previous chapters are finer, more exacting, the crest here is boldly cut. Wide variations are much more acceptable in this style of carving. The lengths and widths of design components shown in the drawing, and the depths suggested in the text, need not be adhered to precisely. They are only guides to insure an attractive, well proportioned crown for the frame. This type carving should show smooth-flowing, confidently made cuts. If any cut should be deeper than intended, but otherwise made with assurance, the extra depth will not detract from a pleasing appearance.

First, the design parts are identified for later reference. (Consult Photos 224 and 225 while reading these design terms.) Center ring and button, wing leaves on each side above wing spiral head scrolls. Inside C scrolls bordering cut-outs. Outside C scrolls joined to inside C's by solid-head intermediate scrolls. V-cut ribs on the extreme ends. Channeled ribs under ring and bottom.

Photo 221 shows carving started on the panel's right side. Complete button relief and rounding, depth about ⅛ inch. Half of the ring has been relieved and rounded, about the same depth. Partial relief of spiral head scroll, final depth on underside about ⅜ inch. The tool is making relief clearance cuts on the right inside C scroll. The solid head-scroll is finish-cut with greatest depth of relief (about ⅜ inch) below the head. This scroll is not cove-cut on the inside edge but has a sheer wall with all rounding toward the outside. Rounding continues over the head with the greatest slope at the cut-out.

Both ends of the outside C scroll are in balance, whereas only one end of the inside C's are full-cut. When cutting the outside C scrolls, part with the ⅜-inch veiner instead of the usual gouge chop. This tool is suggested for two reasons: first, because the depth is little more than ⅛ inch; and, secondly, because it leaves a desirable sharp slope from the ridge downward. Before determining the course the ridge is to follow, gently slope the C tips to about ⅛-inch depth. Now pencil in the ridge line from the actual tip (which is about the center of the scroll width), gradually curving it over to blend in with the veiner parting ridge. Study carefully Photo 221. Observe how the wood on the outward side of the ridge is sharply sloped on a convex curve, using a No. 3 gouge. Choose the No. 7 gouge for the cove cut which starts at the tips, gradually increasing in depth to about ⅜ inch. Grain direction necessitates cutting from each end of the scrolls.

The entire length of edge wood bordering the frame must be chamfered with a No. 3 gouge ⅛ inch deep and about ¼ inch wide. This is done to equalize in thickness the panel edge to the square frame edge before it starts to round (Photo 222). Also, this photograph shows the V-cut rib area as having been sloped before dividing with the ⅜-inch No. 41. Another veiner cut breaks the chamfered surface from the bottom edge to the area under the C scroll. Farther in toward the center (determine the location on the drawing, page 107), chop-part two leaf ends, one round and one pointed. Depth increases as the background nears the solid head scroll. Use the ⅜-inch veiner to part the leaves and isolate the lower side of the round-tipped leaf. (All these instructions are pictured in Photo 222.) Convex the end of the round-tipped leaf. Scoop out its center with a No. 7 gouge, starting about ¼ inch from the tip and gradually decreasing the depth of cut. Complete this leaf with two veiner cuts in the hollow. Instructions are given in the singular, but as each cut is made on one side, a balancing cut should be made on the other side of the panel.

Directly below the solid head scroll (Photo 222), slope the background from a high ridge (at the chamfer) down to the ⅜-inch-deep relief cut. Using a No. 11 gouge, break this plain surface with three channel cuts. Break the chamfer at about this point with a veiner cut, first crossing the chamfer, paralleling it for approximately 1½ inches, then recrossing. The tools showing in this photograph are a No. 11 gouge below, a No. 7 gouge upper left, and the ⅜-inch veiner.

Chop-part for relief the two sides of the spiral scroll and the inside C scroll (Photo 223). Relieve the lower side of the spiral to about ⅜ inch, the upper side to ³⁄₁₆ inch. Draw a guide line through the center of the scroll to a tight curl on the head (drawing, page 107). Convex outside this line, continuing around the head to the end of the curl. Scoop out the curl center with a ⅛-inch No. 4 gouge to about ¼-inch depth. Inside the line from head to ring, use a No. 7 gouge to make the cove cutout.

The area intended for wing leaves should be crowned: the lower side sloping to the scroll parting-cut depth, the upper edge to about ⅜ inch. Divide the leaves with a veiner according to the drawing. Each leaf has an off-center ridge line with sides sloped by a large No. 3 gouge. Cut a vein in the wide side of each leaf.

The inside C scroll starts with the shape of the outside C, but the parting veiner cut and the cove taper off when nearing the scroll's other end. Do not cut the cove quite as deeply as the outside scroll.

Crown the wood surface between spiral scrolls, leaving wood full thickness in the center—between the C scrolls, just a slight crown, governed in height by the depth of C scroll relief cuts. The ⅛-inch veiner, to be used next, is shown in the left photograph lying on the panel. Pencil-mark six division lines for ribs. Cut on these lines the full depth of the ⅛-inch No. 41. Channel between the rib cuts with No. 7 gouge. Still using No. 7, chop a sharply sloping cut at the end of each channel. Now lean the tool about the same angle the other way, and chop to form a crude chain line dividing the two central areas.

Below the C scrolls cut across the chamfer, about 3 inches apart, two flaring No. 3 chop cuts, and relieve to form what appears to be a base block. Above and parallel to the chamfer, make a veiner cut to complete the block effect. As shown in Photo 223, chop-part a crescent line ½ inch from each inside C scroll, and slope-cut in relief. Complete the carving with veiner cuts in each crescent and one up the center line.

Near the curve on each end of the frame top rail, drive in a brad for a blind dowel. Cut the brads, leaving about ⅛ inch protruding. Lay the frame flat on the bench or work table, and place the carved crest close to it on the same level plane. Carefully align them, and press together for brad marks. Separate. Remove the brads, bore ³⁄₁₆-inch holes ¾ inch deep in the frame and the crest. Photo 224 shows the holes in the frame part.

Cut two ³⁄₁₆-inch dowels 1⅜ inches long; coat the holes in the crest with glue, enter the dowels and seat them (Photo 225). Glue-coat the holes in the frame, enter the dowels and press the crest in place. Very little sanding is required for the crest carving. A cursory rub-off with No. 3/0 paper is sufficient.

Photo 226 shows the frame ready for finish. It is recommended that you have the glass cut to fit the frame opening before you apply finishing materials. The material list calls for ⅛-inch Masonite to back up the glass. Cut this material to fit, and drill holes very near the edge, about 6 inches apart, for small wood screws. Apply finishing materials to the frame, rub down, and wax. Insert the glass, placing a sheet of brown paper between the glass and the Masonite. Place the Masonite in its groove, and fasten it with screws. A few inches below the curved part of the frame, on the back surface, turn in a small screw-eye on each stile. Thread heavy picture wire through the eyes, leaving enough slack to stretch the wire over a picture hook at about the top rail.

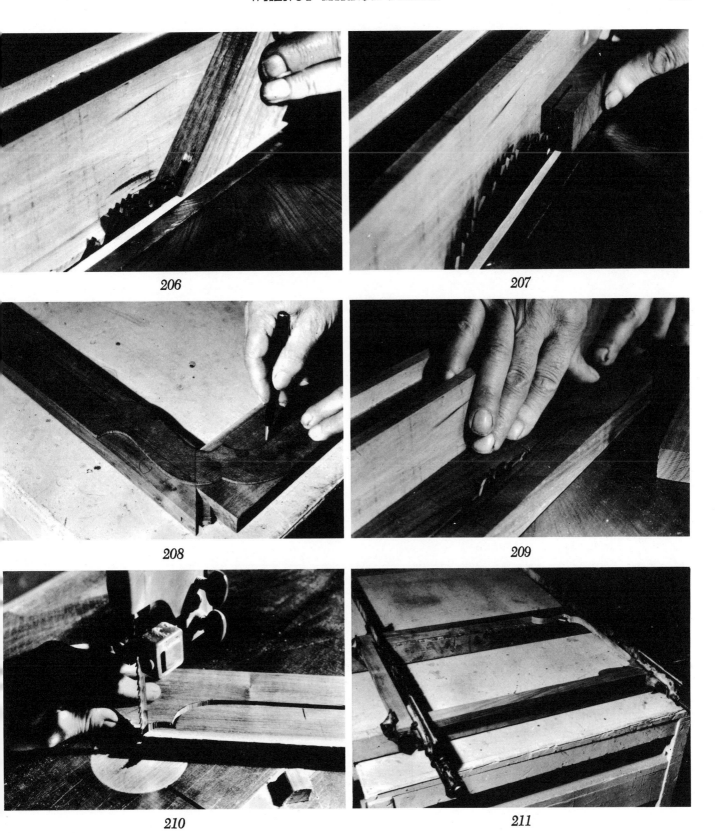

206

207

208

209

210

211

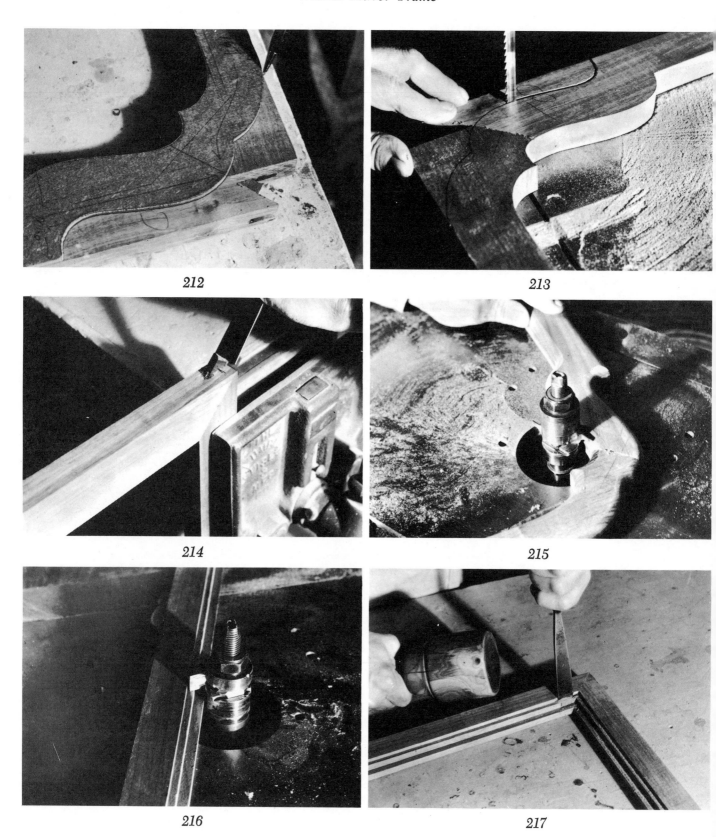

212

213

214

215

216

217

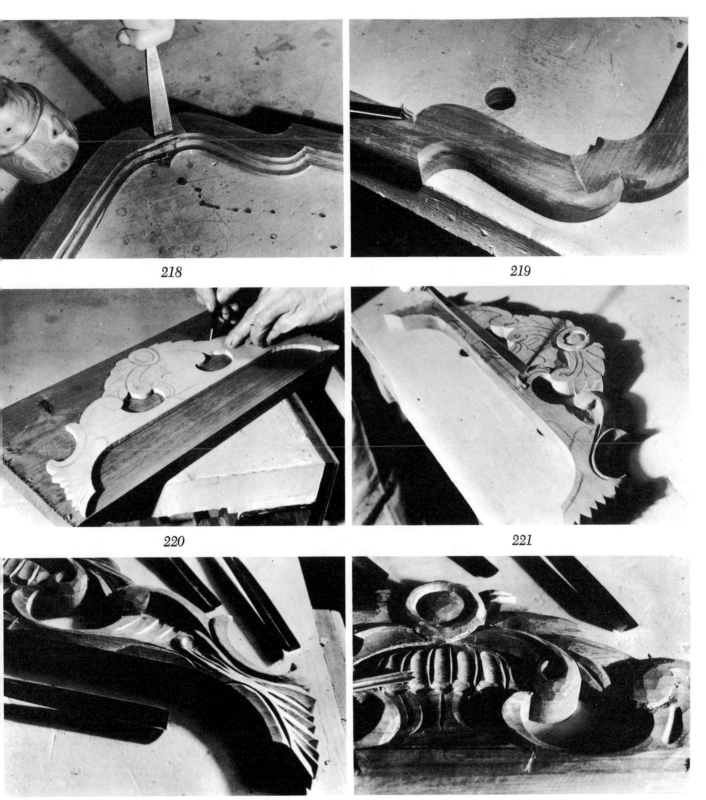

218

219

220

221

222

223

224

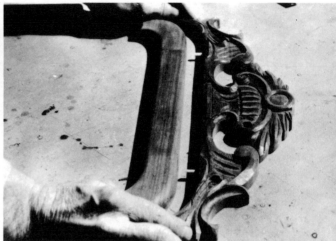

225

226

Paw-Foot Coffee Table

CHAPTER VIII

Paw-Foot Coffee Table

NEW YORK ORIGIN, 1760

Materials (Mahogany, Sizes in Inches)

PIECES	LENGTH	WIDTH	THICKNESS
4	17	2¾	2¾
2	36½	3	$1\frac{3}{16}$
2	16½	3	$1\frac{3}{16}$
8	2½	3½	1¾
2	27¾	$1\frac{3}{16}$	$1\frac{3}{16}$
2	7¾	$1\frac{3}{16}$	$1\frac{3}{16}$
1	40	20	$1\frac{3}{16}$

Coffee tables are modern functional furniture units devised to fill a specific need. Their counterparts in the eighteenth century were "tea tables" light enough to be easily moved from place to place. In socially prominent homes of that era, the tables most used for "tea" were of the piecrust variety. The chair seats were uniformly high, so that table heights of 28 to 30 inches were standard.

To preserve traditional lines, coffee-table design must be adapted from furniture parts of corresponding proportions, such as the front legs of chairs, or stool legs, which are within an inch or two of the coffee-table leg height.

The table designed for this chapter is adapted entirely (except for the wood top) from an eighteenth century New York stool. The stool, of course, is upholstered, with the covering material stretched down over the skirting to meet the carved skirt molding. The table design calls for exposed skirt wood, solid wood top, and submolding. The suggested and illustrated size is 40 inches long by 20 inches wide by 17¾ inches high. Except for the top, the construction procedure follows that of stools.

Mill the legs first. With jointer or hand plane, smooth two right-angle surfaces of each leg. Set the saw fence to cut 2¾ inches plus ¹⁄₃₂ inch for the final smoothing of sawed surfaces. Saw the legs to size. Square the ends to 17-inch finish length. Smooth the sawed right-angle surfaces.

Make a leg pattern, according to the instructions in Chapters IV and V. A scaled block pattern guide is provided in the drawing on page 119. A few words of caution bear repeating: When you place the pattern for outline marking on the front right-angle surfaces, be sure that the knees meet on the front corner.

Set the marking gauge for boring mortise holes. Bear in mind that the leg area adjoining the rails, when band-sawed, will be 1⅞ by 1⅞ inches. Calculate where to center the mark for boring, as follows: Measure from the back corner frontward 1⅞ inches to the presupposed band-sawed line. From that mark, measure backward first 5/16 inch for the predetermined front-rail shoulder width. This is to be the outside mortise line. Now backward another 3/16 inch, or one-half of the ⅜-inch tenon. This mark represents the center boring line and measures 1⅜ inches from the back corner. Set the gauge, and mark the right-angle back surface of each leg from the top three inches downward. On each scratched line, pencil-mark at ½ inch and 3 inches from the top for a mortise 2½ inches high. Use a bit stop on the ⅜-inch bit, setting it to bore 15/16 inch deep. Bore a line of holes between the pencil marks, centering the bit for each hole on the scratched line (Photo 227). Bore mortise holes in all four legs before you proceed further.

Cut the mortise walls to straight lines with a chisel ¾ inch wide. A mallet should not be necessary for this work (Photo 228). Square-cut the half-round ends with a ⅛- or 3/16-inch chisel. A completely cut mortise shows in Photo 228 on the perpendicular back surface. Complete all mortises.

A particularly revealing illustration of the first surface cuts for a cabriole leg is Photo 229. Each cut stops just short of completion, leaving waste wood in place so that the pencil lines may be followed when the block is quarter-turned. The solid bearing surface provided by this waste wood on the back profile assures square cuts when you make the second series of cuts. Stop the saw's motion, to back out of incompleted cuts.

Photo 230 pictures the second (quarter-turned) cuts in progress. These are identical to the first except that each cut is completed. Waste wood severed from the front lies on the saw table as it fell away from the leg block. The back profile cut is being made. Turn the leg back to its original position, and complete the first cuts. Photo 231 shows a leg with all band-saw work finished. Waste wood lies on the table as it was sawed from the leg.

Prepare the four rails by first sawing them to 3-inch width. Square the two long rails to 36½ inches and the shorter pieces to 16½ inches. These lengths were determined by providing for ¾-inch overhang of the top and ⅞-inch long tenons on the rails. Set up the circular saw arbor with the two outside dado head cutters, and place between them a ⅜-inch spacer disc. Adjust the cutting height to ⅞ inch. Set the fence so as to leave a 5/16-inch shoulder on outside surface (Photo 232). All rails must be marked on the chosen outside surface, which is placed against the fence for tenon milling. When the set-up is made, mill all rail ends.

Change to the hollow-ground saw to remove waste shoulder wood. Set it to cut the tenons ⅞ inch in length (Photo 233). Raise the blade to exact tenon height, so as to make a clean-cut corner where tenon and shoulder meet. After you have made the outside shoulder cuts, lower the saw blade and make the inside cuts. There is no appreciable wood to remove from these shoulders— the cuts are made to assure identical tenon length, front and back. Without changing the saw fence, raise the blade to cut ½ inch in height. Edge up a rail so that the chosen edge rests on the saw table, and, with the help of the crosscut gauge, make the first cut to lower the tenon height ½ inch. Keep the end of the tenon tight against the fence when you pass the rail over the saw. Repeat the process for the remaining tenons. Reset the fence to cut ½ inch to the outside of the saw blade. Raise the saw to cut ⅞ inch high. Place a rail vertically with the top edge against the fence and the front or back surface pressed against the crosscut gauge, then pass it over the saw to complete the ½-inch shoulder lowering the tenon. Repeat the process on the remaining tenons.

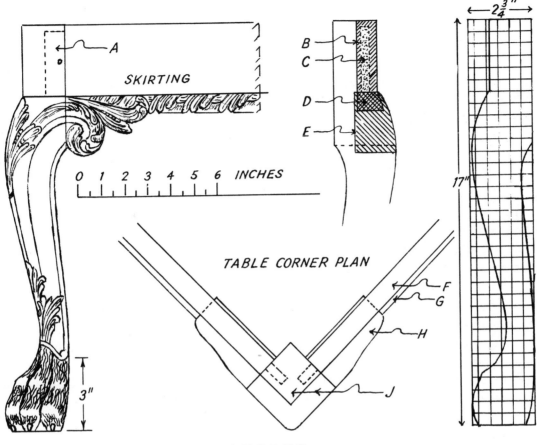

SKIRTING

0 1 2 3 4 5 6   INCHES

TABLE CORNER PLAN

$2\frac{3}{4}''$

17"

3"

LEGEND

A. TENON   F. SKIRT
B. SKIRTING   G. SKIRT MOLDING
C. TENON   H. WING BLOCK
D. SKIRT MOLDING   J. LEG SQUARE
E. WING BLOCK

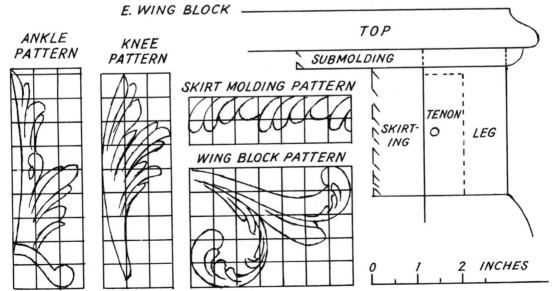

ANKLE PATTERN

KNEE PATTERN

SKIRT MOLDING PATTERN

WING BLOCK PATTERN

TOP

SUBMOLDING

SKIRT-ING   TENON   LEG

0 1 2   INCHES

Photo 234 shows the fitting of a rail tenon into a leg mortise. Trial-fit each mortise-and-tenon joint match-marking it distinctly for quick final assembly. The joints should be reasonably tight. If necessary, mortises may be enlarged by shaving a minute amount of wood from the walls. Perfect fit in a joint is structurally important.

Carving of paw feet is the next operation. The instructions will be worded for a single paw, and should be followed through on the three remaining paws. Set up the bench to hold a leg rigidly for carving. This requires raising the vise dog and inserting a stop pin in the bench top.

Start carving as shown in Photo 235, by chamfering the front and two side corners with the ¾-inch No. 3 gouge. The chamfer cuts should be about ½ inch across and should taper out below the ankle. Mark a stop line 3 inches up from the bottom to indicate where to place a scroll shield after you finish the foot carving. Pencil-mark for four equally divided toes (two on each side of the center).

Divide the toes with the ⅜-inch No. 41 veiner. As shown in Photo 236, the cuts are nearly full tool depth, and they should be made with the help of a mallet for power. To prevent splitting, the tool must cut from the highest point toward the bottom and then be reversed to go toward the ankle.

The next photograph (237) illustrates toe rounding. A large No. 3 gouge, heel up, may be used for this purpose. Remove only as much wood as is necessary on the upper joints. In doing this, follow closely the band-sawed profile of each toe. Observe that the cuts stop safely below the proposed position of the shield.

Follow the rounding process with relief cuts under the upper knuckles (Photo 238), using the ½-inch No. 9 or 10, directly across each toe to accentuate the knuckles. Gently slope each toe from the lower joint upward (Photo 238), retaining the rounded shape meanwhile. Photo 239 shows the profile change clearly.

The division cuts between toes must now be broadened. Use the ⅜-inch No. 11 (Photo 239), and cut in depth to about the tool's full capacity, with mallet blows on the handle. Start the No. 11 cut at the lower knuckles; follow the profile past the upper joints and taper out. Do not continue this cut below the lower joints. Round the toes again as shown in Photo 240. A No. 3 gouge is most suitable for this purpose. Keep its heel up wherever possible.

Deepen the lines that divide the toes with the ⅜-inch veiner, cutting especially deep between the lower and upper knuckles. Do not deepen the cuts below the lower knuckles. Photo 241 shows this work in progress. The use of a mallet gives better control.

The forming of the nails comes next. Pencil-outline the nails ½ inch high by about ¼ inch wide as in Photo 242, centering them in width at the extremity of each toe. Chop-part the half-circle over the nail with the ⅛-inch No. 4 gouge. Part the remainder with a No. 3 gouge (Photo 242). A properly formed nail seems to emerge from deep in the toe. Photos 243, 244, and 246 illustrate the toes particularly well. To sink the upper part of the nail below the surrounding wood, use the ⅛-inch No. 4 gouge, heel up, for sloping cuts on the nail in to the parting line. Deepen the half-circle parting line on a sharp angle (Photo 244). Now, to make the lower half of the nail seem to stand out, slope off the wood on each side so that that part of the nail has necessary relief. Sink the upper part of nails about ⅛ inch. Relieve the lower part about ⅛ inch.

The right-angle back surfaces, still in their rough band-sawed state, may now be brought up in progress to the front. Remove the band-saw marks with the flat-bed drawknife. Form a radius of the back corner, about ½ inch at the ankle increasing to ¾ inch at the bottom. Between the chamfered side corner and the back radius, hollow out a broad depression about ³⁄₁₆ inch deep. As shown in Photo 243, hollowing starts above the upper joint and continues to the bottom. Hollowing is to lend form to the back toe and to help shape the side corner toe. Photo 243 shows the back toenail completely cut.

A front-angle view (Photo 244) shows all nail cuts completed. Parting cuts around the half-circle must be deepened a number of times in sinking the nail. A rough-cut, shaggy look for the foot as a whole is desirable, but the nails should be clean-cut. Removal of tool marks is unnecessary, because all surfaces will be covered with fine veiner hair lines. In fact, the tool marks seem to add a touch of realism.

A pattern guide for the shield scroll and leaf design, labeled "Ankle Pattern," is part of the drawing on page 119. Follow the routine procedure for patterns, using stencil paper. The small size of this pattern, and the fact that it must be pressed to the leg contour, indicate the use of a pliable material. In cutting the pattern outline with scissors, cut on all lines except the long sweeping one that should follow the front corner. Turn the outlined side down, place it properly on a leg ankle, and mark the leg sweep again. Check for variation from the drawing guide line. If there is a difference, cut to the actual leg contour line.

Place the completed pattern on a leg with the shield touching the previously marked cross line 3 inches from the bottom. Hold and mark it as in Photo 245, first on one front surface; then, turning it over, mark the other side. Do the shield and leaf marking now, to provide an accurate line for relief cuts (Photo 246).

Cut the wood below the shield on a gradual slope to give the shield about ⅛-inch relief. To understand terminating treatment, study the toe that is at the right of the center division when in a natural position (Photo 246). A ⅜-inch veiner cut starts at the division line (about the height of the nail) and runs to the bottom on an angle that meets the nail at its lowest point. Make these finish cuts on each side of every front toe, cutting the wood between to a reasonably smooth surface (Photo 247).

With the ⅜-inch veiner, cut "lead" hair lines. They form the pattern for the finer hair lines and should be at least ⅛ inch deep. Photo 246 shows a lead pattern that may be varied as desired. Notice that the hair-line cuts wave from side to side—they are never made on a straight line. Also notice the bare knuckles. Do not cut such lines over the highest part of the knuckles (Photo 247). Bare knuckles are probably not true to life; but they give the joints a prominence possible only through such contrast. Now cover all areas with light ⅛-inch veiner cuts, close together but not running one into another. These lines also weave from side to side and vary in length from ¼ inch to 1 inch (Photo 247).

For accurate pattern placement, the shield and leaf outline is marked on the leg while the front corner is still intact. Using a drawknife, round this corner to a ¼-inch radius (shield included). The shield strap between scroll ends is ¼ inch wide. Complete the upper outline with a pencil. With appropriate tools, part this portion of the shield. Gently slope the wood above to effect a shield relief of ⅛ inch (Photo 248). Study the photograph to understand the side-corner treatment. The corner is chamfered, but not on a 45 degree angle. It shows a cut about ¼ inch wide on the front surface but only ⅛ inch on the right-angle side. Notice an important feature: one leaf tip extends to the corner, breaking the continuity of the chamfer. The leg in Photo 248 is supported by the notched prop described for the Candlestand.

Chop-part the leaf outline with tools of proper curvature for the different radii. Draw a pencil line on the front surface ¼ inch in from the chamfered side edge. Start this line at the shield scroll, and run it upward to the point where the wing block will join the leg. Start another pencil line at a wing tip (second from the top). Compare Photo 249 with the detailed leg on drawing, page 119. For a better understanding of what these guide lines will accomplish, turn to Photo 263. V-cut parting lines on the two pencil marks (Photo 249), starting them only a few inches above the leaf design. They cannot be completed until the knee carving is far advanced. Make these cuts the full ⅛-inch tool depth. The cut nearest the side edge is interrupted by the extended leaf but resumes immediately, continuing to the shield scroll. The cut farther toward the center ends at the leaf tip.

Photo 250 shows the leg illustrated in 249, but in a direct frontal view. Note that the left front (lower) surface is the one pictured in Photo 249. The right, or upper, side has progressed to the completion of the relief cuts. Between the two relief V cuts, make a ⅛-inch-deep flat-bottomed channel, and relieve the leaf outline farther down to the same depth. From the inner V cut to the leg front center, relieve the leaf design to a depth of ¹⁄₁₆ inch.

A central rib extends from the bottom of the knee design downward to the ankle leaf tip, tapering in width from ¼ inch at the knee to ⅛ inch at the leaf. A small part of it shows on the extreme left of Photo 251. The wood surface is sloped from the inside shoulder of the flat-bottomed channel toward the center, meeting the ⅛-inch-deep relief cut of the central rib. Draw leaf division lines on the outlined surface as in Photo 251. The pencil points to a small double petal in-turned leaf that gives contrast to the over-all design.

Leaf carving starts by parting on the division lines with the ⅛-inch No. 41. Strive to make the cuts flow smoothly, without trying too hard to follow the lines exactly. Complete the carving on one side of the design before you start the next side. Chop-part the in-turned leaf outline, sinking an egg-shaped hole (pencil-marked) with the ⅛-inch No. 11. Using this tool to cut roughly a half-circle, place the rounded bottom at the indicated lower edge of the proposed hole, and give it a mallet blow. Do the same at the upper marked edge. Slope the surface of the leaf immediately above the in-turned one for relief. Continue the relief cut past the in-turned leaf, and flow it into the hole, increasing its depth as you near the hole (Photo 252). Slightly round all sharp edges that result from division and parting outline cuts.

Follow on Photo 252 the visual results of the explanations that follow. Starting at the top of the design (left on photo), the first division, or leaf member, is convex. The narrow division which follows is also convex. Hollow out the third division, an extended broad petal, with a No. 7 gouge. Make this cut sharp and deep at the tip, and taper it gradually where it meets the main leaf body. A narrow convex division follows. The petal of the in-turned leaf bordering the hole is convex. Its companion, which is larger, should have a concave inner sweep. Because it is small, the best tool for the purpose is the ⅛-inch No. 4.

The next group of three shows the outside narrow petals as convex. The extended center petal is broad and also convex, but with this difference: its center (lengthwise) dips noticeably. Next to the last, hollow out a rather broad one with the No. 7 gouge (Photo 252). The last, being narrow, is convex. Round the top and bottom edges of the shield strap with a No. 3 gouge. Cut a light crown on the scroll.

With a drawknife, remove any band-saw marks from the back right-angle surfaces of all four legs. Then sand them to finish smoothness. The frame assembly is the same as for the rectangular stool (Chapter IV). Coat all mortises and tenons with glue, clamping each end as a unit. Insert long side rails to make a complete unit of the table base. Span the clamps that hold the end units with two more bar clamps, and draw tight. Allow overnight drying. Bore for ¾₆-inch dowel pins in each joint, glue-coat the holes, and drive in the pins (Photo 253).

The list of materials includes eight wing blocks 2½ by 3½ inches by 1¾ inches thick. At least one of the 1¾-by-2½-inch surfaces of each block must be smooth enough for rub block gluing to a leg. Hold each wing block in place (Photo 253), and mark it along the knee contour. As in the case of the stools, match-number each block and the leg surface to which it will be attached in order to keep each block associated with its intended leg surface. Mark the knee curve on each block, so that all may be band-sawed at one time. Photo 254 shows one wing block with the marked surface turned up on the band-saw table.

A guide marked "Wing Block Pattern" is lined on scaled blocks in the drawing on page 119 for convenience in making the wing-block pattern. Use pliable stencil paper for this design. Mark each block as in Photo 255, where the block shown is one of four for the right side of each leg. When marking the left-side blocks, turn the pattern over endwise. Mark now only the outline to be band-sawed. All other design curves apply to carved decorations and must be marked again after the wing blocks are attached to the legs.

Photo 256 shows a left wing block being band-sawed. Before band-sawing, check all blocks to be sure they are properly marked for rights and lefts. Observe the marking on the block in Photo 256. A short line on the foreground end denotes where band-sawing must stop. This is intended to leave ¹³⁄₁₆ inch of right-angle surface for a neat butt joint when carved molding pieces are fitted between wing blocks.

The band-sawed edges of wing blocks may be sanded before attaching if you wish. Take a block, find the matching leg number, and glue-coat the block surface that will join the leg. Press the block to its approximate position on the leg, and rub it back and forth, bringing it into proper position (Photo 257). When the glued surface seems to "catch," release all hand pressure. It may be asked, Why not coat the edge adjoining the rail? This would create a counter tension when the block expanded or contracted, and would cause one joint or the other to give way.

After overnight drying, shave each knee and wing block assembly with the drawknife to an even surface. The narrow area where rail and knee join, which the drawknife does not touch, may be made even with a No. 3 gouge, heel up. With this tool and a mallet, cut the protruding dowel pin waste wood flush with the leg square. Use a hand plane to bring all adjoining leg squares to an even, continuous rail-line surface.

Make a pattern for knee carving of pliable stencil paper. Mark the pattern material with ½-inch squares as for all previous patterns. An outline guide is included on drawing (page 119). Follow the same procedure for the knee pattern as for the ankle pattern, that is, check the sweep knee contour line with the actual knee shape. If the pattern is placed in position and marked along the knee curve, any variation will show as two lines. Cut on the line that follows the actual curve. Place the pattern with the top leaf tip at the junction of rail and knee, and mark the outline.

Place the wing block pattern in position, and mark the carving outlines. For some sweeping division lines the pattern makes only partial provision. An important sweep curve that starts in the scroll center is not indicated on the pattern but shows plainly in Photo 258. Sweeping around as indicated, it passes within ¾₆ inch of the lower extended knee-leaf tip. It continues down the leg, nearly paralleling the side edge, and joins its lower extension, termed (in carving the ankle design) the flat-bottomed channel's inner shoulder.

Extend the line originating as the last inner scroll feather, to sweep in an arc ending at the upper knee leaf, about ¼ inch from the tip. From the band-sawed scroll outline, pencil-mark its continuance to merge gradually with the scroll-feather curve. Finally, continue the side edge rib line which started at the shield and is to end at the wing scroll (Photo 258).

Carving progress, as illustrated in Photo 259, is explained as follows: The side edge chamfer starts at the wing scroll ½ inch wide by ³⁄₁₆ inch deep and decreases in width to meet its continuation at the foot. Use the ¾-inch No. 3 gouge shown beside the interrupted cut. Next, chop-part the knee design outline with appropriately curved tools and mallet. Then chop-part the inner scroll feathers to and including the last feather tip. Cut on the sweeping line from the last feather tip to the extended knee leaf, using the ¼-inch No. 11 which shows on the photograph near the cut it has completed. The third tool showing in Photo 259 is a No. 6, used for some chop-parting curves. In the foreground is the knee design pattern.

Study Photo 260 in reading the following comments. The scroll feathers have been relieved to about ⅛ inch, with background wood forming a ridge on the sweep line drawn for that purpose. Notice how the side-edge chamfer continues up around the scroll, showing as a preliminary relief cut. A No. 3 gouge is making relief cuts at the knee design outline. Below the ¼-inch No. 11 sweep cut, the relief is deeper because of lower background level, clearly shown in Photo 262. The long curving line near the rail can be parted first with the ⅜-inch No. 41, then made wider and deeper with a No. 7 gouge. Bear in mind that all tool work on this line tapers out when reaching the rail (illustrated well in Photo 261). The narrow No. 3 shown on the left of Photo 260 was used for cutting relief background in small areas.

At this time prepare the pieces for carved molding between the wing blocks. A cross section shows in the drawing (page 119) as D. Size these parts to ¹³⁄₁₆ inch thick, 1¼ inches wide by lengths cut for neat fitting between wing blocks. Photo 261 shows a fitted end piece being marked along the top and ends for hand-plane shaping. Most of the waste wood was removed by an angle circular saw cut. Vise-grip each piece and hand-plane it to slightly below the pencil marks on the ends. Plane to the top surface line. Bore three holes in the short pieces for attachment to rails, five holes in the longer pieces. Holes should start about 1 inch from the ends of each piece.

Photo 262 shows the completed sloping relief cut which started (Photo 260) as scroll feather relief and continues on a sweeping curve past the knee carving. On the ridge formed by these slopes, cut a No. 41 dividing line. Where there is no ridge, follow the penciled line. The other side of the ridge dividing line is the upper end of what started at the ankle as a flat-bottomed channel. The flat bottom gradually gives way to a concave surface formed by gently rising side edges (Photo 263). A No. 7 gouge is deepening the long sweep, which had much waste wood removed above it for clearance. Notice what apparently is a solid head scroll terminating the long curve. After relief cuts are made that will be relined for three feathers (Photo 265).

An excellent over-all picture of a leg is presented in Photo 263. The two decorations under the long curve (which can be termed only narrow leaves) are being divided by the ⅜-inch veiner. Observe the knee decoration, with all its dividing lines cut by the ⅛-inch No. 41. This carving follows closely the procedure adopted for the ankle design. Scroll feathers and added knee carving details will be explained in connection with Photo 266.

Now carve the skirt molding, which has been fitted and shaped. First make a stencil-paper pattern of about two sections, following the guide on the drawing (page 119). Mark a center line on the piece to be carved; place the longest leaf of the second section beside the center line to start the repeat design, and mark. Move the pattern for two more sections, and mark. The short pieces will accommodate only about two sections on each side of the center line. Until these pieces are permanently in place with screws, do not cut the design nearer the ends than ½ inch. After marking a piece full length, chop-part the full length with a No. 7 gouge (first partial section on the right of Photo 264). Relieve the design to a depth of ⅛ inch (first full section from the right, Photo 264). The leaves of this section have also been divided by ⅜-inch veiner. In the second full section from the right all carving is completed. Further progressive cuts are rounding the leaf edges with a medium-width No. 3 gouge, heel up. Make the divisions sharp by recutting with the ⅛-inch veiner. Alternate leaves have one vein cut down the center; intermediate leaves, a shallow flute done with the ¼-inch No. 11, shown at the right center broad leaf.

Photo 265 shows the molding fastened in place on one end of the table. The scalloping effect is accomplished by chamfer cutting on a 45° angle, with a No. 3 gouge. Vary the depth of the cuts so as to border the design evenly. What was originally a solid head scroll at the wing tip has been relined, and three feathers have been cut for decoration. The feather carving varies little. It can be explained as three progressive operations: first, chop-part the desired curve; second, round the outside, or larger, radius; third, concave the smaller, inside, radius.

The feather carving is illustrated on the scroll in Photo 266. A No. 7 gouge is used for concave cutting. The transition from hollow to flat-bottom channeling is clearly pictured here, where more details of knee carving may be studied. After background relief, leaf cutting follows the general pattern set for previous leaf designs. Narrow petals or ribs are rounded; some of the broader ones are rounded on both sides while, for contrast, an occasional leaf is hollowed out on one side. The carving of the knee differs most from that of the ankle in the notched narrow petals. These are simple cuts made with the ⅛-inch No. 4 gouge. Place the tool across a narrow rib, perpendicularly with the heel toward the rib tip, and press it into the wood. Reverse the tool (cutting edge toward the tip), and place the cutting edge about ⅛ inch below the first parting cut. Lower the tool, directing it on an angle so as to make a clean-cut notch. The ribs to be notched are plainly discernible in Photo 266.

Photo 267 shows how the molding leaf design is carried over to the wing block, its continuity interrupted by the three-feather decoration. Place the pattern for repeat sections as for the molding pieces. Mark the outline, eliminating the leaves that would fall on the three feathers, and repeat the carving procedure.

Sanding should now be a familiar part of furniture building. No. 3/0 is sufficiently coarse for all carved surfaces. As before, in sanding the flat rail surfaces close to leg and mold carving, fold the sandpaper and press it with your fingers to sand in the corner where leg contour and rail meet. Otherwise, use the paper-covered cork for rails. Photo 268 presents an over-all sanding picture.

Process the 20-by-40-inch table top next. After squaring it to size, mold the edges to the approximate S curve in the drawing (page 119). This may be done on a shaper or with hand tools. Before inverting the top and placing it on the work table, cover the work area with an old rug or other heavy woven material, to prevent scratching or denting of the coffee-table top while you attach the base. Bore slanting screw holes in the rails, three in short ends, four in longer side rails. Scribe a line ⅞ inch down from the rail top edges where screw holes come through on the inside. With a large No. 11 gouge, cut screw-head clearance up to these lines. End the No. 11 channel cuts on the ⅞-inch mark to provide screw-head seats of uniform depth. Center the inverted base on the top, and drive in 1¼-inch No. 7 screws as shown in Photo 269.

To finish the construction, make and attach the submolding. If a shaper is to be used for the molding, saw strips to double the width plus the saw-blade width. That will be ⅜ inch thick by not less than ⅞ inch wide by an inch more than the finished length of ends and sides. Mold a quarter-round the full length of each side of the strips. Sand to finish smoothness, and saw two pieces from each strip, ⅜ inch wide. Miter the longer side pieces to accurate length, and attach them with about six thin beads in each piece. Miter the end pieces to fit neatly in their positions, using about four brads. Photo 270 shows the inverted table with molding in place on one side, and the end piece being attached. Turn the table upright, and sand its top surface thoroughly—first with No. ½ paper, then with No. 3/0. Combine inspection for flaws with a quick No. 7/0 paper rub-off. The table is now ready for the finishing materials. An important item of instruction was unintentionally omitted in the preceding chapters. Undoubtedly this piece of furniture, like others, deserves to have the maker's name and date (year) cut in an inconspicuous place. Use the ⅛-inch veiner to cut (in capitals) the name, city, state, and year of completion. Photo 271 shows the table ready for the finishing materials.

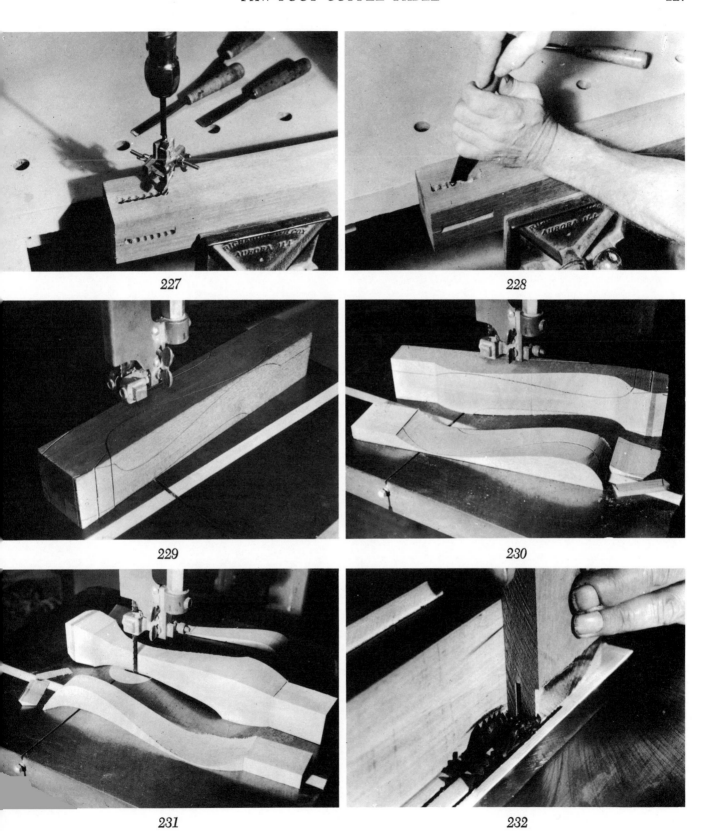

227

228

229

230

231

232

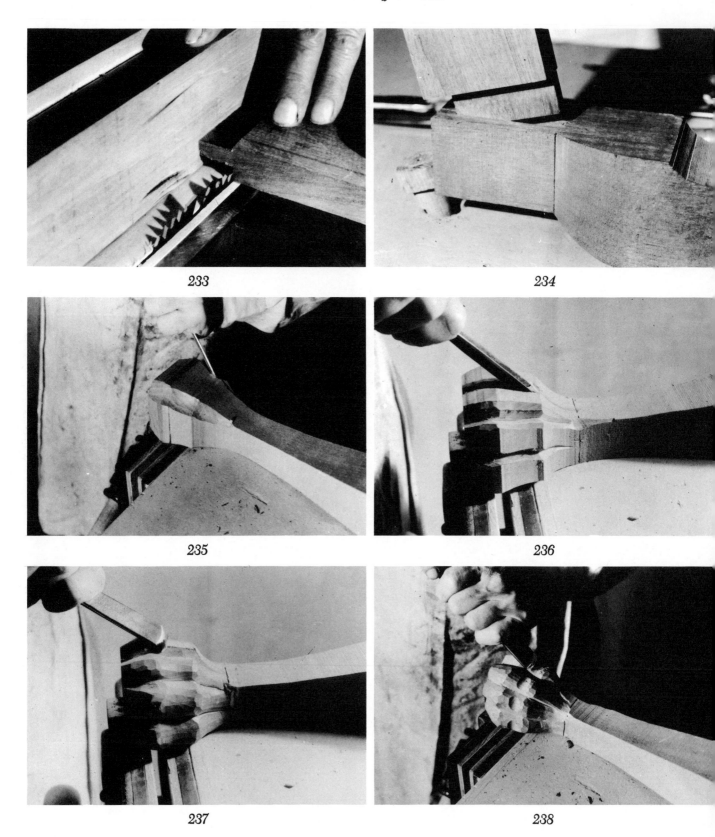

233

234

235

236

237

238

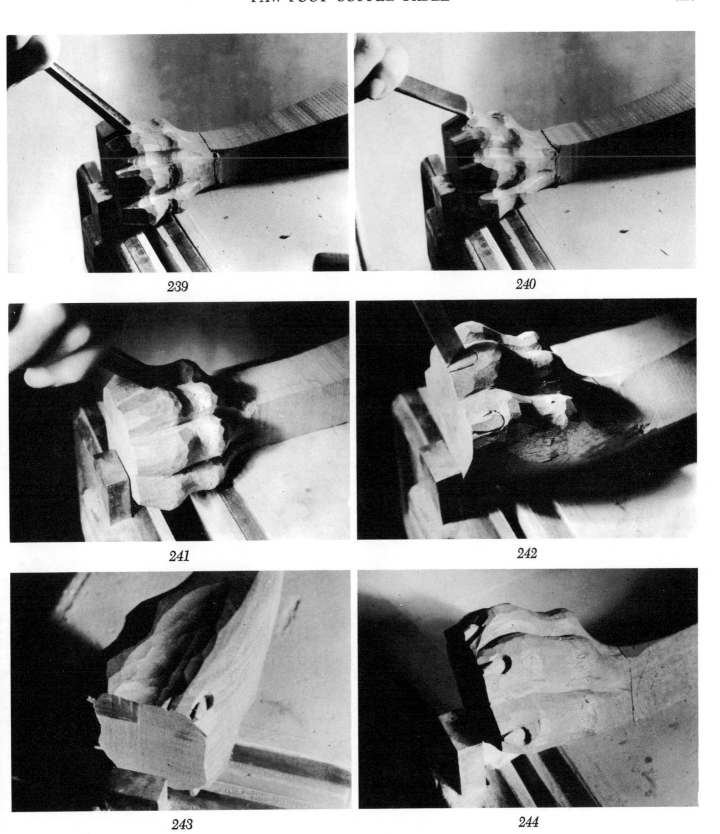

239

240

241

242

243

244

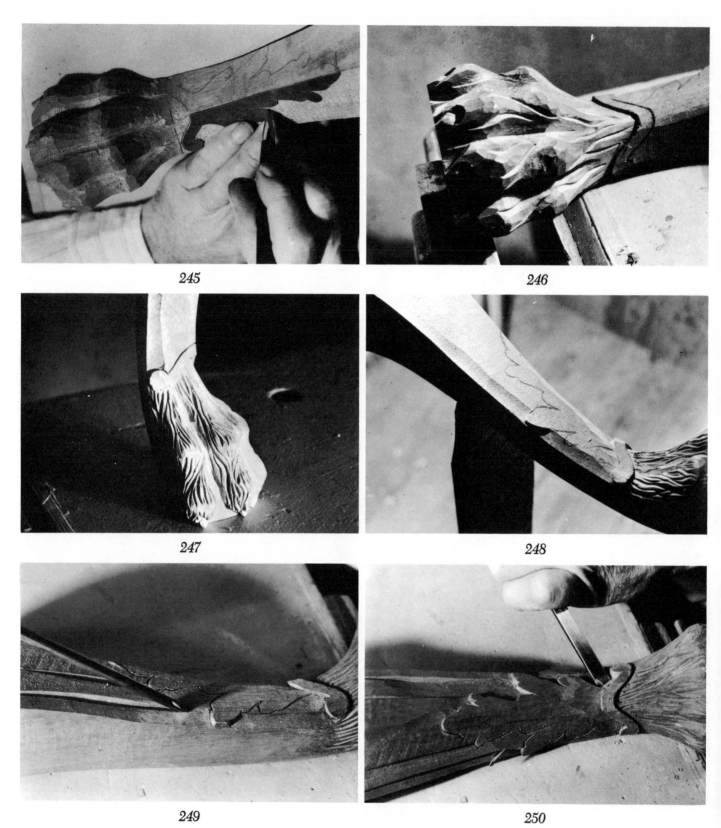

245

246

247

248

249

250

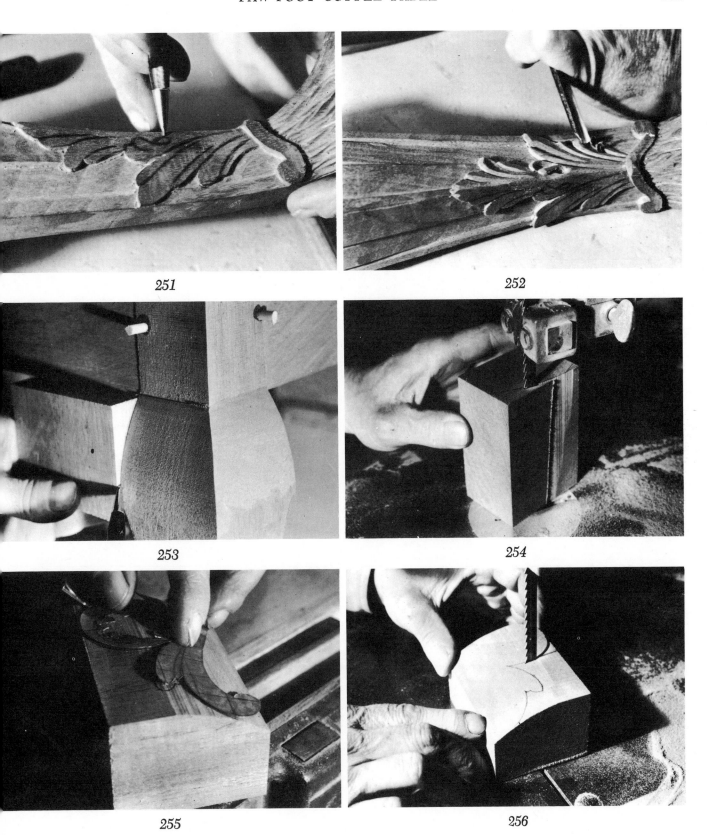

251

252

253

254

255

256

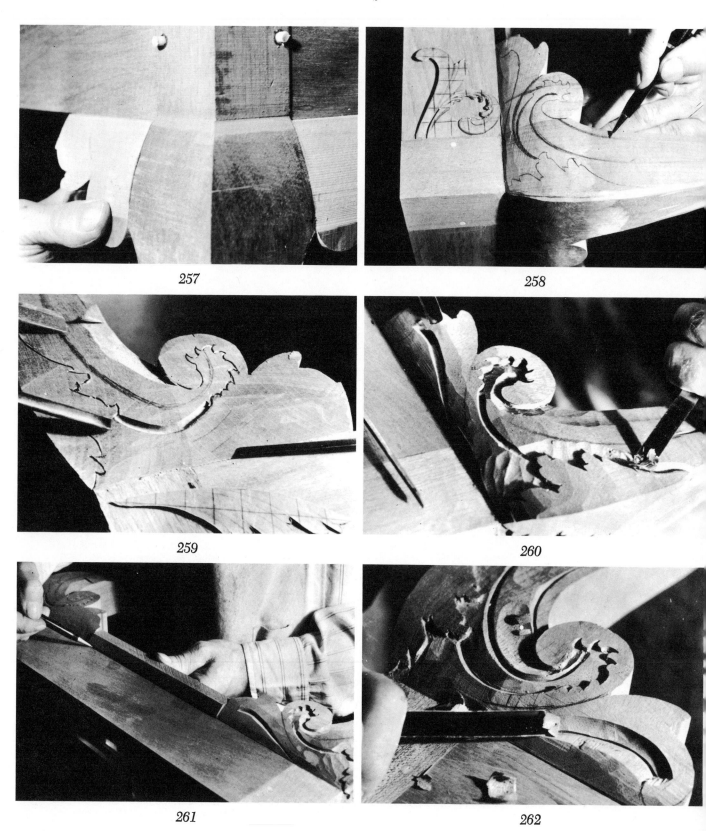

257

258

259

260

261

262

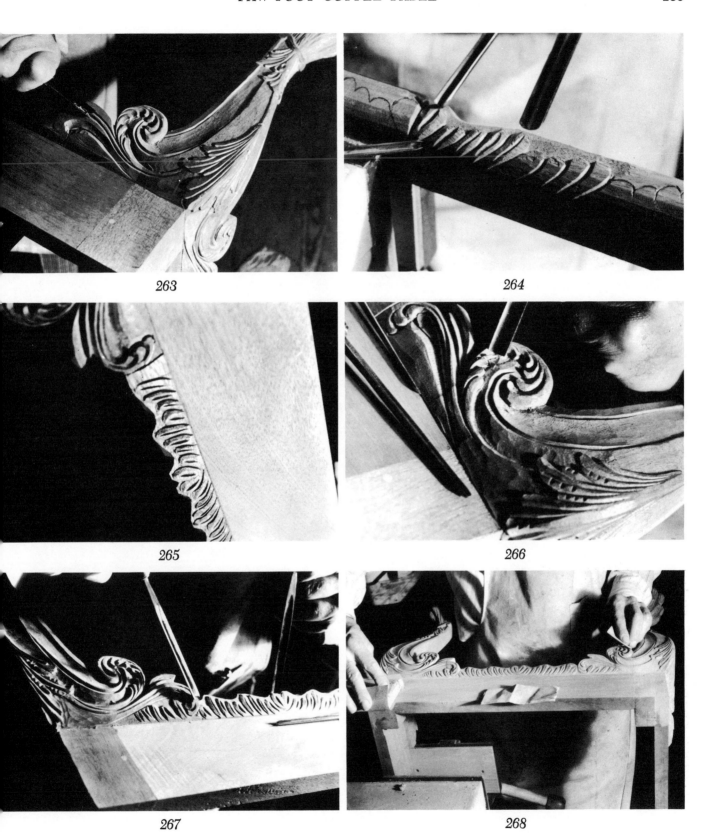

263

264

265

266

267

268

269

270

271

Small Chests of Drawers

CHAPTER IX

Small Chests of Drawers

AMERICAN ORIGIN, 1770

Materials for One Pair—Sizes in Inches

MAHOGANY	PIECES	LENGTH	WIDTH	THICKNESS
Side panels	4	22½	21¾	¹³⁄₁₆
Division frame fronts	10	14¾	3	¾
Base frame fronts	2	15¼	3	¹³⁄₁₆
Base frame sides	4	22¼	2½	¹³⁄₁₆
Base frame backs	2	13	2½	¹³⁄₁₆
Chamfer overlay	4	22½	2½	⁹⁄₁₆
Drawer fronts	2	14½	3⅞	1½
Drawer fronts	2	14½	4⅜	1½
Drawer fronts	2	14½	5	1½
Drawer fronts	2	14½	5⅜	1½
Top panels	2	18½	22¾	⅝

8 lineal feet, 3 inches wide, 1¾ inches thick

YELLOW POPLAR				
Division frame sides	20	17½	2	¾
Division frame backs	10	14¾	2	¾

Drawer sides, backs, and bottoms, about 38 square feet of ⅜ thickness.

¼" mahogany-faced plywood, 2 pieces, 22½ by 15¼ inches

16 rosette bail drawer pulls, 1⅜ inches boring

Serpentine-front chests of drawers were made in profusion during the colonial period, and many fine examples are still in use. The functional qualities of small chests of drawers make them especially welcome for modern living. Small chests made to the size illustrated here may well replace end tables at the davenport or beside a lounge chair; and, as bedroom pieces they make ideal night tables. The only radical change from the original chest selected for reproduction is in size. Whereas the old chests were much wider than deep, these are deeper than they are wide; otherwise they follow traditional design, ornamentation, and construction methods.

Except in drawers and feet, the list of materials calls for pieces of exact size. Where gluing is

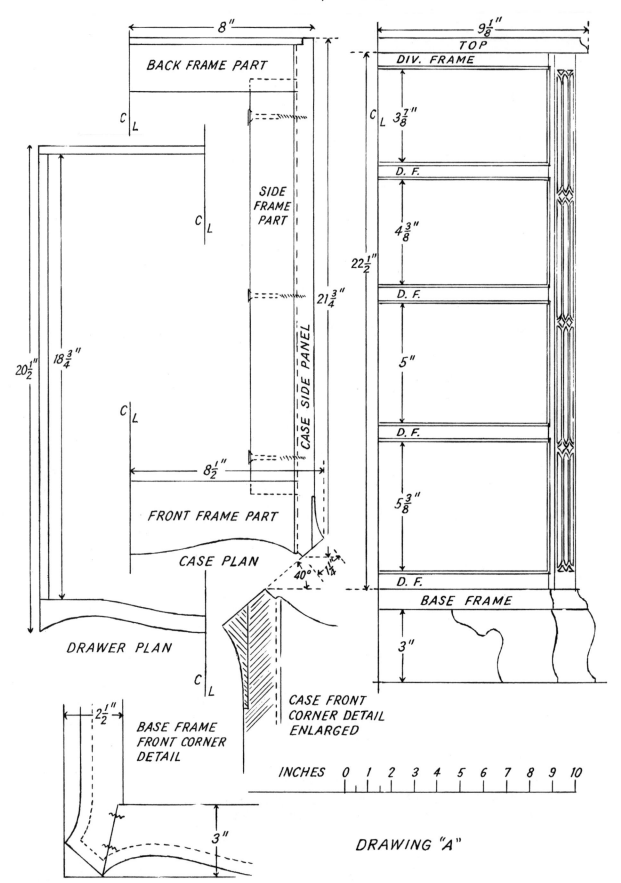

8"

BACK FRAME PART

C L

SIDE
FRAME
PART

C L

CASE SIDE PANEL

21¾"

C L

8½"

FRONT FRAME PART

CASE PLAN

40°   1¼"

20½"   18¾"

DRAWER PLAN

C L

2½"

BASE FRAME
FRONT CORNER
DETAIL

3"

CASE FRONT
CORNER DETAIL
ENLARGED

9⅛"

TOP

DIV. FRAME

C L   3⅞"

D. F.

4⅜"

D. F.

5"

D. F.

5⅜"

22½"

D. F.

BASE FRAME

3"

INCHES   0 1 2 3 4 5 6 7 8 9 10

DRAWING "A"

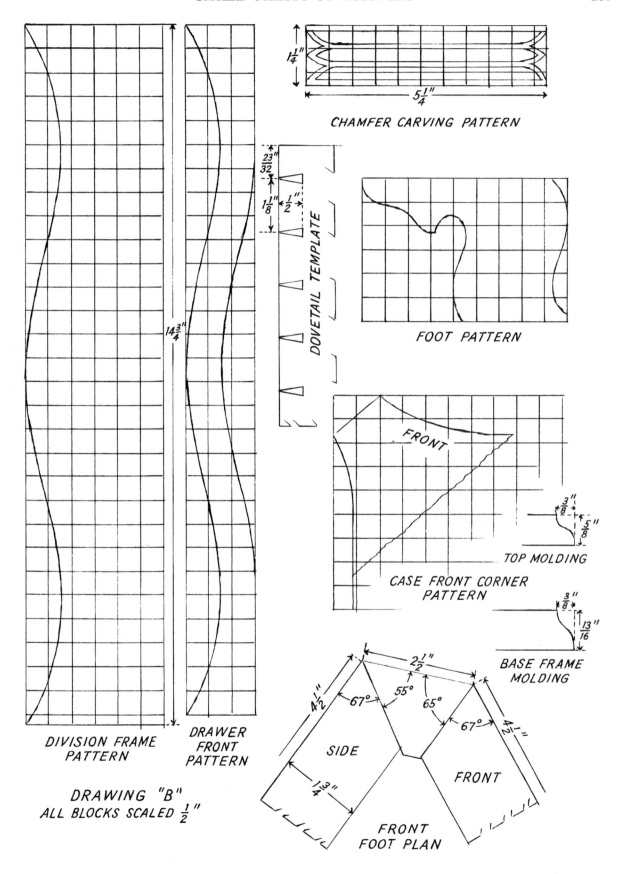

CHAMFER CARVING PATTERN

DOVETAIL TEMPLATE

FOOT PATTERN

FRONT

CASE FRONT CORNER
PATTERN

TOP MOLDING

BASE FRAME
MOLDING

DIVISION FRAME
PATTERN

DRAWER
FRONT
PATTERN

DRAWING "B"
ALL BLOCKS SCALED ½"

SIDE

FRONT

FRONT
FOOT PLAN

necessary to make up the panel widths, cut the wood one inch longer for eventual squaring of ends. Start the construction by gluing to width four mahogany side panels and drying them overnight. Then square them to the exact length, and rough-sand or hand-plane the joints to make all panel surfaces even. Lay off the inside surface of a panel for drawer division frame channels, as follows. From the panel top, measure down and mark ¾ inch for the first frame. Then measure 3⅞ inches from the first mark for top-drawer space, and another ¾ inch for frame thickness. Next, allow space for a 4⅜-inch drawer, space for frame thickness, and so on, continuing to the bottom edge with provision for four drawers and five frames as shown in the drawing (page 138).

Set up the dado head to cut frame channels ¾ inch wide by ⅛ inch deep. Set the saw fence so that it barely touches the dado saw teeth. Place one of the panels on the saw table, with inside surface down and top edge against the fence, and push it over the saw to cut the top frame channel. Do the same with the bottom edge, and repeat the whole process for the corresponding ends of the other panels. Reset the fence for second frame channel from the top. Wood blemishes may make it advisable to place a particular side edge toward the front. This decision must be made before cutting the next division channels. Mark the chosen front edge, and, holding the panels in pairs, mark the top edge of each. The second frame channel down from the top may now be cut in each panel. Reset the fence and cut the third frame channel in each panel (Photo 272). Cut the last frame channel, holding the bottom panel edge against the reset saw fence.

Cut a rabbet in the back edge of each side panel to receive the ¼-inch plywood back boards. The rabbet size is ¼ inch deep from back to front and ⅜ inch wide. Photo 273 illustrates the last machine operation on the side panels. Set the jointer fence so that the knives will cut a width of exactly 2½ inches. Adjust the bed for ³⁄₃₂-inch depth, and, while you hold the front edge against the fence, make this rabbet cut the full length of the outside surface of the side panel. Repeat the process for the remaining three panels. As Drawing "A" (page 138) shows, these rabbets, when worked down to side-panel level, avoid the undesirable feather edging of overlaid pieces.

Prepare all division frame parts by first sizing ten front pieces to 14¾ inches long by 3 inches wide by ¾ inch thick. Ten backs 14¾ inches long by 2 inches wide by ¾ inch thick. Twenty side pieces 17½ inches long by 2 inches wide by ¾ inch thick. The length of the side pieces allows for ½-inch end tenons. Set up the dado head with a ¼-inch spacer between the outside cutters (Photo 274). Adjust the height for a strong ½-inch cut. Set the fence for a tenon approximately in the center of wood thickness. Mark one side of all frame parts for identification. In milling the tenons, place a squared end firmly on the saw table with the marked side against the fence, and pass it over the cutters. Do this at each end of all side pieces. Front and back parts are milled to receive the tenons.

Replace the dado head cutters with a hollow-ground saw to cut the tenon shoulders (Photo 275). Set the fence exactly ½ inch from the outside cutting teeth of the saw blade. Check the setting on a piece of scrap wood. Adjust the height of the saw to about ¹⁄₁₆ inch below the tenon as it lies flat (Photo 275). Cut the shoulder on both sides of every tenon.

Change again from the saw blade to the dado head outside cutters, but without the spacer between them (Photo 276). Adjust their height to a strong ½ inch. When you set the fence for grooves to match the tenons, upend a side piece, with the marked side toward the fence, and move it up to the motionless cutters. Adjust the fence for perfect alignment. Start the saw, and, to check the fence setting, move the tenon until it barely touches the cutters. With perfect alignment, no wood will be left standing on either side. Move the front and back parts over the cutters in a horizontal position with the marked surface against the fence, and cut grooves on the inside wood thickness surface (Photo 276). A stop block may be clamped to the fence to assure uniform length of grooves when you mill the forward ends. The block, clamped behind the saw, serves as a starting point for the other groove in each piece. To groove this end, lower the wood onto the cutters, and push it completely past them.

On the drill press, edge up each side piece in turn, drilling three holes for 2½-inch No. 9 screws: two end holes about 1 inch in from the shoulders and one hole in the center. The screws are to fasten the frames securely to the side panels. The frame parts are now ready for assembly. Place two bar clamps on the work table, paralleling them about the width of the frames. Glue-coat the grooves in one front and one back piece. It is important that the marked surface of each piece forming the unit face the same way, either up or down. Glue-coat the tenons of two side pieces; enter them in their front and back receiving grooves; draw the clamps reasonably tight, then release them a half-turn. With a hammer, move the side pieces so that their edges are flush with the ends of front and back parts. Again draw the clamps tight. Check with a large square, and if the frame is not in perfect rectangle, release one clamp, move it a little out of line, and tighten it again. Do the same with the other clamp if necessary. Allow fifteen minutes for the glue to set. Then release both clamps simultaneously and, with care, set the frame aside for complete drying. Repeat the whole process with the remaining nine frames.

Make a division frame pattern of rigid material, following the usual routine of ½-inch squares, and using division frame pattern (page 139) as a guide to draw in the outline. When the pattern is completed, place it on the front frame piece (Photo 277). Position and hold the straight back edge of the pattern on the junction lines of the front and the side pieces, and pencil-mark the outline. Band-saw each frame to the pattern line. Remove the saw marks with the round-bed drawknife.

A bead ⅛ inch wide by 1/16 inch deep borders all drawer openings. Two methods of forming a bead are illustrated. Photo 278 shows hand tools in use. Draw pencil lines ⅛ inch in from the edge. Part on these lines, using the ⅛-inch veiner to cut 1/16 inch deep. The right side of the photograph shows the veiner making its cut. Remove the wood between bordering beads with a No. 3 gouge, cutting the background to a flat surface. Follow the same procedure in forming the single bead on each side panel edge. A medium-width No. 3 gouge may be employed for bead rounding.

Photo 279 shows the second method of forming a bead—with a shaper. The steel of the shaper is ground to form the desired size bead. Grind the remaining steel above the bead on a taper for smoother bead cutting. As the photograph shows, the center of intervening wood is not cut, and it acts as a depth gauge when pressed against the shaper spindle. Set the cutters with care, allowing them to protrude just far enough to cut a full rounded bead. Do not start or end a shaper cut at the extreme end of a frame front, because the possibility of splitting off a portion of the tip wood is too great. Another reason for stopping the bead short of the end is the need for a straight outside wall where the beads form a right angle (see Photo 281).

Adjust the spindle height for bead cutting on the bottom or shaper table level of the wood to be beaded (Photo 279). This height assures a perfect edge bead, regardless of wood thickness. Check the setting of the shaper on scrap wood. Shape first one edge of a frame, then the other, and continue until all the frames are beaded. Before changing the spindle height, reset the bead cutters to protrude 1/16 inch farther. Beads may now be run on the inside front edges of the side panels. The new tool setting positions the side-panel beads far enough back from the edge, permitting a full serpentine sweep to the peak point. Study the case front corner detail in Drawing "A" (page 138) until you thoroughly understand the point involved. Cut side beads the full length of panels.

Replace the bead cutters on the shaper spindle with ½-inch steel ground to straight edges (Photo 280). This set-up is to cut a smooth, flat background between the edge beads of frames. Take care in setting the cutters for depth to allow for the removal of background wood to the full depth of the beads. The spindle height should be adjusted so that no part of either bead will be cut away when the background wood is removed. A reminder: Start and stop this operation before you reach the ends. Choose four frames for tops and bottoms. Now either raise or lower the shaper spindle, to remove one of the beads on each of the four frames. Make these cuts, exerting very little pressure when frame and spindle collar come into contact. Remember, a single small bead is now acting as a depth gauge. Sand all beaded frame edges to finish smoothness.

Case parts are now ready for assembly (Photo 281). Lay a side panel on the covered work table, turning the inside surface upward. Attach with screws either the top or the bottom frame, positioning it for bead alignment (Photo 281). These end frames have only one bead which must border the drawer opening. Next insert in the grooves three double beaded frames. Carefully bring the beads into line, and fasten the frames securely with screws. Attach the remaining end frame, making sure that the bead borders the drawer opening. Replace this assembly on the work table with the other side panel. Invert the assembled portion, and position all the frame sides in their respective grooves. Align each frame separately, and fasten it with screws. Repeat the assembly steps with the second case.

About the center (in width) of the shallow 2½-inch-wide overlay rabbet, and directly over each frame channel, bore a screw hole. Countersink the holes sufficiently to assure recessing of the screw heads. Drive in 1-inch No. 6 screws (Photo 282).

The list of materials includes four overlay pieces 22½ inches by 2½ inches by 9⁄16 inch. The surface of each piece to be glued to a side panel, and the edges joining rabbet shoulders, must be smooth and straight. Photo 283 shows how these pieces are clamped in place. Prepare for this glue job by setting four C clamps for each side. Set them to include a supporting board, which will help distribute the clamp pressure evenly on the entire overlaid piece. Glue-coat the wide surface and the abutting edge of the overlay piece, and place in position, keeping the ends flush with the case. Position the supporting board, place the clamps and tighten them lightly. Using a hammer and a block of waste wood, tap on the overlaid piece for a tight rabbet shoulder joint. Tighten clamps, and check for satisfactory shoulder joint. The number of overlay pieces to be glued at one time depends on how many C clamps are in the shop equipment.

For a case front corner pattern guide, see Drawing "B" (page 139). Make the pattern of rigid material, and lay it off in ½-inch squares. Front and side radii are not alike. Therefore, mark the front for identification. The apex, or junction, of the serpentine front and the chamfer is about 3⁄16 inch from the side panel bead. Pencil a straight line the length of the side panel, to indicate this peak point. Place the front corner of the pattern on it, and adjust the front curve flush with the case line (in Photo 284 the chamfer has been completed). Hold the pattern, and outline the chamfer angle and the side radius line, which is intended to continue an unbroken side surface to the chamfer (Photo 284). Mark the other corner end in like manner. Hand-plane on the chamfer angle, removing wood down to the penciled line on each end (Photo 284). Check for a straight longitudinal chamfered surface. The corresponding work on the remaining corners may be brought up in progress to the pilot corner at the craftsman's convenience.

Draw a straight pencil line on the chamfer face to allow a width of 1¼ inch, and meet the pattern mark point on the top and the bottom of the case. With the ¾-inch No. 3 gouge, driven with a mallet, chip off the waste overlay wood as shown in Photo 285. The pencil line on each end indicates the cutting depth and the radius at these extremities. To assure radius uniformity, make a reverse pattern, using the side curve of the original pattern for an outline. Check the depth and the contour of the newly cut surface frequently with the reverse pattern. When you have nearly reached the final surface level, dispense with the mallet, and finish cutting by hand thrust for fewer deep tool marks. The more smoothly this radius is worked down, the less time will be required for sanding.

Photo 286 shows the side panel, including the newly cut radius being sanded. Make a rounded-edge block, shown in the photograph, and cover it with No. ½ sandpaper for removing radius tool marks. Use a cork block with No. ½ paper for the flat-side panel surface. Follow the now familiar sanding routine. In sanding the radius with No. 3/0, check carefully for very slight tool marks that the No. ½ paper may not have completely removed. These shallow depressions will not show until the surface is sanded with the finer grit paper. If you discover any marks, sand again with No. ½ paper.

With hand tools, work down the frame ends to their ultimate level and contour (Photo 287). Use a veiner to part for bead width, a No. 3 gouge for background and bead rounding. Take sufficient time to do a satisfactory job on bead right-angle corners, and sand these recently worked areas to finish smoothness. Of the case proper, only the chamfered corners remain unfinished.

Drawing "B" has the chamfer carving pattern laid out to scale. Transfer it, full size, to stencil-paper pattern material. All cutouts will be neater if they are parted with appropriate carving tools instead of scissors. Lay the pattern material on a piece of flat scrap wood for solid background when pressing the tools through the stencil paper. Mark a transverse line ¾ inch from each end. Place the end of the pattern on this line, and mark cutouts with a finely pointed pencil. Indicate also where the first section ends and the pattern is to be placed for the second sectional marking. Four sections make up the carved length of the chamfers. Photo 288 shows the first section on the right as being design-marked only. The diamonds dividing the first and second sections are chop-parted with an appropriately curved gouge. The second sectional cutouts are being parted to a depth of ¹⁄₁₆ inch by the ⅛ inch No. 41. The second pair of diamonds (at the left of the photograph) are cut to ¹⁄₁₆-inch background depth. Strive for the straightest possible cutout parting lines. These cuts play an important part in the final symmetry of the design.

In Photo 289 nearly all the background wood has been cut to a uniform depth of ¹⁄₁₆ inch. A ³⁄₁₆-inch chisel is removing wood from the last cutout in the second section from the left. Diamonds and half-diamonds have also been reduced to the lower level. Clearly visible is the stippling work started in the left section. The stippling tool shown is a converted screw driver. (Chapter III explains in detail its conversion.) No sanding is required on the lower areas. Use No. 3/0 paper with cork block for the design surface.

Make the base frames next. Check the list of materials for size and number of parts. Study the base frame front corner detail in Drawing "A" (page 138) until you understand where these joints should be placed. The angles were determined to make the joints coincide as closely as possible with the point of molding angle change. Angle the ends of the front piece first. Set the circular saw crosscut gauge to 89 degrees, angle the front piece to a length that will bisect the front corners of the chamfers when it is placed in its proper position under the case. Parallel the two side pieces, with the outside edges 19 inches apart. Position the mitered front piece on top of them, and mark where to cut the matching butt joints. Carefully cut to these lines on the band saw. Glue the four joining edges, and hold the joints together with corrugated fasteners. Measure for butt joining, the length of the back piece, cut to size, glue-coat the ends and the joining side-piece areas, fasten in the manner used for front joints (Photo 290). Position the case on the completed frame, and mark the case outline. Measure ½ inch outside the outline on sides and front. A straightedge may be used to make a continuous line on the straight sides. Measure and mark about every inch around the curved portion (Photo 290). Connect the broken lines into one continuous outline. Band-saw to outline as in Photo 291. Remove saw marks with a drawknife.

Grind a pair of shaper cutters to a shallow ogee curve, suitable for ½-inch extended molding. That means the top, or deepest part, of curves reaches into the wood about ⅜ inch farther than the lower ends. (See the drawing page 139). Set up the shaper spindle with the bottom edge of the cutters flush with the lower grooved collar—allowing the lower collar to act as a depth gauge. Adjust the spindle height to cut a balanced ogee curve on this-thickness wood (Photo 292). Mold both frames while the shaper is set for this operation. Sand the molding to finish smoothness. Bore four screw holes in each side part, three in the front piece, and two in the back, for attaching the frame to the case. The two central screw holes in each side piece must be ⅞ inch in from the edge, for fastening to the side panel wood. All other holes may be located farther in, for screw attachment to the division framework. Invert the frames and countersink holes for screw heads. Set the base frames on inverted cases, position them for even borders, and drive in 1¼-inch screws (Photo 293).

Make the ogee bracket feet next. An ogee is a reverse or S curve and refers here to the shape given to the front surfaces of the feet. Eight lineal feet, not necessarily in one piece, are needed to produce the eight bracket feet. Size the mahogany to 3 inches wide by 1¾ inches thick. Smooth the four surfaces with a jointer or hand plane. Each back foot consists of two blocks 4½ inches long, 3 inches wide, and 1¾ inches thick. Miter one end of each block to 45 degrees (see Photo 298 for a view of both front and back feet). Study the front foot plan in Drawing "B" (page 139) in conjunction with Photo 294. Because of the unsymmetrical nature of the front corners, different mitering angles must be observed for proper wing spread in relation to the chamfer line. The drawing shows the two main blocks of each front foot with the same mitered angle, 67 degrees. If they are to be cut from a long piece, one miter cut will serve for two blocks. Miter eight such blocks. The drawing also shows the proper angles for cutting the chamfer corner blocks. Remember that the feet must be assembled as rights and lefts, so place a distinguishing mark on either the side or the front mitered end of each corner block. For safety, allow considerable waste when you miter corner blocks. Set the crosscut gauge (or tilting arbor) to the 55-degree side angle. Miter one end of the stock piece. The finished block will be 2½ inches. Therefore, allow an extra 2 inches for hand hold when cutting the front miter. Move the piece of stock wood (having one end mitered to 55 degrees) 4½ inches, and make another 55-degree angle cut. Repeat, making four blocks. Reset the saw equipment to cut the indicated front angle of 65 degrees. Cut the four blocks to this angle, with the long sides measuring 2½ inches. Photo 294 shows the three blocks that form a front foot.

Make a foot pattern of rigid material, by the usual pattern-making process. A guide is provided in Drawing "B." To prevent errors when marking, stand the three parts of each foot together, and mark the top surface of each piece, respectively, F for front, S for side, and the chamfer block F at the front miter and S at side angle. Remember—assemble these parts for right and left feet. All marks being on the top surfaces, no mistakes will be made when the pattern is placed for outlining. Position the pattern's ogee high points even with the block's straight mitered end, and mark the outline. Referring again to the eight back-feet blocks, use the same pattern for outlining. Mark four pieces with one pattern side up, four more with that side down, remembering rights and lefts. Photo 295 shows a front foot block being band-sawed to outline. Retain one of the waste blocks for use when molding the face surfaces of the back feet. Sanding band-sawed surfaces before the foot assembly will be found more convenient.

A solid surface such as the circular saw or shaper table top is necessary for assembling the feet. A glance at Photo 298 will make the following instructions clear. Glue-coat two joining miters, rub them together, and place the parts upright on a solid flat surface. Place a ⅜ × 4 corrugated fastener midway on the joint and drive in flush, with a heavy hammer. If this is a front foot, fasten the other mitered joint in the same way. One joint completes each back-foot assembly.

Temporarily, rest a case on its four feet. Move the front feet into such a position that ⅜ inch of foot wood protrudes along the chamfer line and at each wing tip (Photo 296). Outline the base-frame contour on the top surface of the foot. Next, draw a line parallel to the base-frame shape, ⅜ inch outward (see the photograph). This step may be omitted for the back feet.

Photo 297 shows a front foot being band-sawed on the ⅜-inch extended line. This cut is preliminary to giving the feet an ogee shape, in order to border the base-frame contour evenly.

The feet in Photo 298 are at varying stages of progress. The one at the upper left, a front foot, shows the outline and the extended outline. The other front foot, at the upper right, has been band-sawed on the extended line. The back foot at the lower right shows no progress beyond assembling of parts into a unit. The ogee curve has been band-sawed on the face sides of the back foot at the lower left.

Before you mold the face surfaces of the back feet to the desired curve, position the pattern on one foot side and mark the ogee outline, which meets the corner at two points. Observe the set-up for band-sawing in Photo 299. The wing edge of a foot rests on the waste-wood block retained for this purpose. The foot extends over the block about ½ inch, for saw-blade clearance. Band-saw on the ogee outline. Rest the other wing edge on the block for the next surface cut. It is unnecessary to outline the pattern in sawing this side, because the mitered joint serves the same purpose as a pencil line. Repeat the sawing on the remaining three feet.

Wrap rounded block with No. ½ paper, and sand the concave parts of the back feet (Photo 300), making sure that saw marks are obliterated. Cover cork blocks with No. ½ paper, and sand the flat surface at the bottom edge and the convex areas, removing all saw marks. Cover the same blocks with No. 3/0 sandpaper, and sand the four back feet to finish smoothness.

The curved surfaces make it necessary to mold the front feet with hand tools. Mark the ogee outline on the chamfered surface as in Photo 301, and place the pattern so that the high points at the knee and the foot bottom are even with the mitered joint. To mold the convex areas, use the ¾-inch No. 3 gouge, with its heel up whenever possible. Because of grain direction, the tool must cut from each end in turn (Photo 302). For the concave curved parts, use the largest No. 4 or 5 gouge you have, and cut toward the center from each end. The convex curve from the knee to the top surface must end at the base-frame outline. Therefore, do not cut beyond this line. Examine carefully for uniformly deep curvature. A reverse template may be made to determine the progress of the foot molding. Use the joint at each end of the chamfer block as a guide line in molding the chamfer.

Longitudinal curvature makes it impractical, in sanding the front feet, to support the paper with blocks. Fold coarse sandpaper, and sand with finger pressure only (Photo 303). Some tool marks will be deeper than others, and you will have to guard against the tendency to follow these depressions with the sandpaper. Sand long enough to obtain longitudinally even surfaces.

To attach the feet to the base frame, bore one screw hole in each wing—through the small radius area shown by the screw driver in Photo 304. Invert a case on the work table. Carefully position a foot so that the top edge of the face curve meets the edge of the frame. Hold the foot in place while you drive in the two screws. Choose a screw length that will imbed itself ⅜ inch deep in the frame. The back feet should also be positioned without overlap, and secured in place with screws.

There is little need for progressive illustrations of the top-panel processing, because this kind of work has become routine. A number of boards glued together will probably be necessary to make up the panel widths. After overnight drying in clamps, hand-plane or sand (across the grain) for even surfaces. Invert a top panel on the work table, and place an inverted case on the panel. Position the case, allowing for ½-inch top overhang along the back. Pencil-mark the outline of the case. Measure ½ inch outside this line, following the instructions given for base frames. Band-saw on the larger outlines. With a drawknife, remove saw marks.

Grind another pair of ogee cutters for the shaper. Like the pair ground for the base frames, they should cut from the collar ⅜ inch in horizontal depth. Unlike frame cutters, they should be ground 3/16 inch less in height. (See the drawing on page 139.) Mold all four edges of each top panel, and sand the moldings to finish smoothness. Bore screw holes through the top division frames for attaching the top panel. Angle the holes so that the screw driver will clear the frame above and still be in line with the screw. Bore two screw holes through the front and back frame pieces, about 1½ inches from the side panels and ½ inch from the outside edge. Bore two holes through each top-frame side piece, about 5 inches from front and back edges and ½ inch from the inside edge of the side piece. Countersink for screw heads, using a large No. 11 gouge. Center a case on its inverted top (Photo 305), and drive in one-inch screws for attaching the top. Fasten the top to the other case in like manner. Place the cases on the floor, right side up, and sand the top surfaces first with coarse paper, then with No. 3/0 for finish smoothness.

Construction of drawers starts with sizing the fronts to fit their openings, less about 1/32 inch in width and height. The mahogany for the drawer fronts should be not less than 1½ inches thick. Next, make a drawer-front pattern of rigid material, guided by drawing (page 139). Mark one side of the pattern "Top," and place the pattern on each drawer front with the marked side up (Photo 306). Pencil-mark each drawer front, keeping pattern ends and straight-line parts of the back edge even with the wood edges. Set the marking gauge to scratch a line exactly the thickness of the side and back wood. Gauge-mark each drawer front as in Photo 308. Using the back corner as a gauge stop, scratch a line on the ends and on the back surface at each end. Reset the marking gauge to scratch a line ½ inch up from the bottom on the ends of each piece. These lines pin-point the top edge of the grooves into which the drawer bottoms are to slide.

Now make a dovetailing template of thin sheet metal that has at least one straight edge and is long enough for use on deeper drawers. The template is laid out in the drawing on page 139. Uniformity of cutout spacing and of tail widths is unimportant, because all template marking is done from one end. Whatever variations occur in the pattern will be transmitted to the front and the side pieces when they are marked. The template drawing calls for cutouts ½ inch deep, so that it can be used also on drawers that require side wood ½ inch thick. With a needle-point scriber to mark the lines, lay off the metal according to the drawing. Cutouts are 1/16 inch wide at the edge and 3/16 inch at the ½-inch-deep mark. Cut out wedge-shaped openings with tin shears. To complete the template, scribe a line at right angles to the edge 1 1/16 inches from the starting end. Scratch a corresponding line on the other side of the pattern (this line shows clearly on the template in Photo 307).

Read this paragraph carefully. It explains two template positions: why one is chosen for a particular drawer, and why scratch lines are ½ inch up on wood and 1 1/16 inches up on metal. In scratch marking for dovetails, use the ½-inch-gauge mark on wood as a starting point. The two template positions will be called "high" and "low" because the high position has the first tail marked just above the groove for the bottom panel (Photos 310, 312). When the template is placed "low" the 1 1/16-inch mark on the metal is matched to the ½-inch mark on the wood. This position puts a tail or rather a half-tail below the groove for the bottom panel (Photos 308, 309). The height of the drawers determines which position is to be used on each drawer. To understand the necessity for two positions, study the drawer front in Photo 310 (it is marked "high"). Suppose this width of wood were marked "low," shifting the template about ¼ inch to the right. The shift would add ¼ inch to the uncut portion at the top of the drawer front and give the dovetailing an extremely unbalanced appearance. Choose the position for each drawer height that will leave the top half-tail between ¼ and ½ inch in width.

When the template is held in either position, the straight edge is to be even with the 3/8-inch gauge mark on the wood. When marking "high," place the widest part of the first cutout just above the ½-inch groove line. Mark with a needle-point scriber. When marking "low," as in Photo 307, align the two marks. After the drawer fronts are template-marked on the ends, pencil-line the back surface, showing the position and width of tails (Photo 308). These lines are for convenience when you are chop-cutting between tails.

Photo 309 shows a front being chop-cut. The line ½ inch up from the bottom indicates that the template was held in the low position for marking. A solid base and a drawer front held firmly on it are essential for satisfactory chop-cutting. Clamp a drawer front on the bench top, face side down, with the end to be cut seated firmly on the bench. For this work, use a ½-inch-wide chisel driven by a mallet. Limit the bites to 1/8 inch. Hold the chisel in a perpendicular position, and give the handle a number of mallet blows. The cutting depth of the chisel will be indicated by the protruding waste wood. Chop in depth to about the 3/8-inch gauge line, but not below it. Chop the full width between the tails. Move the chisel back 1/8 inch and repeat. The last chop cut is, of course, on the 3/8-inch line scratched on the back surface by the gauge. Dovetailing is made more interesting if the tails are completely cut on one drawer front before another is started.

Vise-grip the front with an end up (Photo 310). The front pictured was marked with the template in the high position. Place the ½-inch chisel exactly on the scratch lines, hold it vertically, and press to cut the tail sides. A mallet is not necessary. Cut a vertical wall at the ⅜-inch gauge mark in the same manner. (The photograph shows the No. 2 chisel which is used to clean out corners at the tail points.) Complete the dovetail cutting on all drawer fronts.

Now band-saw the fronts to the serpentine shape marked on the top of each piece. The drawer front in Photo 311 has both the back and front saw cuts made. Waste wood lies on the saw table. Band-saw all drawer fronts at this time.

Grind two pieces of ¼-inch-wide shaper steel with one square cutting end on each piece (Photo 312). Mount them in the shaper collar grooves, measuring their protrusion for ¼-inch cutting depth. Adjust the spindle height exactly ½ inch to the top of the cutters. The drawer front in Photo 312 was marked and cut for dovetails in the high position. Observe that the bottom-board groove is in line with the lower edge of the first dovetail. This groove cutting operation completes the machine work on the drawer fronts.

Size all drawer sides to 19½ inches in length, and (in pairs) to the different heights of the drawer fronts. The drawer backs are to be sized ½ inch narrower than the sides (one back to each pair of side pieces). Square all back pieces to the length of the drawer fronts. All interior drawer parts may be sanded, but not necessarily with the thoroughness required by exterior surfaces. Mount the saw arbor for the bottom grooves in the side pieces (Photo 313). Set the fence so a ¼-inch-wide groove will be cut ½ inch from the bottom to the groove's top edge (side grooves should match in height those cut into the fronts by the shaper). Set the dado cutters to cut ¾₁₆ inch above the saw table. Groove all side pieces.

Sort out, match, and keep together the four parts that make up each drawer, in order to prevent errors when you match-mark the sides and the backs for dovetailing. Follow with care the following directions. Both ends of the side pieces intended for drawer fronts, with tails cut in the high position, have the same marking as the front. The sides for "low" positioned fronts must be placed together as a pair, with one end of each identified for front fitting and marked like the front. The back piece does not extend below the bottom groove; therefore, the back ends of side pieces for the low half-tail cutouts should not be marked (see Photo 316). The part shown is the back end of a side piece marked "low" because no cutout is provided below the groove. Were it marked "high," the first full tail would be placed just above the bottom groove. As soon as you understand these directions and explanations, proceed with side-piece dovetailing.

Reset the marking gauge to side and back wood thickness. Scratch-mark both sides of both ends of every side and every back piece. Work on the sides of one drawer at a time. Check the front for high or low marking, place the template (edge to edge) in the corresponding high or low position. Photo 314 illustrates template placement for low marking. The scriber points to the 1¹⁄₁₆-inch scratch line that must be placed on the top edge of the bottom groove. Template-mark the inside surface of side pieces. In marking sides with the template in the high position, place the widest part of the first dovetail cutout on the top edge of bottom groove (Photo 315). Mark cutouts on the side pieces of the pilot drawer with a needle-point awl. Carefully jig-saw to these scratch lines, keeping the width of the saw cut on the "tail" side of the lines. The waste wood of the top cutout can be completely severed by the jig saw as in Photo 315. This also applies to bottom cutouts when the sides are so marked.

To remove waste wood from the tail cutouts, hold the ⅛-inch chisel vertically and give it a mallet blow of sufficient force to cut about halfway through the wood thickness. Cut the inside surface first, turn over the side piece and chop cut the remaining wood thickness for complete severance (Photo 316). Photo 317 shows a side, with cutouts made, held close to the drawer front for comparison and trial fitting.

Marking the back pieces for dovetails follows closely the technique established for drawer fronts. Marks are scratched on the end surfaces, and the template straightedge is held to the *outside* corner of the back piece instead of (as with drawer fronts) the ⅜-inch gauge marked line. When positioning the template for marking, keep in mind that the bottom edge of a back piece corresponds to the top edge of the bottom groove and the 1⅟₁₆-inch scratch line on the template. The back piece in Photos 318 and 319 is marked in the high position, meaning that the widest part of the first tail is placed at the bottom edge. When marking backs for the low position, align the 1⅟₁₆-inch template scratch mark with the bottom edge of the back piece, and then scratch-mark for the tails, pressing hard enough to leave a clearly visible line on the end wood. Pencil-mark the position and width of tails on the inside surface of the back piece (Photo 319).

Jig-saw on these pencil lines, keeping the width of the saw cut in the waste portion of the wood. Stop the saw cuts on the ⅜-inch gauge-marked line (Photo 320). Remove the wood between the tails by making two jig-saw cuts (the first cut is shown in Photo 321). Make the saw cut in a curve to meet and follow the gauge-marked line. Saw on the line to the next tail, severing that part of the waste wood. Turn over the back piece, and saw on the line to the starting tail, completing the straight recessed line and forming two square corners at the tails.

Vise-grip the back piece vertically. Place the cutting edge of a ½- or ¾-inch chisel on the *outside* edge of scratched lines, and press for a cleanly cut tail side. The waste wood will lean over, but it is not completely severed (Photo 322). Place the chisel in a horizontal position to cut away this waste wood. The back shown is for the high position. When all the drawers have been brought to this stage, they may be assembled.

Glue-coat the tails and the side seating shoulder of one end of a drawer front. Pick the matching end of the proper side piece, and tap it into place with a hammer. Glue-coat the end of the back piece that matches this side, place the back vertically on the work table, enter the tails in the side piece, and tap to seat the joint firmly. Next, coat both the front and the back dovetails for the other drawer side with glue. Place the side piece in position, and tap both its ends for proper seating (Photo 323). Front and back low position dovetail joints are shown in Photo 324. Note that the bottom of the side piece for the back joint does not have a half-tail cutout. As each drawer is assembled, slide it into its case opening, and align the front with the bordering beads before the glue sets. If it fits too tightly for eventual free movement, make the final fitting after overnight drying of the glue.

Remove the drawers, one at a time, for final fitting. Try to determine which areas cause a drawer to bind. Hand-plane these, and trial-fit, as many times as necessary for easy movement. Binding is usually more pronounced on the top edge of a drawer than at the side. If the drawer becomes tight when it is halfway in, examine the back opening for a clue to the binding area.

Smooth the drawer fronts with a drawknife, removing all band-saw marks (Photo 325). Replace each drawer in its opening to check surface evenness with the bordering bead. If any part of the drawer front surface is too high, shave it gradually to the desired level, maintaining the sweeping curve of the front. Bring all drawer fronts to this stage.

A cork sanding block with one surface slightly rounded is a useful part of shop equipment. A rounded block covered with No. ½ sandpaper performs much more efficiently on serpentine shapes and other curved surfaces. Sand thoroughly each drawer front in turn—first with coarse paper, then with No. 3/0—using the cork to support the paper. When they are sanded to finish smoothness, examine them carefully for unobliterated tool marks. Go over again any area where you find these, with both numbers of sandpaper. Remove the sharp bordering edges of the drawer front with folded 3/0 paper.

Glue up the drawer bottom panels of ⅜-inch-thick yellow poplar boards 20½ inches long. Panels to be ⅟₁₆ inch narrower than the groove depth opening across the drawers. After overnight drying, sand the panels to the degree acceptable for drawer sides and backs. Square one end of each panel. Place a panel on the work table, rest a drawer on it, allowing the squared end to extend ¼ inch past the back piece of the drawer (Photo 327). Center the drawer on the panel width, that is, the position the panel will assume when tongued and slid into place. Pencil-mark on the bottom panel for each drawer the back contour of the drawer front (Photo 327). Band-saw the panels separately on this outline.

Make the groove-cutting shaper set-up as for the drawer fronts, allowing the cutters to extend at least ⁵⁄₁₆ inch past the collars. Place an inverted bottom panel on the shaper table, adjusting the cutter height for a tongue that will slide freely into the bottom groove (Photo 328). Cut this tongue on both sides, and the front of bottom panels. Slide each individually marked bottom into its drawer when tongued (Photo 329). Tap it with a hammer for solid seating in the front groove. Drive three nails about 1¼ inches long through the bottom panel into the back piece, to hold the bottom in place permanently. The photograph also shows the maker's name, the city, and the year of completion cut on the lower surface of the top drawer panel. Do this on the top drawer of each chest.

Cut sixteen drawer stop blocks, about 2 inches long, ½ inch wide, and ¼ inch thick. Move a drawer into its opening so that the front surface is recessed to the same depth as the background wood on the other side of the bordering bead. Make a rub block joining to the side panel at each side of drawer, rubbing the block to a contact position with the drawer (Photo 330). Allow the glue to set, then drive two ¾-inch nails through each block into the side-panel wood. Cut the ¼-inch backing plywood to fit neatly into the case-back rabbets provided. Bore about five small screw holes in the long sides, very close to the plywood edge, three holes in the top and bottom ends. Fasten in place with ½-inch No. 2 screws. If the backs of these chests will be visible in their intended positions, use brass wood screws for back attachment. After the final examination and a rub-off with No. 7/0 sandpaper, the chests are ready for the finishing materials. Drawer interiors may or may not be coated with the finishing materials. Photo 331 shows a completed chest. Bore holes for the drawer handles after the finishing materials have been applied.

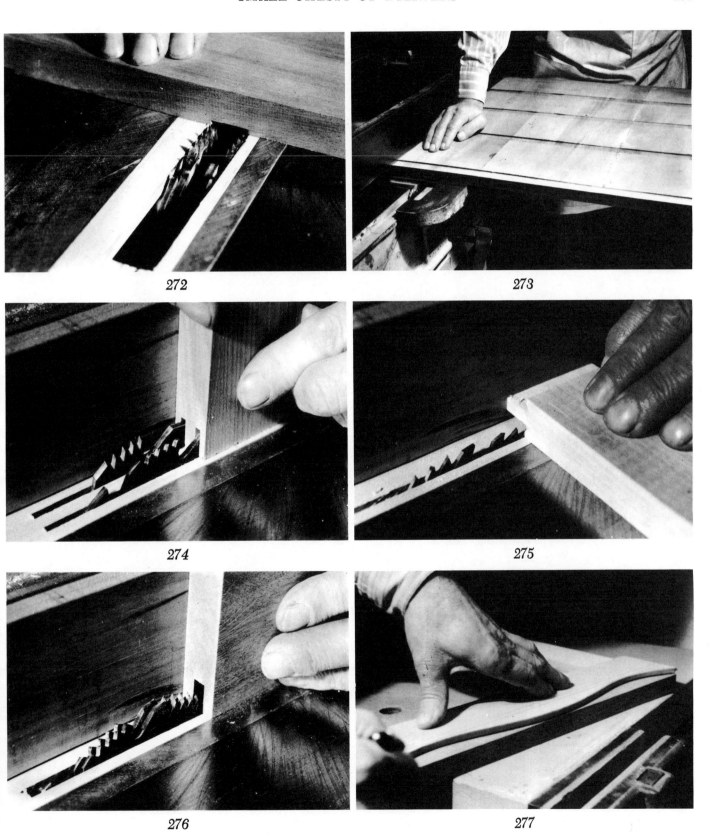

272

273

274

275

276

277

278

279

280

281

282

283

284

285

286

287

288

289

290

291

292

293

294

295

296

297

298

299

300

301

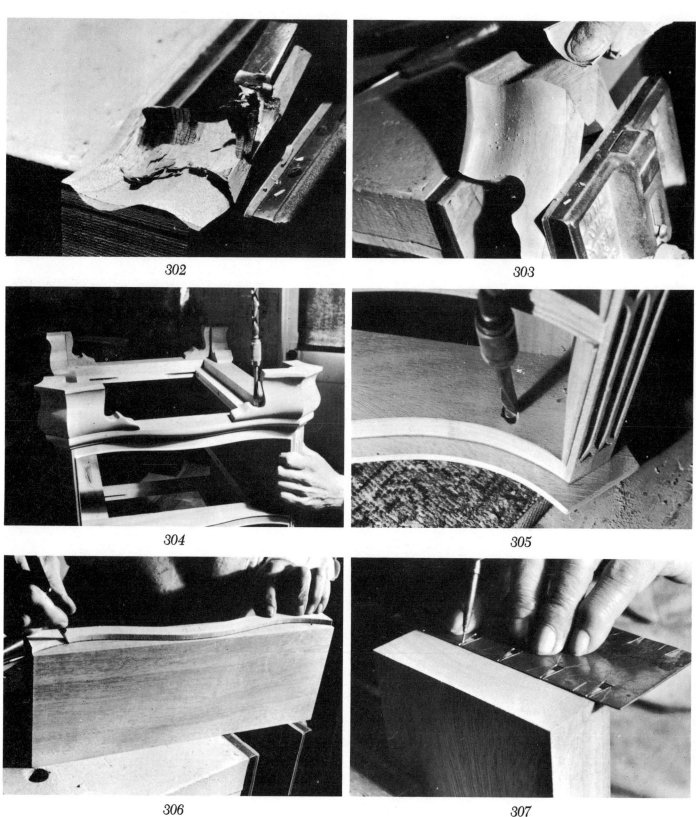

302

303

304

305

306

307

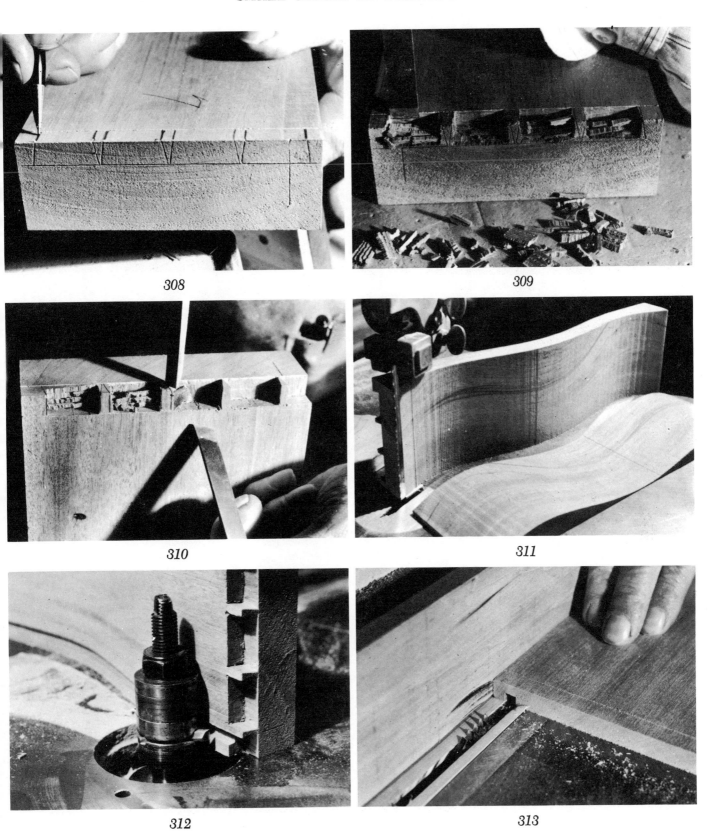

308

309

310

311

312

313

314

315

316

317

318

319

320

321

322

323

324

325

326

327

328

329

330

331

Piecrust Table

CHAPTER X

Piecrust Table

PHILADELPHIA ORIGIN, 1770

Materials (Sizes in Inches)

MAHOGANY	PIECES	LENGTH	WIDTH	THICKNESS
Post	1	22	4	4
Three legs	1	20	14	2½
Crow's-nest	1	9	8	$^{13}\!/_{16}$
Crow's-nest	1	8	8	$^{13}\!/_{16}$
Battens	2	31	1½	$^{13}\!/_{16}$
Top	1	36	36	1¼

1 brass table catch

Philadelphia artisans provided many of the piecrust tables exhibited in museums, and the interest shown in them by persons who ordinarily pay little attention to furniture is not surprising. The graceful lines, pleasing proportions, and elegant carving of the piecrust table make it truly a pièce de résistance of any home.

Start construction with the post, or column—4 by 4 inches, and 22 inches long. Measure and mark a center in each end for mounting in the lathe. Check the mounting for sufficiently embedded centers. The size and weight of the post make this safety check important. Slow speed is also wise. Use the reduced speed until a cylindrical shape is attained; then increase the speed. Photo 332 shows the large gouge removing the corners of the post.

Consult Drawing "B" (page 167) frequently for diameters, shapes, and lengths of sections. First turn the uniform 3⅞-inch diameter section at the lower end of the post in the following manner. While the lathe is in motion, pencil-mark from the lower end of the cylinder 4½ inches upward. Make a parting-tool cut on the lower side of this line to the depth of 3⅞-inch diameter. Cut to this same diameter at the lower end, still using the parting tool. Remove the intervening wood to the uniform 3⅞-inch depth with the ¾-inch gouge. Pencil-mark two more sections, both ¾ inch in length, while the post is in motion. On the line between the two, part with the skew to a depth of about ⅛ inch, keeping the lower wall of the parting cut as close as possible to a right angle. Leave the first ¾-inch section flat at the full 4-inch diameter. Place the parting tool on the upper side of the line ending the second ¾-inch section. Part to 3¼-inch diameter. Form a bead

of this section with the skew (Photo 333). Before parting for the cove section which follows, turn that area down to an oversized diameter. This preliminary work permits better manipulation of the tool. The distance across the cove, including both parting cuts, is $^{13}\!/_{16}$ inch. Pencil-mark accordingly. Part on the cove side of the upper line to 2¾-inch diameter. Turn the cove, using the ¾-inch gouge as instructed in Chapter VI, Candlestand. Drawing "B" shows the small diameter to be 2⅜ inches. The shape of the cove shows on the drawing and in Photos 336 and 337.

Pencil-mark for the vase length 3¾ inches. Starting on the pencil mark, turn a flat recess to 3⅝-inch diameter for about an inch on each side. This recess cut provides the proper diameter at the upper vase turning, and lessens the depth of the next two parting cuts. The best tool for turning the vase is the ¾-inch gouge. Turn this section to a well balanced ogee profile, as indicated in Drawing "B" (page 167). Measure and mark ½ inch above the vase for the quarter round (which is actually part of the vase). Part on the upper side of this line to a 3-inch diameter. Use the skew for rounding. A small ogee, or S curve, follows the quarter round and has the 3-inch diameter parting cut as its base. When measuring up the post ⅜ inch (as shown on the drawing), include the width of the 3-inch parting cut, and pencil-mark. Part on the upper side of this line to a depth of 2¾ inches. Use the ¼-inch round-nose tool for the concave portion of the S curve; the skew for the convex curve. The 2¾-inch diameter parting cut represents the base of a straight tapered section.

For the rest of the turning, make all measurements from the top end of the post. Measure 4¼ inches downward from the end for the length of the pin around which the crow's nest will revolve. In making this parting cut, keep the tool on the upper side of the line. Slightly undercut the wide shoulder, or bearing surface, so that the base square of the crow's nest will rest on the periphery. Carefully turn the pin to a uniform diameter of 1¼ inches. Measure ⅝ inch below the shoulder, pencil-mark, and part (keep the parting tool on the lower side of the line) to a 3-inch diameter. Quarter-round this section with the skew. Include the last parting cut when you measure ½ inch for the next fillet section. Part the lower side of the new line to 2⅜-inch diameter. This cut represents the upper end of the straight taper and forms its finished diameter. With the ¾-inch gouge, form the fillet to the size and the shape indicated on Drawing "B." Return now to the lower end of the straight taper. As shown in the drawing, a shallow fillet precedes the straight line of the taper. The fillet ends on the 2⅝-inch-diameter straight-line starting point. Turn this section down to size with the ¾-inch gouge, and finish the square-cut corner with the horizontally held skew (Photo 334). Sand the post first with coarse paper, then with No. 3/0. As before, do not hold the sandpaper in one place. Keep moving it back and forth, even if the distance of travel is short.

Lay off the vase circumference in six equal parts, in the following manner. Strike a true longitudinal line the length of the vase, to be used as a starting point for dividers. Set the dividers, and mark six equal sections around the vase base. Divide the larger diameter at the vase top in the same way. Mark the divisions from a starting line corresponding to that of the base. Draw pencil lines from base to top terminal marks.

Make a stencil-paper pattern for the vase-carving outline. The length of the pattern, from top to bottom, may vary from that in Drawing "B" (page 167). It is suggested that you press a piece of pattern material against the vase contour, marking it along the base and top lines. Cut the material with scissors on these lines. Replace the stencil paper on the vase, paralleling the newly cut border lines with the vase extremities. The outline imposed on the scaled blocks, Drawing

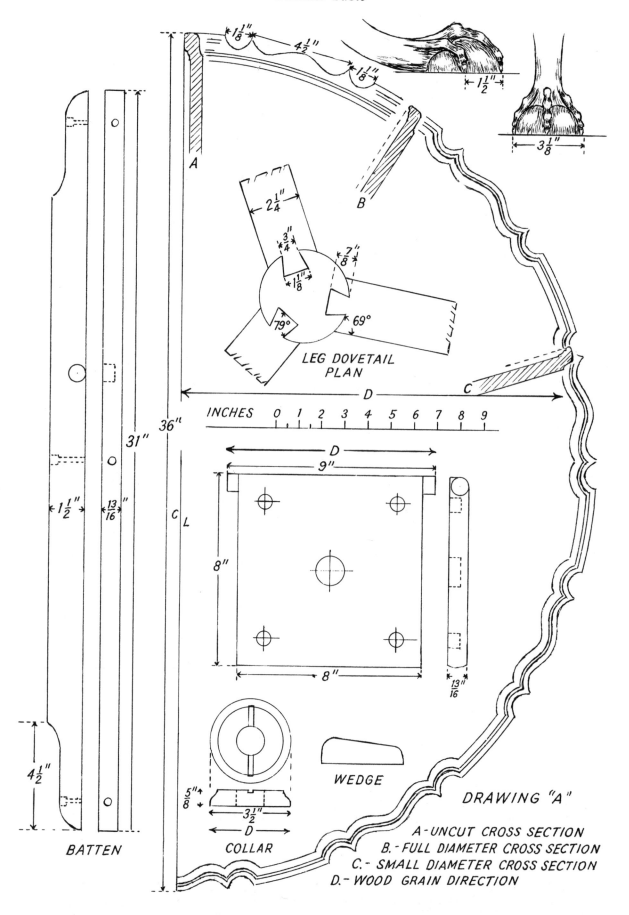

$1\frac{1}{8}''$ $4\frac{1}{2}''$ $1\frac{1}{8}''$ $1\frac{1}{2}''$ $3\frac{1}{8}''$

A

B

$2\frac{1}{4}''$ $\frac{3}{4}''$ $\frac{7}{8}''$ $1\frac{1}{8}''$ 79° 69°

C

LEG DOVETAIL PLAN

D

INCHES   0 1 2 3 4 5 6 7 8 9

D

9''

8''

8''

$\frac{13}{16}''$

36''

31''

$1\frac{1}{2}''$ $\frac{13}{16}''$

C L

$4\frac{1}{2}''$

$\frac{5}{8}''$ $3\frac{1}{2}''$ D

WEDGE

BATTEN

COLLAR

DRAWING "A"

A - UNCUT CROSS SECTION
B. - FULL DIAMETER CROSS SECTION
C. - SMALL DIAMETER CROSS SECTION
D. - WOOD GRAIN DIRECTION

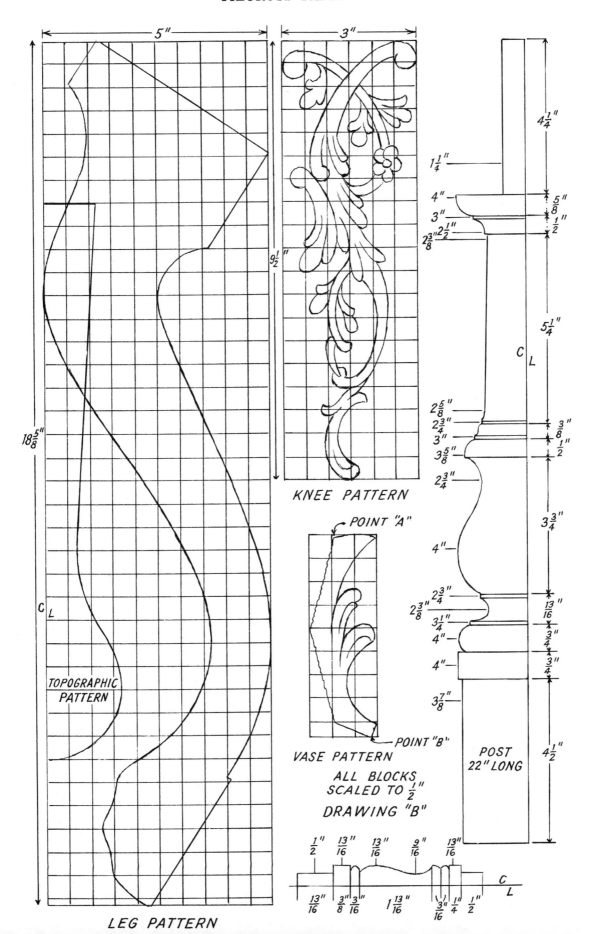

5"

3"

KNEE PATTERN

$9\frac{1}{2}$"

$18\frac{5}{8}$"

C L

TOPOGRAPHIC
PATTERN

LEG PATTERN

POINT "A"

VASE PATTERN

POINT "B"

ALL BLOCKS
SCALED TO $\frac{1}{2}$"

DRAWING "B"

$4\frac{1}{4}$"

$1\frac{1}{4}$"

4" $\frac{5}{8}$"
3" $\frac{1}{2}$"
$2\frac{3}{8}$" $2\frac{1}{2}$"

$5\frac{1}{4}$"

C L

$2\frac{5}{8}$"
$2\frac{3}{4}$" $\frac{3}{8}$"
3" $\frac{1}{2}$"
$3\frac{5}{8}$"

$2\frac{3}{4}$"

$3\frac{3}{4}$"

4"

$2\frac{3}{8}$" $2\frac{3}{4}$" $\frac{13}{16}$"
$3\frac{1}{4}$"
4" $\frac{3}{4}$"

4" $\frac{3}{4}$"

$3\frac{7}{8}$"

POST
22" LONG

$4\frac{1}{2}$"

$\frac{1}{2}$" $\frac{13}{16}$" $\frac{13}{16}$" $\frac{9}{16}$" $\frac{13}{16}$"

$\frac{13}{16}$" $\frac{3}{8}$" $\frac{3}{16}$" $1\frac{13}{16}$" $\frac{3}{16}$" $\frac{1}{4}$" $\frac{1}{2}$"

C L

"B," has two points marked "A" and "B." Point "A" is at the upper end of a division line; Point "B," at the lower end of the division line to the right of "A." Mark the positioned stencil paper accordingly. Use these two point marks on the pattern material as measuring points for the ½-inch block layout. Transfer the scaled-down outline from the drawing to the full-size blocks on the stencil paper. Cut on the outline with scissors.

Position the pattern on the vase as in Photo 335, holding Point "B" (the lower end) at a section line; Point "A" at the section line to the right. The accuracy of the pattern may be checked by measuring from the lower leaf tip to the Point "B" division line. The distance should be about 5/16 inch. If the pattern is satisfactory, mark its outline. Turn over the pattern, position it in the next section, and mark this for one complete leaf design. Three designs cover the full circumference.

First chop-part the three-quarter circle that lies between two designs (Photo 336). Use a No. 3 or 4 gouge, holding the tool on an angle that will produce a sloping side wall (Photo 337). Remove some waste wood for tool clearance, and then chop-part again. Relieve to a depth of 3/16 inch, striving for the background curvature that would result if this smaller diameter were turned on the lathe. Chop-part the leaf outlines on each side of the circle. Relieve the leaves, gradually lessening the background depth. The upper leaves in Photo 337 have been relieved. Only one lower leaf has been chop-parted. The quarter round above the vase will be called the leaf curl, for identification. On the sectional line dividing two designs, make a wide V cut as deep as the turned parting cut above the curl. This also shows on Photo 337.

Study Photo 338 in conjunction with Photo 343. Before leaf-tip shaping, widen the space between the leaf curl of two designs to ¼ inch. Now slope off the largest diameter of the leaf curl, curving it down to about ⅛ inch above the ¼-inch dividing-space background. Slope and round the upper outline of the leaf curl. Smooth the resulting flared background with a No. 3 gouge to the turned parting-cut diameter above the leaf curl. Photo 339 presents at the upper right another view of this carving. Notice in Photo 343 how the wide leaf curl swings down and around to meet the second petal tip.

Divide the first and second petals with the ⅛-inch veiner, as in Photo 338. Now divide the upper half of the first petal into two parts. Chop-part the small, round secondary tip of the second petal. Use the ¼-inch No. 11 gouge for petal channeling. Photo 338 shows two of these channels partly cut. The lower one will blend in with the secondary tip parting line. The upper channel forms one side of the second petal.

The right side of the leaf design (the lower half in Photo 339) has the two channels mentioned, cut through to completion. The one that joins the small rounded tip parting line ends abruptly at the small tip. All cuts feather out before reaching the base. Also in the lower half of the photograph, the central rib is sloped from the peak to meet the channel which forms one side of the second petal. A No. 3 tool is used to smooth this background. Now an explanation of the progressive steps taken in the upper half of Photo 339: The top, or first, leaf has its half nearer to the circle sloped and rounded toward the second half. But the wood height along the ridge should not be lowered. The other half of this petal is cut on a long slope toward the tip. Slope the angle to continue around the end of the first half with its lowest point (at the tip) about 1/16 inch above the background surface. This shows particularly well in Photo 343. Slope the corresponding part of the second petal in like manner, but let the side ridge nearer to the center rib remain high. Sloping takes place in width as well as length.

Photo 343 presents the best picture of leaf curl. Hollow out with a No. 7 gouge at the sides, where the whole broad leaf tip appears to curl over; and, with it, modify the unnatural point, which was formed in sloping the leaf outline, to a sweeping curve of the leaf edge. Begin at the leaf edge by cutting deeply (almost undercutting) with a gradual lessening of depth that will blend with the second petal relief channel. Now change to the ¼-inch No. 11 gouge and cut a flute, close to the leaf edge, from the leaf curl to the second petal tip. Beside this flute, cut another which will form a continuation of the second petal relief channel (see Photo 340). Change again to the ⅛-inch veiner and, between the flutes on each side, divide the leaf width into a series of ribs. Make the veiner cuts quite deep on the peak, or high point, because they will follow over the quarter-round area. Photo 343 shows the veiner rib cuts, feathering out in the direction of the central rib. With the ¼-inch No. 11 gouge, cut a short flute in the center of each rib, below and above the peak. As in carving the vase base, feather out all cuts when you near the turned parting line at the leaf top.

Now finish carving the first and second petals. A channel, or flute, runs the full length of the second half of each petal (see the upper half of Photo 339). Cut a short flute on the secondary rounded tip of the second petal, and make a final decorative cut that boldly transverses each petal tip. Cut deliberately across the flutes, imparting character to the petals. A short flute separates the bordering petal from the three-quarter circle (Photo 343) by starting on the circle side wall, passing up over the ridge, and feathering out at the base. Round the circle ridge slightly with a No. 3 gouge. Photo 340 shows the vase carving from the base of the post upward.

Groups of three spiral ribs, centered directly under each leaf carving and under the circle between carvings, decorate the large bead below the vase. Three ribs together are about ⅞ inch wide. Mark the bead circumference accordingly. Mark the outside and dividing lines for the ribs of each group, and make the divisions with the ⅛-inch No. 41 veiner (Photo 341). Although these cuts are not very deep, a mallet will give better tool control in cutting up and over this bead surface. Round the edge of each rib slightly with a small No. 3 gouge. Flute the center of each rib with the smallest available No. 11 gouge. With a No. 3 gouge, heel up, lower the background wood surface between rib groups, retaining the bead contour as closely as possible (Photo 342). For a neater appearance, let the bead carving feather out before you reach the border lines.

Photo 343 shows the vase and bead carving sanded with No. 3/0 sandpaper. Because of curvature, few carving cuts permit the use of shaped wood blocks to back up the sandpaper. In sanding the flutes, roll the paper to a convenient diameter, and keep the roll tight so that it will support more finger pressure. Retain the sharpness in sanding.

Next, make a leg pattern of rigid material. Lay it off with the usual ½-inch squares, consulting the scaled-down model in Drawing "B" (page 167). When the pattern outline is completely drawn, use a large square to check the foot bottom line with the post line for perfect right-angle relationship. Band-saw the pattern on the marked outline. Photo 344 shows the leg pattern being nested and marked on a piece of mahogany 20 inches long, 14 inches wide, and 2½ inches thick. (Mahogany of this thickness should be obtainable 14 inches wide. If a lesser width must be used, nest the pattern as well as possible, for a minimum waste.)

Band-saw the legs on the marked outlines. Save the larger pieces of waste wood, for later use to widen the feet. If the wood is in the rough state, smooth one side of each leg with a jointer or hand plane (Photo 345). Set the circular saw fence for 2¼-inch leg width. Adjust the saw blade to about half the height of the leg, and place the smoothed side of a leg against the fence. Make the saw cut; then turn the leg, end over end, and saw the remaining half. Do the same to the other two legs of the set (Photo 346). Smooth the sawed side of each leg by hand plane or jointer (Photo 347).

To transfer the post curvature to the top leg surface for dovetail positioning, vise-grip the post, bottom surface up. Invert a leg and place it on the post in its ultimate position ⅞ inch in from the deepest point of the post arc. Hold it in this position and mark the post curve on the top surface of the leg. This line shows on the leg in Photo 348.

Study the leg dovetail plan in Drawing "A" (page 166), which provides the measurement and angles necessary for milling the dovetails. Mount the hollow-ground saw on the arbor, and tilt to 79 degrees. Set the fence so that a saw cut from each side of the leg will leave a dovetail 1⅛ inches wide at its widest point (Photo 348). Adjust the blade height to meet the penciled post outline. Saw the three legs in turn, holding first one side of the leg against the fence, then the other side. These cuts size and outline the dovetails.

Reset the blade angle to 69 degrees, and reset the fence so that the blade will cut entirely on the dovetail side of the post arc line (Photo 349). Adjust the blade cutting height to meet the dovetail outlining cut. Lay one of the three legs on its side, pressing it against the fence as shown in the photograph, and make the saw cut. Then turn the leg over on its other side and make a corresponding saw cut. Bring the other two legs up to this stage.

The 69-degree saw cut was, of course, a straight saw-cut line, but these shoulders must be shaped to fit the post curvature. With a No. 3 gouge, the shoulders may be radius-cut for neat fitting. Mark both the top and the bottom surface of each leg with the post arc for guides in radius shaping. Chip the wood in the general direction from bottom to top (with the grain) for ease of tool handling. Photo 350 is practically self-explanatory.

Now lay off the post bottom surface, marking where the receiving grooves for the leg dovetail are to be placed. A starting point must be determined. Carry through, to the post bottom, one of the longitudinal division lines used for the *center* of a vase carving design. This will be the center of the starting leg dovetail. Set the dividers as in Photo 351, adjusting the points to the post radius. This setting divides the periphery into six nearly perfect sections.

Place one point of the dividers on the starting mark. Step the dividers around the circumference, marking every other step for a leg center (Photo 352). Draw a pencil line from each of the three leg center marks to the post center (also shown in the photograph). Now center-mark each leg dovetail on the wide surface, drawing it to the top right angle edge. Position a leg on the post bottom, matching the leg center mark to the one drawn on the bottom (Photo 353). The positioning includes the two side edges, which must meet the post perimeter. Mark the dovetail outline with a needle-point awl or scriber. Identify each leg and its place on the post with matching numbers.

Adjust the combination square to mark the post as in Photo 354. From the points where the scribed dovetail lines break the side surface of the post, continue them in pencil down the side to the leg cap shoulder. Do this for each dovetail. Also pencil a center line between the two side lines for centering the bit.

Mount the ¾-inch bit in the brace. Use of a bit stop is impractical, because of the shoulder at the upper end of the receiving grooves. In boring the first hole, which cuts through the bottom surface (Photo 355), count the number of brace revolutions for the desired depth. Bore a line of holes up to the shoulder, determining their depth by the number of brace revolutions. In working on this part of the post, grip it in the vise with the larger shoulder diameter free from vise pressure. If you hold the post in the vise with the center line at the top of the radius, you can align the brace and bit vertically for proper angle boring.

Shape the receiving dovetail grooves with chisels. First cut the walls vertically, starting the chisel cuts on the side lines. With the ½-inch chisel, level the bottom of the groove to the desired depth. Now hold the ¾-inch chisel on an angle that matches the dovetail mark on the post bottom, keeping its heel toward the groove. Chop-cut, using a mallet. The amount of waste wood to be removed by this angle cut will probably create too much resistance for the chisel to reach the bottom level in a single attempt. Chop as deep as you can, making side-by-side chisel-width cuts the full length of the groove (Photo 356). Cut the other groove side in like manner. Remove most of the waste wood from each side angle, holding the chisel in a horizontal position as you enter the groove from the post bottom opening. Repeat the side-wall chisel cuts, using enough force to sink the chisel to the bottom of the groove. Cut both side walls to the bottom. Level off the full width of the groove bottom for dovetail clearance. For this operation, the chisel must enter the bottom opening of the post.

Trial-fit the leg that has the matching number (Photo 357). Many fittings may be necessary before the leg slides into position satisfactorily. Whenever it binds, look in the groove ahead of the leg to discover the binding area, remove the leg, and shave off some of the side-wall wood. As the fitting of each leg is completed, keep it in position until you have drawn a line on its top surface to indicate the bordering cap edge. This line is for use in carving the knee design. In making the initial side-wall cuts it is possible to remove too much wood, especially near the upper end of the groove. If the leg fits loosely at the top, prepare a suitable wedge ½ inch long by ⅞ inch wide, tapering the length from a necessary thickness to a feather edge. When you fit the leg permanently with glue, glue-coat the wedge and press it against a side wall, feather edge toward the post bottom. If the lower end of the leg needs to be wedged, tap a wedge into the open joint after the leg is in final position. Depend on fit instead of force. Trial-fit the remaining two legs.

Waste-wood blocks must be glued to the feet, to increase their width from 2¼ to 3⅛ inches. Size the blocks from the waste wood saved from the legs, with their grain direction parallel to that of the feet. Lay one block on a foot side surface, with the grain parallel to the leg grain. Mark on the underside of the block along the straight foot bottom edge. This is the only important edge surface. Foot contour may be followed for height, and length in excess of 3½ inches. Process the other thick block at the same time. Smooth one side of each block by hand plane or jointer for glue joining to the side of the foot. Set the circular saw fence for resawing blocks ⁷⁄₁₆ inch thick. Hold the smoothed side of the thick block against the fence, and cut a thinner block from it. Resurface the sawed side of main block, and repeat for two more sized blocks. Smooth the opposite side of the other block, and resaw to produce three more blocks. Of the six blocks now ready for gluing, three are for the right side of the legs and three are for the left. Glue-coat a right and a left block surface, rub them into position on a foot, keeping the bottom edges flush with the foot surface. Place a C clamp approximately at the block centers, and apply pressure (Photo 358). Attach blocks to the other two feet in like manner, and allow overnight drying.

Refer to the drawing on page 167 for the topographic pattern needed for the top profile of leg and foot. Make a scaled block pattern, and place it on the top surface of the leg and foot, pressing to contour. Be careful to center the pattern in the leg width. Outline the three legs in pencil.

In band-sawing on the outlines, start at the tip of the foot, holding the leg in a natural position, that is, with the foot bottom in contact with the top of the saw table. Keep the leg in this position until the saw reaches the ankle area, and then gradually drop it to the position shown in Photo 359. In this photograph the far-side cut has been made, and the saw has nearly completed the fore-side outline. Saw the other two legs on the marked outlines.

Smooth the sides of the legs with the flat-bottomed drawknife as in Photo 360. Grip the upper end of a leg in the vise as in the photograph. Support the ankle area with the notched prop described in Chapter VI. Smooth each side of the three legs down to the ankle, removing all saw marks.

Photo 361 shows a foot with claws outlined. Start by drawing a center line on the top surface from above the ankle to the foot tip. Draw the center claw outline on each side of the center line for total widths: at the nail extremity, $\frac{3}{16}$ inch; at all knuckle joints, $\frac{1}{2}$ inch; and between knuckles, $\frac{3}{8}$ inch. A guide for side-claw marking is provided in Drawing "A" (page 166). It shows the side claws starting at the bottom line $1\frac{1}{2}$ inches from the foot tip. They are to be drawn on a slight backward angle to the first joint, which is one inch above the base line. The side claw's second joint is approximately $\frac{1}{2}$ inch farther from the foot tip than the third, or high, knuckle of the center claw and is $1\frac{1}{2}$ inches above the base line. Draw the side-claw widths about the same as those of the center claws.

Carving instructions will be given for one foot. The remaining two may be cut at the same time or held over until the completed first can serve as a pilot. First, part the center claw on its outline to a depth of about $\frac{3}{16}$ inch, using the $\frac{3}{8}$-inch No. 41. Mallet blows will permit better tool control. A change in direction of cutting will be necessary at about the second knuckle. In the upper left foot shown in Photo 362 one side of the center claw has been parted, and the other side is partially cut. The center and side claws of the lower foot have been parted, and preliminary work on the ball is in progress. Make each progressive step of ball and claw carving on both sides of the pilot foot.

The ball will ultimately have a shape reasonably close to a half-sphere. The center claw has been band-sawed to follow this contour, but the side claws must receive this relative gripping impression. So, as the side claws rise, they must bend inward to keep their gripping position on the finally shaped ball. The illusion of gripping must be created with carving tools. Photo 363 illustrates side-claw contour. Notice a slight inward slope starting just above the nail area and extending to the first joint. Now the inward slope continues from the first joint to the second, combined with a concave or dip curve between knuckles. Study the front view of the foot, Drawing "A" (page 166). To give the second joint prominence, make a concave side cut from this knuckle, and blend it with the ankle line. Photo 364 illustrates clearly the full lateral contour, as explained. Remove some waste wood now from the ball and the web between front and side claws for tool clearance. Refine the claw outlines, and deepen the parting cuts in one operation. Do not rough out the ball shape behind the side claws (Photo 363) until the front part has been reduced to size.

The fore part of the ball in Photo 364 has been shaped to finish size with the No. 3 gouge, heel up. The claw relief given here is approximate: at the nail extremities, $\frac{1}{8}$ inch; at the first knuckles, $\frac{1}{4}$ inch; at the second knuckles, $\frac{5}{16}$ inch; at the center third knuckle, $\frac{3}{8}$ inch. A sharp right-angle corner where the claws grip the ball is desirable, from the center second joint and the side first joint down to the base line. Above these knuckles, use the $\frac{1}{4}$-inch No. 11 instead of the veiner. This area will be represented by a web, joining the claws with a fillet instead of a sharp corner.

The front part of the ball now shows a finished radius line on the bottom surface. Shape the back part of the ball to a continuing arc (Photo 365). Strive to give it the rounded shape that would blend with the front part if the side claw were not superimposed. The ball and leg side line meet under the second joint and curve downward, following the ball contour, to the bottom leg surface (Photo 367). The side of the leg must be lowered to provide claw relief, and a more delicate appearance. Treat this meeting of leg and ball as a web overlap. That is, the leg ending seems to lap over the ball with a shoulder of not more than 1/16 inch.

In giving the claws their final form, start with the nails. Place a No. 7 gouge, heel upward, across the claw extrusion 3/8 inch up from the bottom line, and press for a parting. Slope the nail to this parting line by pointing the gouge on a slant upward. Keeping the heel of the gouge in the same position, slant it toward the bottom, and give the cuticle a sharp slope (Photo 366). Now give the nail more taper by narrowing the width at the bottom line to about 1/8 inch. Slope the nail ending to about 1/8-inch relief. Round the nail with a small No. 3 gouge.

With this gouge, continue the sloped cuticle down each side of the claw. Between the cuticle and the first joint, hollow out the wood for a noticeably smaller diameter (Photos 367, 368). Carry this refinement down the sides, changing the outline where it meets the ball. Form similar claws between the first and second joints. Round the knuckles as the formation progresses upward. Remove just enough wood from the knuckles to erase the decided peak line which results when two angles meet. Above the second knuckle, hollow slightly and round, gradually lessening the curve to blend in with the ankle line. After completing the two side claws, repeat the successive steps on the center claw. The only difference is an added knuckle.

Study Photo 368. The ball has its approximate final shape as far up as the second joint of the center claw and the first joint of the side claws. From these areas up to the ankle, remove much more wood, to relieve the bony structure effectively. For deepening the claw relief in these areas, use the 1/4-inch No. 11 gouge. For other surface cuts, use No. 3 gouges of varying widths.

Photo 369 shows two feet in different stages of development. Both show web lines that start at the third center knuckle and travel in an arc across the ball to a point midway between the first and second side-claw joints. Draw web lines accordingly. Chop-part on these lines with an appropriately curved gouge. With a 1/2-inch No. 3 gouge, heel up, refine the ball shape up to the web parting cuts (the right foot in the photograph). Below the webs, the claws grip the ball on a sharp right-angle line. The webs join the claws with a fillet cut by the 1/4-inch No. 11 gouge. The webs overlap the ball with a shoulder of not more than 1/16 inch. With a drawknife, remove band-saw marks from the four surfaces of the ankle area, and round the ankle (the left foot in Photo 369). The underside of the leg where it meets the ball is also to be rounded, smoothed, and sanded.

Shape the front surface of the legs next. Hold a leg in the vise (Photo 370). Start at the top, where the cap radius has been marked, chipping the wood to follow this radius 1/8-inch oversize. It is necessary to leave extra wood standing on the juncture area of leg and cap for final leg shaping (illustrated in Photos 373 and 374). Use a large No. 3 gouge for preliminary removal of wood from the top surface to the change of curve which starts the knee. From knee to ankle, do the shaping with the drawknife. The knee is to be crowned rather than rounded, showing a distinct edge where side surface and crown meet. The crown is approximately 3/8 inch high. From the lower knee area (about where the drawknife is held in Photo 370), make the corner radii progressively smaller, gradually changing to a true round as you approach the ankle. The change is so gradual as to be unnoticed. Use the No. 3 gouge to blend the knee crown with the hand-tooled radius at the top of the leg.

Sand the feet and ankles next (Photo 371). Supporting blocks cannot be used here. Instead, fold small pieces of No. ½ sandpaper to three thicknesses, and carefully remove all tool marks. Avoid dulling the sharp cuts, especially in the cuticle and nail area, and in the web overlap. Always sand the length of the claws, and from bottom to top of the balls, never crosswise or from claw to claw. Sanding from the other direction would scratch the wood deeply, and then much time would be required in removing the scratches. After the coarse paper, use No. 3/0 with the same technique.

Mark a piece of stencil paper 9½ by 3 inches, with ½-inch blocks for pattern transfer. Taking the scaled-down model in Drawing "B" (page 167) as a guide, draw the knee-carving design outline. Transfer also to the stencil paper the petal division lines of the model. You will find these lines very helpful in familiarizing yourself with the main carving cuts of the design. Cut the pattern to outline with scissors, and make cutouts with appropriate carving tools for more satisfactory results. Make the center line on the pattern particularly heavy, for identification.

Grip a leg in the vise, as in Photo 372. Center the pattern in width, placing the right, or high, scroll ⅞ inch down from the top edge. Transfer the pattern outline to the leg, marking small sections at a time while you press the pattern close to the wood. Before marking any section, make sure that the pattern has not moved off center. Pattern-mark all three legs.

Chop-part all design outlines on a pilot leg with appropriately selected tools. A mallet is unnecessary, inasmuch as narrow tools are used and parting depths do not exceed ³⁄₃₂ inch. Reasonably heavy hand pressure on the tools is enough. Photo 373 shows the complete design outline parted on the pilot leg. Vise-grip the leg progressively in positions most convenient for the work. The photograph also shows a No. 3 gouge forming the final shape on the upper leg edge which joins the cap. From the cap radius line, which you marked in pencil when you fitted the leg, to a parallel line ⅜ inch down the leg, scallop the intervening surface.

Transverse the leg with a ⅛-inch veiner cut (Photo 374) on the ridge formed in scalloping the ⅜-inch surface. Below the veiner cut, start sloping the wood to the parting line, relieving the carving design to a depth of ³⁄₃₂ inch. The scrolls ending the design are spread to a width that makes them extend down the sides of the leg. Relieve these portions by extending the crown farther down the leg. Photo 375 shows the new and lower side line. Photo 374 calls attention to carving progress; the veiner is placed to make its cut on the ridge across the leg width, and a No. 3 gouge is cutting background wood to relieve the carving design. Portions of the design have been relieved.

Photo 375 shows the complete design, relieved and ready for surface cuts. In addition to the widely spaced scrolls, other design parts extend to the crown edge, necessitating a lowering of the crown farther down the side walls. Without any abrupt crown-line changes, alter the lines on a long sloping basis.

The following detailed instructions for design surface cuts are to be read with frequent reference to Photo 376.

Crossed leaf stems start at the top and end in scrolls which are slightly crowned. Immediately below the left scroll, a small three-petal leaf shoots out from the stem. With the ¼-inch No. 4 gouge, part the two small side petals for only a short distance in from the outline. Sharply slope the parting cuts to accentuate the division. With a No. 7 gouge, hollow the main petal from stem to tip. Make this a bold cut, even if it includes parts of the side petals. The left stem crosses under the right and is rounded on both sides to the point where a pair of leaves shoot out. Cut the left leaf of the pair much as you have just cut the three-petal leaf. For the right leaf of the pair, use the No. 7 gouge to concave-cut the outside edges of the side petals. Round the stem between the leaves, and the flower decoration farther down the stem.

Carve the flower by first parting the center button. Bear in mind the small, delicate design, and handle the tools with care. If a tool does slip, glue the broken piece back into place and let the glue dry. As you look at the flower from the center button upward to the petal tips, the left side of each petal is high, seeming to overlap the next petal to the left. Part the left side of each petal with a No. 7 gouge. Starting at the high side of the petal, use a No. 4 gouge to dish it out, and chop this concave cut to relieve the next petal on the right. From the flower, the stem circles to join decorations that emanate from the other stem. Round this part of the stem.

Now start with the right stem at the top. From the scroll to the first leaf offshoot, concave-cut its lower side, as shown in Photo 376. A pair of leaf petals shoot out at this point. Use a No. 3 gouge to cut a sharp division line between them (this tool will produce a much sharper division than the veiner). Use the veiner to outline the left side of the second petal. Refer to the photograph, and hollow out the first petal with either the No. 7 or the ⅛ inch No. 4 gouge, retaining its high left side. Hollow out the second petal also, but remove more wood, to put it on a lower plane than the first petal.

Continue down the right side of the stem, where another pair of petals (larger than the first) are outlined. Divide these with the ⅛ inch No. 41. The first of the pair is narrow and has both sides rounded. The second should be hollowed out rather boldly, but not quite as much as the wider petals described and shown above. Next comes a single petal, which is long and narrow. Divide it on the lower side with the ⅛-inch veiner, and hollow it slightly with the No. 4 gouge. From here to the scroll ending, the design changes from a decided stem to a long, narrow petallike tail, which we shall describe soon.

Where the left side of the stem is concerned, consult the knee pattern outline in Drawing "B" (page 167), which shows more design detail than the photographs, especially in this area. After crossing over the left stem, the right broadens to swing into an in-turned scroll, which is slightly crowned. Following this is an isolated scroll that ends in a three-petal leaf. Crown the scroll, round the leaf stem adjacent to the scroll, and hollow the outside edges of the side petals. Hollow the center petal, starting near the scroll and deepening the cut to a bold finish at the tip. To fill the space between the last described leaf and the main stem, fashion a short petal and round both its sides. (This is illustrated fairly well in Photo 378.) Next comes a long narrow petal, to be rounded on both sides. For a portion of the main stem, from the first petals to the one just described, cut a vein that feathers out at both ends (Photo 376).

We now return to the petallike tail, mentioned in an earlier paragraph. Cut its upper half to leave a ridge in the center. With a No. 4 gouge, heel up, give the outside a slightly convex slope. Concave-cut the inside, feathering out about halfway down (Photos 376, 377, 378). As the lower half gradually changes, both sides become rounded. From the petal immediately above the tail, a secondary stem emerges, swinging to the right and ending with an oddly fashioned decoration that faintly resembles an acorn. Round this stem, crown the acorn, and make closely spaced veiner cuts across it. To the left of the stem (right side in Photo 377) a stubby two-petal leaf carries the design to the edge of the crown. Sharply divide the petal tips for a short distance, and boldly hollow the center.

Between the leaf and the acorn, another stem emerges, ending in a crown scroll. We have now reached the vicinity of an unusual scroll ending for the tail. The scroll is conventional, but attached to it and pointing up the leg is a leaf petal that makes the whole look like an inverted comma. Round both edges of the petal, and hollow the center, carrying this cut through the scroll. Cut a vein down the center of the petal and the scroll (Photo 377).

A short scroll tip links the tail's end and the last scroll, completing the design. It is concave except on the lower side of the tip, which is convex. Slope the larger radius of the lower scroll, and concave more than half its width with a No. 7 gouge. Cross the lower tip with a bold ¼-inch No. 11 flute cut, which will complete the knee design carving.

The background wood surrounding the carving may be sanded lightly with coarse paper to remove tool marks. Sand the background again with No. 3/0, and sand the carving also. Carefully avoid any dulling of the sharply carved features.

Assemble the legs and post, with glue. If an upper wedge is included with a leg fitting, have it conveniently close in the assembling. Glue-coat first the receiving groove, then the matching numbered leg dovetail. Enter the leg, and tap it into a solid seat. Assemble the remaining legs similarly.

Make an angled scallop cut on each side of the three legs (Photo 379), with the largest No. 7 gouge available. On the bottom edge of the post, between legs, make a V cut (three cuts, in all) with a large No. 3 gouge. To do this, first make a parting cut down in the V form, convexing the surfaces with the No. 3 gouge, heel up. After you sand the newly made cuts, the table base is complete.

Prepare the top and bottom crow's-nest squares next. The bottom is a true square, 8 inches by 8, and 1¾₆ inch thick. Cut the top one inch longer to provide a ½-inch-long hinge pin on each end. Mount the hollow-ground blade on the arbor, and adjust the saw fence for a ½-inch-wide cut to the far side of the saw blade (Photo 380). Press one end of the block against the fence and saw within ¾ inch of the other width edge. The blade radius will cut farthest at the table level. Therefore, pencil a mark on the saw fence at right angles to this extended cutting point to assure accurate cutting distance. Saw the other end in the same manner.

Set the fence ¾ inch from the saw, adjust the blade to cut ½ inch in height. Place the top piece on end, supported by the crosscut gauge, with the intended pin-side edge against the fence (Photo 381). Make the saw cut. Do the same at the other end, holding the same side against the fence. Pencil-mark a continuation of the ½-inch saw cut to the hinge-pin blank on each end. Carefully band-saw on these extended lines, to sever the waste strips of wood.

Photo 382 shows the two squares clamped together, with all edges perfectly aligned. The intended top square (with the pin-blank extensions) is placed underneath for boring because none of the holes will be bored completely through this block. In clamping the two blocks, make sure that the grain of one runs in the same direction as that of the other. Mark both blocks for identification so that, after separation, they may be assembled in the same relative position. Mark for ½-inch post-hole centers 1⅛ inches in from the edges at each corner. Mark the exact block center for boring a 1¼-inch hole that will fit over the post pin. Align brace and bit for true 90-degree holes. Bore the holes completely through the inverted bottom square and to a depth of ⁹⁄₁₆ inch in the top block. Remove the clamp, hand-plane a chamfer of about ⅛-inch on all right-angle edges of the bottom block.

Sand all surfaces to finish smoothness. (The top block edges in Photo 383 are being chamfered to the hinge-pin blank.) Chamfer all edges of the top square except the upper hinge-pin right angle, which must be planed to the pin radius.

Scribe ¾-inch circles on the hinge-pin ends, keeping the radius lines even with the top surface of the block. This is important because the upper outside quarter of the circle must be hand-planed to form a continuous radius length from end to end (Photo 384). After the pin circle line is marked on each end, the upper quarter-circle radius may be planed before the pins are formed to full rounded shapes. In forming the pins, use a fine-toothed wood saw or a hack-saw blade held flat on the block's straight edge line. Saw to the approximate radius of the pins. Chip off the waste wood to the scribed circle with a No. 4 or 5 gouge (Photo 384). For a neat fit, bore a ¾-inch hole in scrap wood to be used for trial fitting. If necessary, continue to work down the pin to a free-turning, but not loose, fit in the scrap-wood hole.

The four corner posts may be turned from two pieces of mahogany 10 inches long by 1¾₁₆ inch square. Mark the centers in the ends, and mount one piece at a time on the lathe. In the usual way, turn each piece to a full-length cylindrical shape. Leave sufficient wood at each post end for dowels, and indicate the shoulders, measuring 3 inches between. Mark for two posts from one 10-inch piece (Photo 385). Mark for the two top ends of posts that are to face each other. Use the parting tool to undercut the shoulders slightly to a ½-inch-diameter depth. Turn the dowels to ½-inch finished diameter. Mark lines on the revolving wood in accordance with the measurements on Drawing "B" (page 167). Make parting cuts with the skew on all lines except the one that indicates the vase top. In shaping post profiles, check with the drawing and Photo 385. Round beads with the skew, vases with the ¾-inch gouge. Sand to finish smoothness. Turn the other 10-inch piece to match. Saw apart each pair of posts, cutting the dowels to length at the same time.

Turn a collar according to the specifications in Drawing "A" (page 166). The underside (attached to the faceplate screw) need not be turned—only smoothed by jointer or hand plane. Turn the edge to an ogee shape, true up the top surface, and sand the top and the edge to finish smoothness. Remove it from the faceplate, and bore a 1¼-inch hole through the center. The hole must be bored exactly at 90 degrees to the bottom surface; otherwise, when the collar is slipped on the post pin, its circumference will not bear evenly on the bottom square.

Assemble the crow's-nest next. Make sure of the position of the blocks in relation to each other, glue-coat the corner holes in the top square, enter it, and seat the four posts. Glue-coat the corner holes in the bottom square, position it, and seat it on the four posts. Slide the nest on the 1¼-inch post pin, and check for an even bearing on the periphery of the post shoulder. Raise the nest far enough to slide the collar on the pin. Check this turning for even distribution of bearing surface. At the top surface level of the collar pencil-mark on the post-pin circumference a line for a starting point in wedge-slot marking and boring. Mark a longitudinal line upward on the pin for centering the bit. Place another mark across the centering line 1⁄16 inch below the circumference line. From this newly made cross line, measure one inch up the pin, and mark this for slot height. Bore a ¼-inch hole for slot bottom ending. Center the bit so that its radius will cut exactly on the lower cross line, and keep it in a true horizontal position for this hole.

Now bore the upper slot ending hole. Center the bit, for its radius to cut the upper cross line. Instead of holding the bit horizontally, angle it downward to come through the pin for a slot height of about ¾ inch. Bore as many holes as you find convenient in the intervening slot wood (Photo

386). Cut the slot walls straight with a ½-inch chisel. Square-cut the bottom surface of the slot, but leave the bit radius shape on the slot's top end.

Make a ¼-inch-thick wedge, allowing about an inch extra wood at each end. Taper its height from about 1½ inches to ½ inch. Insert it in the slot, and check it for accuracy of taper. Make any necessary changes in the taper for perfect slot fitting. Turn the collar so that its grain will run at right angles to the wedge. Mark the wedge thickness on the top of the collar, each side of the post pin. Remove the wedge, raise the nest, and slide the collar off the post pin. Cut a shallow groove between the wedge thickness lines on the top of the collar. The depth of the groove should bring it to the exact level of the slot bottom. Photo 387 shows a complete assembly consisting of nest, collar, and wedge.

Although a 36-inch one-piece board for the top excites the imagination, do not rule out the possibility of procuring it. If you are unsuccessful, glue together as many 1¼-inch-thick boards as necessary to make up the width, matching grain patterns at each joint. Scribe a 36-inch circle on the chosen bottom surface, pressing the center point deeply into the wood for later identification. Hand-plane (Photo 388) the bottom, checking often with a straightedge for an even, flat surface. The slightest warp or twist will seem to be magnified many times when the top is mounted on the lathe faceplate. Even with a reasonably true bottom surface, the top's final thickness after truing up will probably be about ⅞ inch.

For a turning of this size, build up the faceplate diameter to at least 20 inches with a ¾-inch plywood disc (Photo 389). Bore six screw holes close to the edge of the faceplate, center it accurately on the table top, and attach it with screws of sufficient length to embed themselves about ½ inch in the wood.

The initial r.p.m. of the turning will depend on the rigidity of the faceplate shaft mounting and on the accuracy of centering of the top on the faceplate. Play safe: until the bottom, the edge, and the top have been trued to near finish size, revolve the disc at a low speed free from vibration. After surface truing, place the tool-rest standard close to the bottom surface (Photo 390). With the ¾-inch gouge, cut a fillet ⅛ inch deep, 1 inch in from the edge. Cut this lower level on a straight line to the edge of the circle. Round the bottom edge corner to a ½-inch radius, moving the tool rest when necessary so as to keep it close to the work.

Place the tool rest for face cutting (Photo 391). While the top is in motion, make a pencil line ¾ inch in from the edge and another 1⅛ inches from the edge toward the center. Place the parting tool inside the ¾-inch line, and make a cut ³⁄₃₂ inch deep. In Photo 391 the parting tool is held on the flat resulting from this cut. Part inside the 1⅛-inch line to a scant ¼-inch depth. Round both edges of the ¾-inch flat. Cut away some of the waste center wood nearly to the lower level, to provide tool clearance for cutting the final rim. With the ¼-inch round-nose tool, form a small cove, leaving a flat ³⁄₃₂ inch wide at the first parting cut and a shoulder of less than ¹⁄₁₆ inch at the bottom level. (See Cross Section A in Drawing "A," page 166.)

Turn off the waste wood of the entire center area with the large gouge. Keep the tool rest as close as possible to the work. If the speed of the faceplate has not been increased, step up the r.p.m. to what seems safe for the better balanced turning. This is a time-consuming job. If it is not hurried, there is little likelihood that the gouge will "pull in" and cut a channel deeper than the intended surface level. When you near the final surface level, have a straight-edged stick ready to place against the top surface as a means of checking for high spots (Photo 392). Gradually turn the top to a satisfactory flat surface, then to the desired depth. Sand the flat top with coarse paper supported by a cork block, checking frequently with the straightedge for retention of flatness. Fold coarse paper to sand the rim, the edge, and the underside. Sand in the same way with No. 3/0 paper for finish smoothness. Remove the table top from the faceplate.

Next, lay off the circumference in eleven sections. Adjust dividers to a trial setting of 10¼ inches, and step them around the top's periphery, resetting if necessary for making uniform sections. Before marking the sections definitely, place the top on the work table, and turn it so that the grain runs from side to side. This position corresponds to the layout in Drawing "A" (page 166). Mark a sectional starting point at the table top or at right angles to the grain direction (comparable to the top in Drawing "A"). Pencil-mark this starting point. Place one point of the dividers here, step off one section, and pencil-mark. Repeat this section marking for the full circumference. As in the drawing, the area not scalloped, which we will call the uncut section, is centered at the top. Because of the odd number of sections, a scalloped section is centered at the bottom.

Make a pattern of rigid material to receive the scallop, or piecrust, design. First, mark the radius lines on the pattern material. To do this, lay the pattern board on the bench top, set the compass to an 18-inch radius, and mark the pattern board with this largest-diameter arc. Without moving the pattern material or disturbing the compass center, reset the compass for a 17½-inch radius, and mark this line. Reset for a 17¼-inch radius, and mark. If the dividers are still set for sectional divisions, place them on the largest pattern radius line exactly as for marking the top circumference. Pencil-mark the divider point impressions. This will be the exact length of the pattern.

Divide the largest radius line of the pattern in the following manner: starting at one pencil-marked end, measure half of the 3½-inch uncut section, or 1¾ inches, and mark this measurement. Next, make a 1⅛-inch mark for the first scallop cut. Then, a 4½-inch serpentine, and the second 1⅛-inch scallop. The pattern should end with another half-length uncut section of 1¾ inches. Use Drawing "A" as a guide for filling in scallop and serpentine outlines. In depth, these outlines do not extend beyond the 17½-inch radius line. Band-saw the outline of the pattern. Now follow the outline with a parallel line ¾ inch less in radius. Band-sawing on this line produces a pattern similar to that in Photo 393. Place the pattern on a section of the top (Photo 393), and mark both the outside and the inside pattern outlines. Repeat at every section. Band-saw the table top on all scallop and serpentine outlines (Photo 394).

Chop-part on the inner design line (Photo 395), with appropriately curved tools. The wood thickness to be parted varies with the curvature of the design. Therefore in some areas, after parting, waste wood must be chipped away with a No. 3 gouge, and then they must be parted again to reach the desired lower level. Photo 396 shows the removal of waste wood, extending the flat surface line to the raised rim design. Strive, in the flat surface work, to leave the fewest possible tool marks. Less sanding will then be required for a satisfactory job.

Parallel the piecrust edge with a line ¼ inch in from the edge for the bordering bead width. This may be drawn with ease by holding the pencil between the thumb and the second and index fingers. Place the index finger, in relation to the pencil point, so that its nail touches the table edge while allowing the pencil point to mark a ¼-inch parallel line. Pencil-mark the entire table-top circumference. Chop-part on this line to the first lathe parting-cut level. Chip off the waste wood to this level (Photo 397).

Photo 398 shows on the right a No. 3 gouge rounding the bordering bead, outside and inside edges. On the left a No. 7 gouge is cutting the small cove, allowing a ³⁄₃₂-inch ledge or flat to parallel the bead while permitting a scant ¹⁄₁₆-inch shoulder to stand at the bottom. The grain direction changes as the work progresses around the top, and the tool cutting must change direction just as often.

Now form a ½-inch radius on the underside of the band-sawed edge to match the turned radius that remains on the uncut sections (Photo 399), using a large-size No. 3 gouge. It will be necessary to change the cutting direction of the tool frequently. Remove tool marks on these radius cuts with a sandpaper-covered length of wood (Photo 400) before sanding with folded coarse paper in a direction parallel with the table edge. Follow with folded No. 3/0 paper to obtain finish smoothness. Now sand, with the two grits of sandpaper, the bead and cove on the top surface edge; and finally sand (with the grain) the entire top flat surface with No. 3/0 paper wrapped around the cork block. This will remove the faint scratches left when sanding was done while it was mounted on the lathe faceplate. Sand thoroughly the flat surface areas that were brought to the final level with hand tools.

Mill the battens next. These are the two supporting pieces attached to the underside of the table top (Photo 401). Specifications are provided in Drawing "A" (page 166). Counterbore and bore the necessary screw holes, shown in the drawing. Positioning the holes for the crow's-nest hinge pins is important. Lay the two battens together, long edge to long edge, determine the center in length, and mark. Measure from the center mark half of the crow's-nest size, or 4 inches, and mark the batten. Now measure back toward the center ⅜ inch, or half of the planned ¾-inch hinge-pin hole. This is the bit center point in length. Square a line across both battens, bisecting this center point. Now measure, from the long edge upward, ⅜ inch for bit center height. Bore these holes ⁹⁄₁₆ inch deep. Sand all batten surfaces (except the long edges) to finish smoothness.

Before attaching the battens to the top, flush-fit the table catch strike plate (Photo 402). The plate must be fitted on the top surface of the top square and centered on the edge opposite the hinge pins. Set the plate in its proper position, and scratch-mark its outline with a needle-point scriber. Chop-part (as in carving designs), and remove the waste wood to a depth equal to the plate thickness. Mark for, and cut, a chamfer for spring-latch clearance in line with the plate opening. Fasten the plate in place with ½-inch brass wood screws.

Enter the crow's-nest hinge pins in the batten holes, and place the assembly on the bottom surface of the top (Photo 401). Position the battens so that the hinge pins will be on the lower side of center when the top is tilted. Do *not* glue-coat bottom edge of battens. Center the top uncut section in a direct line between the two battens. Center the bottom scalloped section between battens also. Check the distance from the battens to the side edges—they should be equal. If necessary, shift the batten assembly slightly to one side or the other. Measure for equal distance of top overhang at the batten ends. Attach the battens with screws of such length that they cannot be embedded in the table-top wood more than ½ inch (Photo 401).

Fill the ½-inch counterbored screw holes with plugs made by the method explained in Chapter II (under "Covered Bowl"). Align the table catch with the spring latch entered in the strike plate opening (Photo 403), check the top button for free movement, and fasten the catch in place with ½-inch brass wood screws. Sand the counterbore plugs flush with the surrounding batten wood. Assemble the top unit on the base, and press the wedge in place for a final check. This completes the table construction. Give it a final examination for marks or scratches that can be erased. At the same time, give it a quick rub-off with No. 7/0 sandpaper.

332

333

334

335

336

337

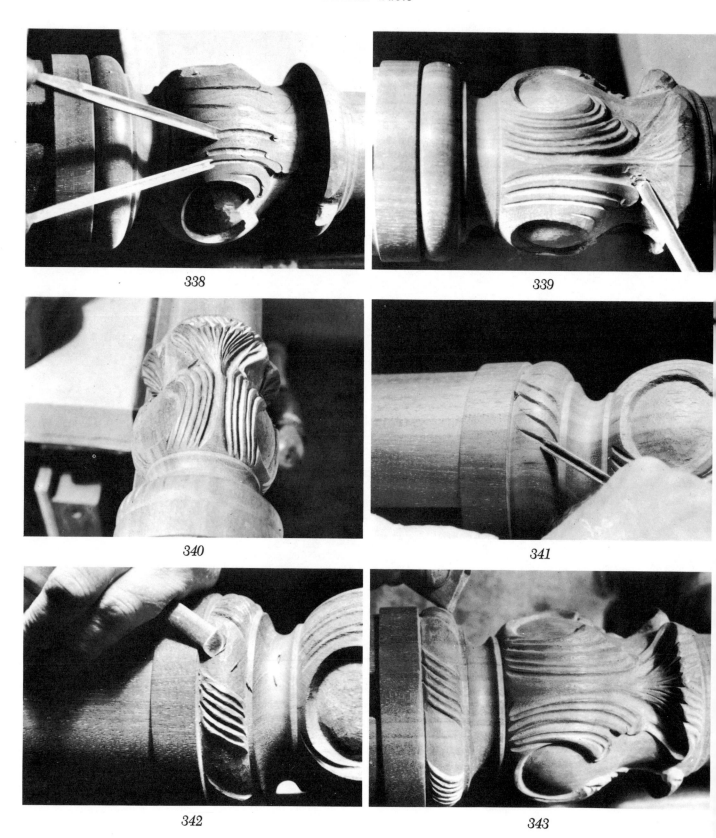

338

339

340

341

342

343

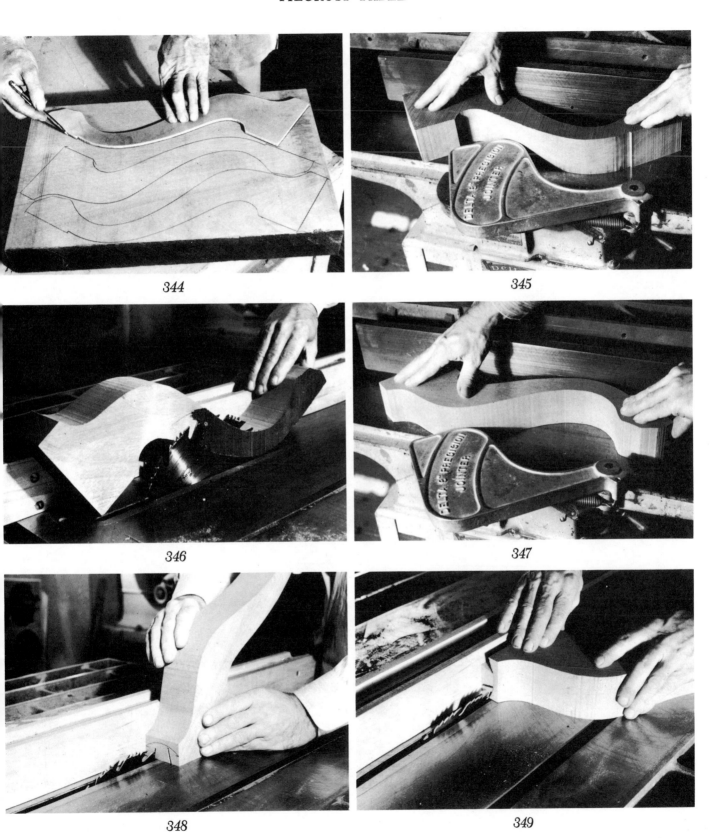

344

345

346

347

348

349

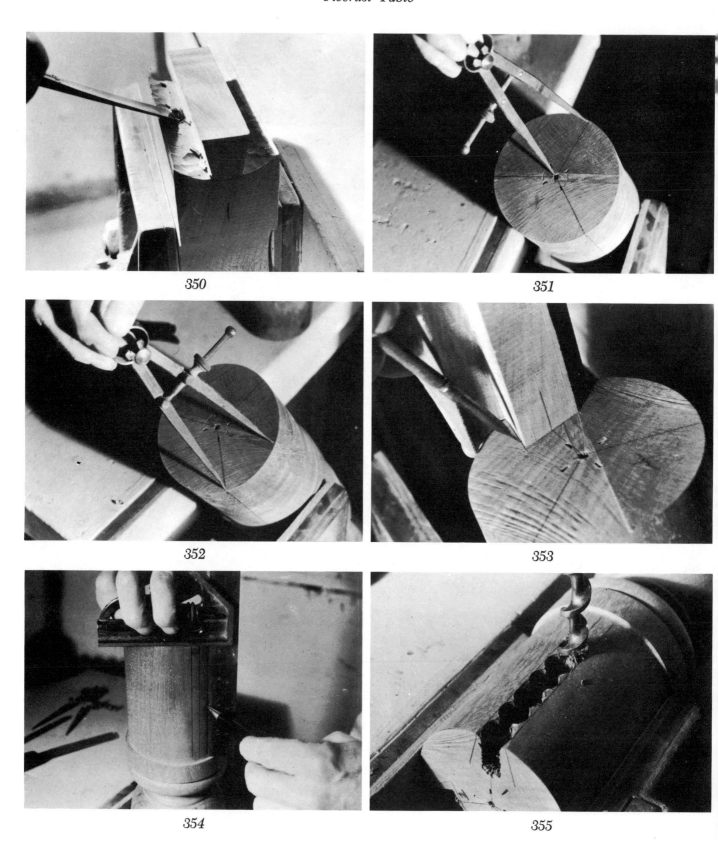

350

351

352

353

354

355

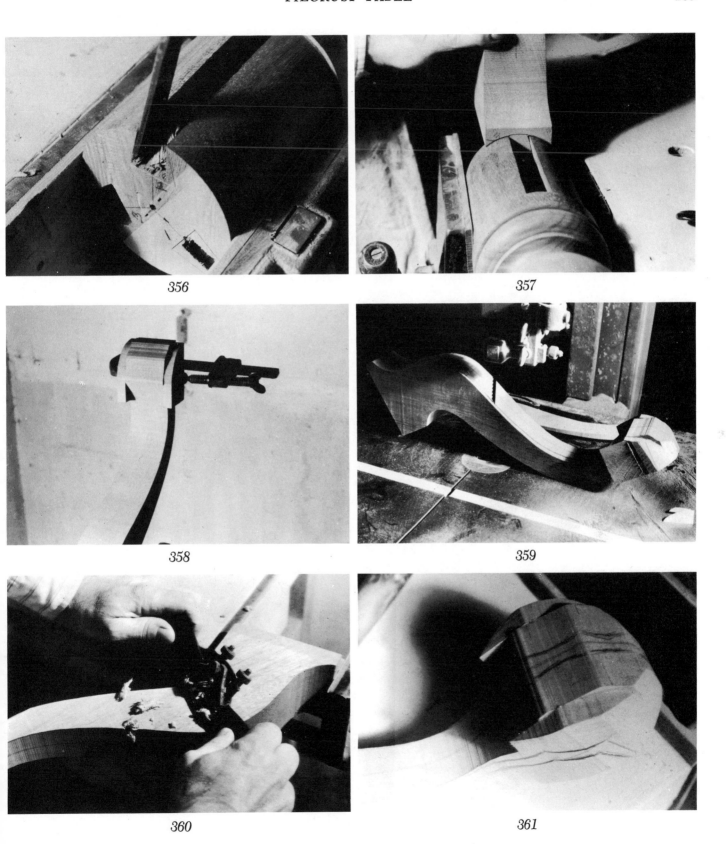

356

357

358

359

360

361

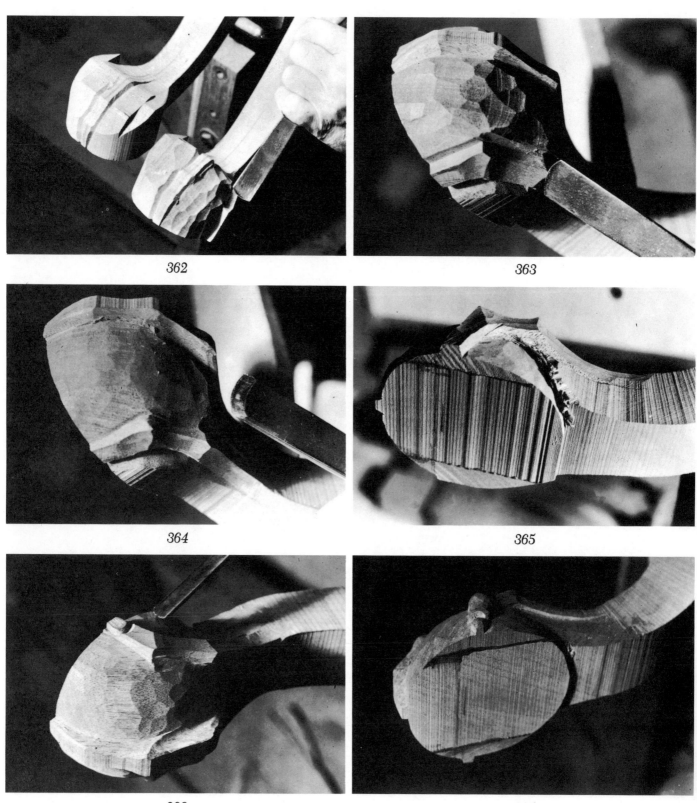

362

363

364

365

366

367

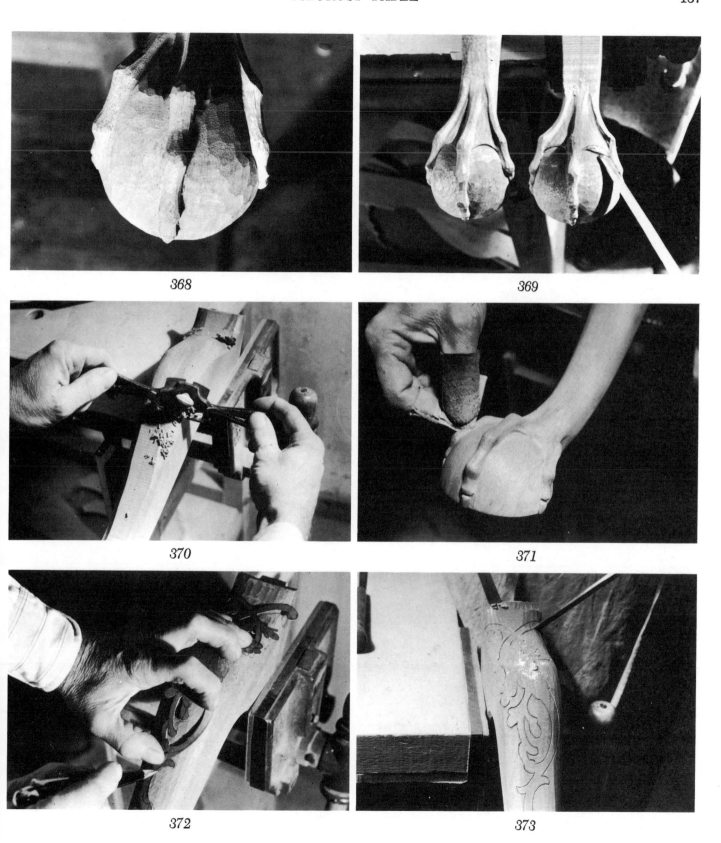

368

369

370

371

372

373

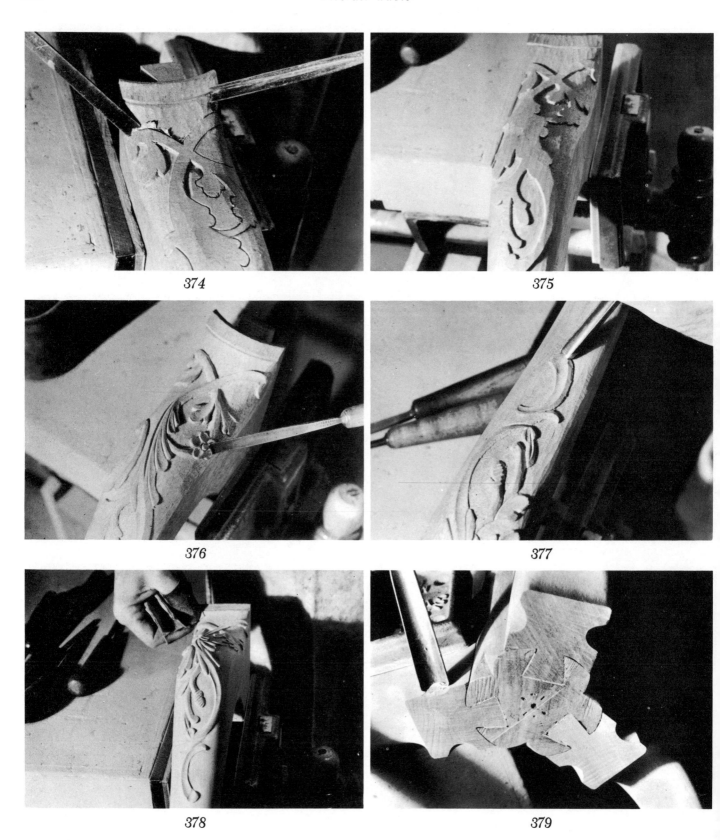

374

375

376

377

378

379

380

381

382

383

384

385

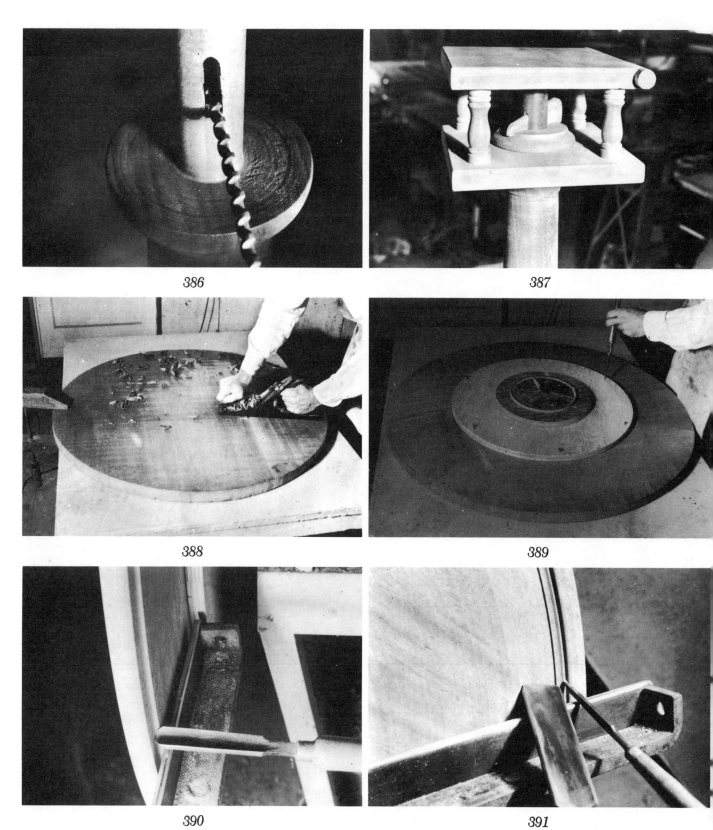

386

387

388

389

390

391

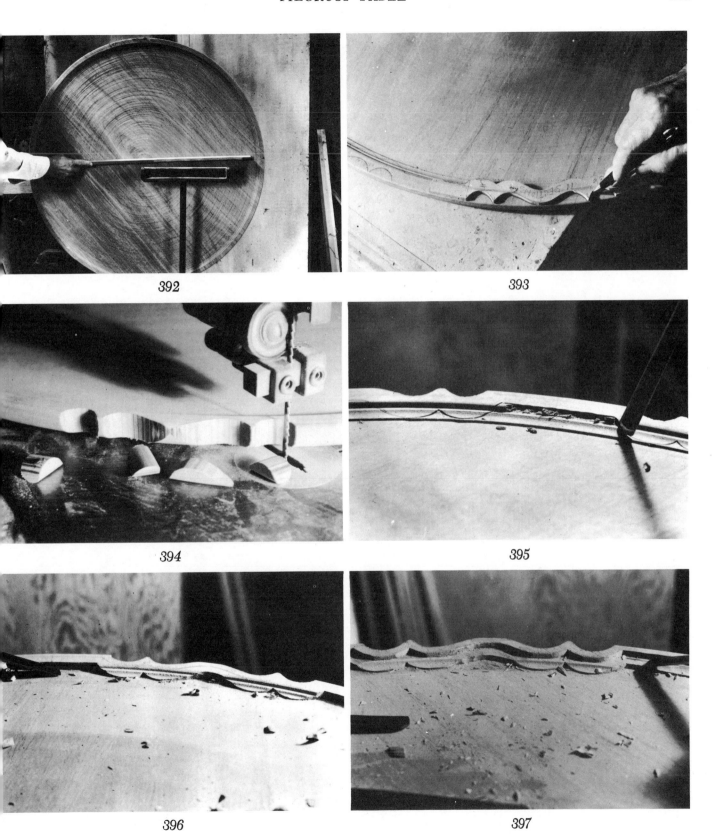

392

393

394

395

396

397

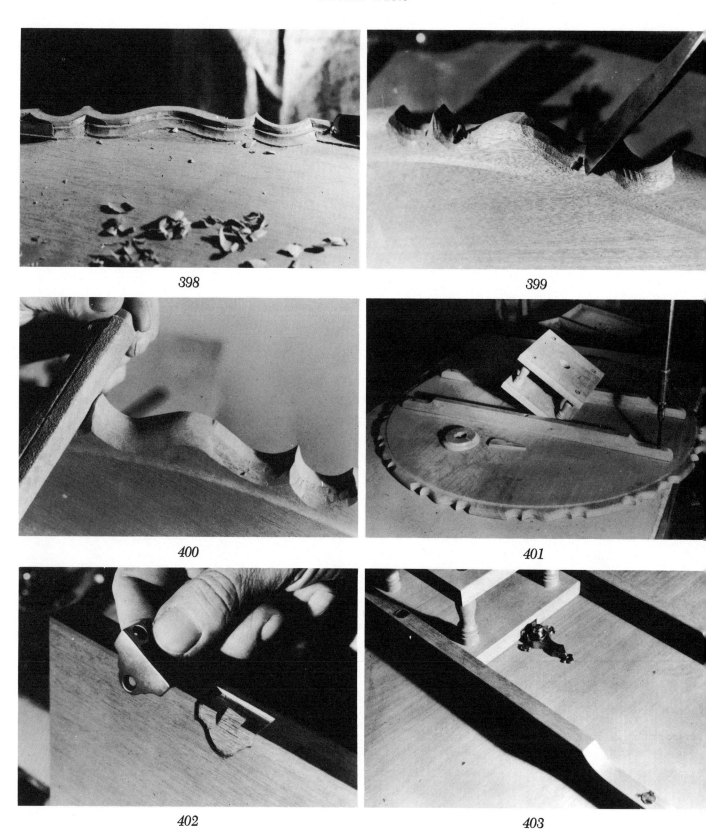

398

399

400

401

402

403

Contributory Processes

CHAPTER XI

Contributory Processes

SANDING

Flat surfaces. Bruises, often found on flat surfaces of wood, are indentations caused by extreme pressure on a small area and should be treated before sanding. Application of water to the affected parts will swell the fibers and bring them back to a normal position. Many pieces of otherwise fine furniture made in hobby shops have brought disappointment because this remedy is not known.

Thorough sanding is all-important. Marks such as the circular saw makes are easily discernible to the very point of disappearance. Most difficult of all marks to remove are those of the planer, which cover the entire area of flat surfaces. Soon after sanding starts they become no longer noticeable; but if sanding ends at this point the waves will reappear when the finishing materials are applied. This rule is safe: When the planer marks vanish, continue to sand just as long with coarse paper.

The suggested grits of sandpaper for use in cabinetmaking are No. ½ Garnet Cabinet paper for coarse work; No. 3/0 Garnet Finishing paper to follow the coarse; No. 7/0 Garnet Finishing paper for the final rub-off.

Garnet paper comes in sheets 9 by 11 inches, and a quarter-sheet is a convenient size to use with a block or cork 2¾ by 4 inches and ⅞ inch thick. If cork is not obtainable, soft wood may be substituted. Bend the paper up the sides of the block, and grip it hard enough to keep the block from shifting. In sanding a surface of considerable area, start at one end, using a natural stroke (12, 14 or more inches long), work the block slowly across the surface and back again. A distinct line of wood dust will accumulate to show where the strokes of this section have ended. Move ahead the length of a stroke less about 3 inches overlap, and repeat the cross-over. Overhard pressure on the block will tire the worker too quickly. Always sand with the grain. (These instructions also apply to the next operation with No. 3/0 paper.)

Curved surfaces. For sanding curved surfaces such as cabriole legs, fold one quarter-sheet of sandpaper three times, and use it with pressure of the fingers instead of the block. Sand with the grain wherever possible, and remember: quality sanding practically assures a quality finish.

Sanding with No. ½, then with No. 3/0 should be done at the most convenient stage of construction; that is, before an obstruction is added that will make sanding into a corner difficult. A quick rub-off with No. 7/0 is desirable when the piece is completed.

Carved surfaces. Opinions differ on the sanding of carvings. I think they should be sanded—but *properly*. Sanding is not difficult if all conditions are kept in mind. Most important of all, sharpness must be retained. High points and ridges should be carefully *approached* with sandpaper, without dulling by a direct pass over the apex. Veins, rib divisions, stippled background, and other depressions need not be touched. The coarsest paper used for small carvings is No. 3/0 Garnet Finishing paper. Use a quarter-sheet, folded three times and creased to a sharp edge. As long as the paper has a certain amount of stiffness, sand the contours where the fingers cannot be used for pressure. After the paper becomes soft, sand the high, easily accessible surfaces. For channel cuts of all kinds, roll a piece of sandpaper to the desired diameter.

For the preservation of well groomed hands, cut fingers from old lightweight leather gloves, about 1½ inches long for use on the thumb and the first finger of the right hand. These will protect the fingernails from abrasion.

A quick, light rub-off with No. 7/0 Garnet Finishing paper follows the No. 3/0 operation.

FUNDAMENTAL FINISHING PROCEDURE

Frequently amateurs enthusiastically discuss pet processes for finishing or refinishing furniture. The process most discussed uses wax dissolved in oil or turpentine or both, which is applied freely and allowed to penetrate for a variable length of time. Then the surface is wiped clean. A second coating is allowed to dry for a longer period, and then is rubbed well into the wood pores. The number of rubbed applications may total four, five, or six.

This method gives a beautiful but not too durable finish that requires constant care to maintain a satisfactory appearance. On a table top so finished, a frosted water glass will leave a white mark and will also raise the grain of the wood. Fine sandpaper must be used to remove the resulting roughness, and several applications of wax will be necessary to restore the finish.

A durable, trouble-free finish can be obtained by using lacquer or one of the new synthetics for the final coat. These materials, in drying, form the necessary hard, moisture-proof film.

The beauty of any finish coat depends almost entirely on the quality of work preceding its application. To obtain a professional finish, carefully observe the following procedures.

Dust the piece with a large brush, and examine the quality of the sanding. If you find any faults, correct them immediately. Stain will be more easily applied, with much more satisfactory results, if the surface is dust-free.

Water and spirit stains are not recommended unless you have had considerable experience with them. Oil stain colors of the same brand may be intermixed. Rarely does a manufacturer of stains market colors with the desired mellowness. A good practice is to blend small quantities of chosen colors for the desired effect.

Apply the stain in sufficient quantity to insure an even coat, brushing with the grain. Oil stain, if wiped immediately, leaves the lightest shade possible. If it is allowed to penetrate, the shade deepens to the maximum when the wet, glistening surface becomes dull. Remove the stain residue left on the surface with a clean cloth, always wiping with the grain. In corners, wipe the surface dry in the most convenient way, but finally wipe with the grain.

A word of caution: Do not brush too far in advance of wiping. Predetermine the complete area or part to be stained, and decide whether or not time permits brushing another area before you wipe the first. Allow overnight drying.

Next, brush or spray a wash coat of shellac or shellac substitute. A "wash coat" is a mixture of one part shellac and two parts of alcohol. Many substitutes for shellac that are now on the market were formulated especially for ease of sanding. For best results, allow the wash coat to dry overnight before you sand with No. 7/0 Garnet Finishing paper. When it is thoroughly dry, shellac or the substitute will not adhere to the paper but will leave a fine white powder on the sanded surface. If the paper becomes "gummed up," either the material of the wash coat is inferior or extreme humidity retards its normal drying action. Humidity is the most common adverse influence in the finishing process, at all stages. For sanding carvings choose well worn, soft No. 7/0 paper. New sharp paper will cut through the high spots before it touches the lower surfaces.

For mahogany alone, application of a paste filler is the next step. Readily procurable in most paint stores, the filler is too light. To darken it, mix the filler with Vandyke brown in oil. A desirable shade for filler is dark brown. Brush the prepared mixture on, with a circular motion. After five minutes, using a cloth folded into a pad, rub the surface with a circular motion; then, using a clean cloth, rub it with the grain. Such rubbing forces the filler into the open pores, to accomplish its purpose. Do not leave any residue on the surface. An interval of a few hours is commonly allowed before application of the finish coat. To avoid the cloudy effect that the filler-finish combination often gives, apply a wash coat of shellac over the filler before you proceed with the final coat. Sand lightly.

All materials for the final coating may be had in flat, dull, or gloss. A dull or "hand-rubbed" effect is recommended for furniture. Apply the coat evenly, and let it dry thoroughly before the final rub-down.

The most popular method of rubbing down is to go over the surface lightly with a pad of No. 00 steel wool and thus remove any roughness caused by dust settling on the wet finish, and then to apply liquid or paste wax, which is rubbed dry with a clean cloth.

Another method is to prepare a mixture of linseed oil and powdered pumice stone. Saturate a cloth with it, and rub well all surfaces until they have a smooth, pleasing appearance. The mixture must be completely removed with a clean cloth; otherwise, as the oil gradually dries, the pumice will turn white. The "oil and pumice" method is not recommended for a surface that includes carvings.

Where to Get It

CARVING TOOLS (London Style)

ALBERT CONSTANTINE & SON, INC.
2050 EASTCHESTER ROAD
BRONX, NY 10461

CRAFTSMAN WOOD SERVICE CO.
2727 SOUTH MARY STREET
CHICAGO, IL 60608

GARRETT WADE CO. INC.
302 FIFTH AVENUE
NEW YORK, NY 10001

SCULPTURE ASSOCIATES, LTD.
114 EAST 25 STREET
NEW YORK, NY 10010

LUMBER

Native woods can be purchased from local dealers. Special woods may be obtained through Albert Constantine & Son, Inc. and Craftsman Wood Service Co., whose addresses are listed above.

INLAY

See the comprehensive catalogues of Albert Costantine & Son, Inc. and Craftsman Wood Service Co. Each requires 50¢ in stamps. The addresses are above.

HARDWARE

For catalogues including brass reproductions of drawer pulls, table catches, hinges, and the like, write to:

BALL & BALL
463 WEST LINCOLN HIGHWAY
EXTON, PA 19341
(catalogue $1.00)

PERIOD FURNITURE HARDWARE CO., INC.
123 CHARLES STREET
BOSTON, MA 02114

Also, Albert Constantine & Sons, Inc., and Craftsman Wood Service Co., whose addresses are above.

Summary

This summary is intended to suggest a number of different design arrangements, using only design features encountered in this book. Size variations will be suggested to increase or change the functional qualities of a piece of furniture. Other ideas of interest are brought up for discussion so as to emphasize the versatility of traditional forms.

In studying the small chest of drawers in Chapter IX you may say to yourself: "Perhaps I can make this chest from the plans shown. But I would never attempt the larger one we need in the bedroom." A moment's thought will reveal that not one structural problem is added in the larger chest. Drawers for the larger piece are made in exactly the same manner as those for the smaller ones. The same could be said for the case work. The decorations probably can be made with more ease in the larger size. There are only two items that vary significantly in larger size: the greater amount of material and the longer time required. The same factors exist in any piece of furniture, provided no design change is involved.

It is not unreasonable to imagine the piecrust tray attached to a tripod base such as the candlestand with a shorter post. This would make an attractive table beside your favorite chair. Or the tray, still used as a tray, in a larger size which would only require a change of piecrust edge pattern. Or a plain dish-top tray of any size with the ¼-inch bead provided for the candlestand.

Consider the covered bowl. It could be turned in various sizes or shapes, with or without inlay, and of many different kinds of wood, with or without a cover. If covered, the turning design could be changed, possibly omitting the carving. Ideas for change are almost limitless. With all these changes, the basic wood-turning techniques involved in making the original bowl remain the same.

The size and shape of the cigarette box suggest its possibility for a jewel box. Instead of plastic liners and wood division strips, velvet lining could be substituted. The single portrait frame may well be envisioned on a dressing table, with a mirror instead of the portrait. Or the double frame made in separate units equipped with hanger rings for wall decorations.

Study the rectangular stool. Try to picture it longer and wider, with a coffee table top replacing the upholstered board. Think of it made of cherry wood, which, quite possibly, would blend well with the living-room furnishings, as either a stool or coffee table. A change in leg design, also adhering to tradition, could be made by leaving off the knee tongue carving and omitting the webs on the spoon feet. This change would result in typical Queen Anne style legs with conventional spoon feet. Such a design is popular either as a stool or as a coffee table, made of walnut or cherry. Neither curves nor wood thicknesses need to be altered for this variation. Just add extra inches to the length of long and short rails to obtain the desired size.

The oval stool, minus knee and wing carving, with wing outlines modified, would remain a welcome piece of furniture for the home. Ball and claw feet and mahogany seem to be practically synonymous. Although most mahogany furniture featuring ball and claw feet has carved decorations elsewhere, many examples show that the designer relied entirely on the ball and claw for decoration.

Ideas for change find fertile ground in the candlestand. The rat-claw feet show a marked resemblance in shape to snake feet. In fact, the same leg patterns would be used for either style foot. The post, to be compatible with snake feet, should have little or no decoration. The reeded vase would be permissible, but not in conjunction with the flutes above it. A conservative combination in extremely good taste is a plain turned post (shown in Photo 168) without decoration, combined with snake feet. Another combination that has merit is a plain turned post, retaining the rat-claw feet.

The paw-foot coffee table can also be varied to a limited extent. Paw feet are always associated with leg carving, so that little can be done to vary this table's design. Another style of knee carving, such as that worked on the oval stool knees, would be acceptable. It is questionable whether this combination would be as attractive as the table in its present illustrated form. Of course it could revert to the stool size from which it was originally adapted. Or a stool and a table could be made as companion pieces.

The small chests were discussed to some extent, but ideas of expansion could be carried further. Suppose the drawer space provided by an average-size four-drawer chest was insufficient. How could more space be obtained? Just add another chest on top, making it a "chest on chest." Although it may sound complicated, the addition presents no problems. Instead of attaching a top panel to the lower chest, make another case to contain three or four drawers of gradually lessening height. The only difference between the two cases is size. The upper one would have less height and would be 1¼ inches less in width, ⅝ inch less in depth. This provides a ⅝-inch offset space for division molding. The top of the lower chest would be attached to the upper case. Again no new problems; only additional time and material are required in making two chests instead of one.

Piecrust tables range in diameter from 21 to 38 inches. In making patterns for a size other than the 36-inch illustrated, the leg spread (from the post center to the tip of the foot) is determined as being one inch less than the radius of the table top. The eleven sections forming the circumference of the table illustrated are unusual. Piecrust tops are more often divided into eight segments. In using the eight-segment design the same patternmaking routine would be observed. Design change could also add thirteen flutes to the straight taper post section above the vase on the 36-inch table in Chapter X. The majority of piecrusts have knee and post carving although a few are exhibited with only the scalloped top edge and the ball and claw feet. If a change of post and leg decorations seems to be in order, the builder can either combine or eliminate features.

The reader, if he builds or fashions all the subject pieces illustrated in this volume, will increase his knowledge of furniture making tremendously. With this new knowledge he will have a much deeper appreciation of fine furniture. What is seen in tastefully furnished homes, in the better antique shops, or in museums will inspire a new interest in custom made furniture. He will look for points of quality construction, such as hand-dovetailed drawers, joining details, carvings and moldings cut from solid wood rather than applied. He will find himself comparing his own handicraft with that of the masters.

He will have learned, first hand, the necessary ways of wood joining for furniture work. He will know that rail or skirt attachment to a leg must be accomplished by the mortise-and-tenon method, and will know how to make this joint. He will have learned that interior frame parts are joined best by tongue and groove.

He will have the intriguing know-how of hand dovetailing: drawers that will stay rigid for generations; tripod table legs that cannot be loosened without breaking the post wood. He will have a good working knowledge of wood carving as related to furniture. Even if not complete, this basic training will provide the foundation on which his initiative can build.

Above all, he will have learned how to use woodworking tools effectively. He may have learned to improvise. If a power tool is not available, he will know how to substitute hand tools. He will have learned to fix in his mind how a larger or more elaborate article of furniture will look when built. He will mentally catalogue the extra units, how they should be assembled, what method of joinery to use—and he will find no new structural problems to dampen his spirits. Lastly he will know the pride and satisfaction of having and using furniture that he has made with his own hands.